BELSEN

Other Books on the Holocaust

Holocaust Agendas, Conspiracies and Industries?
Issues and Debates in Holocaust Memorialization
Judy Berman

Remembering Belsen
Eyewitnesses Record the Liberation
Edited by Ben Flanagan and Donald Bloxham

A History of the Holocaust
Saul S. Friedman

Holocaust Memoir Digest, Volumes 1, 2 and 3
Compiled and Edited by Esther Goldberg

Israeli Society, the Holocaust and its Survivors
Dina Porat

Children of the Holocaust
Edited by Andrea Reiter

Approaching the Holocaust
Texts and Contexts
Robert Rozett

History, Memory and Mass Atrocity
Essays on the Holocaust and Genocide
Dan Stone

Belsen 1945
New Historical Perspectives

Editors

Suzanne Bardgett
David Cesarani

Published in association with
the Imperial War Museum

VALLENTINE MITCHELL
LONDON • PORTLAND, OR

First published in 2006 in Great Britain by
VALLENTINE MITCHELL
Suite 314 Premier House, 112–114 Station Road,
Edgware, Middlesex HA8 7BJ

and in the United States of America by
VALLENTINE MITCHELL
c/o ISBS, 920 N.E. 58th Street, Suite 300
Portland, Oregon 97213-3786

Website www.vmbooks.com

Copyright © 2006
Text © Trustees of the Imperial War Museum

British Library Cataloguing in Publication Data

Belsen 1945: new historical perspectives
 1. Bergen-Belsen (Concentration camp) – Congresses 2. World War, 1939–1945 – Concentration camps – Liberation – Germany – Congresses 3. World War, 1939–1945 – Mass media and the war – Congresses
 I. Bardgett, Suzanne II. Cesarani, David III. Imperial War Museum (Great Britain)
 940. 5'31853593

ISBN 0 85303 716 7 (cloth)
ISBN 978 0 85303 716 3 (cloth)
ISBN 0 85303 717 5 (paper)
ISBN 978 0 85303 717 0 (paper)

Library of Congress Cataloging-in-Publication Data:

A catalog record has been applied for

This group of studies first appeared in a special issue of *Holocaust Studies: A Journal of Culture and History*, Vol.12/1–2 [ISSN 1359-1371] published by Vallentine Mitchell & Co. Ltd.

All rights reserved. No part of this publication may be reproduced, stored in or introduced into a retrieval system, or transmitted, in any form or by any means, electronic, mechanical, photocopying, recording or otherwise, without the prior written permission of the publisher of this book.

Printed in Great Britain by Antony Rowe Ltd, Chippenham, Wilts

Contents

List of Plates   vii
List of Illustrations   viii
List of Abbreviations   ix
Foreword by Robert Crawford CBE, Director-General
of the Imperial War Museum   xi

Introduction   *David Cesarani*   1

PART I: THE LIBERATION OF THE CAMP AND THE MEDICAL RELIEF EFFORT

A Brief History of Bergen-Belsen   *David Cesarani*   13

A Survivor's Memories of Liberation   *Anita Lasker-Wallfisch*   22

The First Day in the Camp   *Major Dick Williams*   27

The Medical Relief Effort at Belsen   *Ben Shephard*   31

The Medical Relief Effort: Eyewitness Accounts   51

British Relief Teams in Belsen Concentration Camp:
Emergency Relief and the Perception
of Survivors   *Johannes-Dieter Steinert*   62

Andrew Matthews and the Two Sachselová Sisters   *Rainer Schulze*   79

A Few Words to Explain the Origin
of My Drawings   *Eva Macourková*   84

PART II: COMPILING THE RECORD

The Filming of the Liberation of Bergen-Belsen and
its Impact on the Understanding of the Holocaust   *Toby Haggith*   89

What Wireless Listeners Learned: Some Lesser-Known
BBC Broadcasts about Belsen *Suzanne Bardgett* 123

Lesser-Known BBC Broadcasts: The Scripts 137

'And I was only a child': Children's Testimonies,
Bergen-Belsen 1945 *Boaz Cohen* 153

The Liberation of the Bergen-Belsen Camp as seen
by Some British Official War Artists in 1945 *Antoine Capet* 170

PART III: PRESERVING THE MEMORY

From 'This Belsen Business' to 'Shoah Business':
History, Memory and Heritage, 1945–2005 *Tony Kushner* 189

Forgetting and Remembering:
Memories and Memorialisation of Bergen-Belsen *Rainer Schulze* 217

Abstracts 236
Notes on Contributors 240
Index 244

List of Plates

(plates 1–8 between pages 82 and 83,
plates 9–16 between pages 178 and 179)

1–8. The drawings made in her hospital bed by Eva Sachsel and given to Andrew Matthews, the medical student who looked after her

9. 'Belsen Camp: The Compound for Women', Lesley Cole, oil on canvas

10. 'One of the Death Pits: Belsen SS guards collecting bodies', Lesley Cole, oil on canvas

11. 'Belsen: April 1945', Doris Clare Zinkeisen, oil on canvas

12. 'Human Laundry, Belsen: April 1945', Doris Clare Zinkeisen, oil on canvas

13. Aerial view of Bergen-Belsen

14. The ceremonial burning down of the last hut at Belsen, photograph by Sergeant Bert Hardy

15. The new Documentation and Information Centre at Bergen-Belsen

16. 'Master Plan Bergen-Belsen'

List of Illustrations

1. The twelve medical students from St Mary's Hospital medical school who participated in the relief work at Bergen-Belsen   80
2. Sergeant Oakes and Sergeant Lawrie with their camera next to a jeep   95
3. A dead German officer filmed at Arnhem, probably by Sergeant 'Jock' Walker   97
4. A camp inmate grasps the hand of Lieutenant Martin Wilson   98
5. Sergeant Mike Lewis filming a mass burial   99
6. Prisoners re-enacting the moment of liberation for Sergeant Hopkinson   100
7. A 'corroborating' interview with Franz Hosler   102
8. A former prisoner watches a mass burial   103
9. A 'cross' in the foreground of a scene filmed by Sergeant Mike Lewis   104
10. The corpse of an inmate being dragged into a mass grave   105
11. 'Romance in a Romantic Setting'. A former prisoner with a British soldier at Belsen   105
12. Study of women showering in the Mobile Bath Unit   106
13. Former prisoners selecting clothes in 'Harrods'   108
14. Patrick Gordon Walker   124
15. Patrick Gordon Walker with fellow BBC colleagues   130
16. 'A British Army Bulldozer pushes Bodies into a Mass Grave at Belsen'   171
17. 'The Liberation of Bergen-Belsen Concentration Camp, 1945: One of the Mass Graves partially filled with Corpses'   175
18. 'The Bodies of Victims in Bergen-Belsen Concentration Camp'   180

List of Abbreviations

AFPU	Army Film and Photographic Unit
BBC	British Broadcasting Corporation
BEF	British Expeditionary Force
BRC	British Red Cross
CCS	Casualty Clearing Station
COBSRA	Council of British Societies for Relief Abroad
DDMS	Deputy Director of Medical Services
DP	Displaced Person
EMS	Emergency Medical Services
FAU	Friends Ambulance Units
FRS	Friends Relief Service
IWM	Imperial War Museum
JCRA	Jewish Committee for Relief Abroad
JDC	Joint Distribution Committee
KL/KZ	Konzentrationslager (concentration camp)
NGO	Non-Governmental Organisation
OXFAM	Oxford Committee for Famine Relief
POW	Prisoner of War
RAF	Royal Air Force
RAMC	Royal Army Medical Corps
REME	Royal Electrical and Mechanical Engineers
RSHA	Reichssicherheitshauptamt (Reich Security Main Office)
SAS	Special Air Service
SHAEF	Supreme Headquarters Allied Expeditionary Force
TNA	The National Archives
UNRRA	United Nations Relief and Rehabilitation Administration
WVHA	Wirtschafts- und Verwaltungshauptamt (Economic and Administrative Head Office of the SS)

Foreword

The discovery of the camp at Bergen-Belsen in April 1945, the horrific experiences of those imprisoned there and the effort at restoring order and saving lives in the camp – these events are documented in some detail here at the Imperial War Museum.

Belsen was the only significant Nazi concentration camp to be liberated by the British Army, and the records made in the days and weeks following its opening were compiled in the main by British soldiers, relief workers, cameramen, war correspondents and broadcasters. Many of these records came to the Museum straight after the war; others trickled in over later years, as former soldiers and those involved in the relief operation emptied their attics and realised that the letters and diaries they had written those many years ago had historical value and should be preserved for posterity.

From the mid-1980s onwards, these liberators' accounts started to be augmented by accounts written by survivors, Anita Lasker-Wallfisch's memoir being among the first to be deposited here.

These collections formed the basis of a small exhibition about the camp and the relief operation which opened in 1991. It drew much comment from a public clearly moved and stimulated to know about this subject.

Nine years later the Museum opened its large and detailed Holocaust Exhibition, extending its building to include this major new display. Four years in preparation, it tells the full story of Hitler's war against the Jews, and other groups, and is richly filled with testimony, archive film, photographs and dozens of artefacts borrowed from former camps in Poland or Germany, or given by survivors. The exhibition has brought the Museum new audiences – particularly young people and visitors to London from overseas – and has earned us praise for tackling such a difficult theme. Most importantly it has given well over a million and a half visitors an in-depth understanding of how the Nazis embarked on their programme of mass murder, and what it meant for those they persecuted.

Very rewardingly, too, the Holocaust Exhibition has provided a focus for lectures, academic conferences and seminars on related themes – something we greatly value, both for the intellectual refreshment they bring this institution and the enhancement of our reputation as a place of serious historical study.

In April 2005, on the sixtieth anniversary of Belsen's discovery – in partnership with Royal Holloway, London – we held a one-day seminar to look at recent historical research into all aspects of Belsen in April 1945. Funding came in large part from Their Past Your Future, the major initiative to commemorate the sixtieth anniversary of the end of the Second World War funded by the Big Lottery Fund.

This book is the fruit of that seminar. Within it the editors – David Cesarani and Suzanne Bardgett – have brought together the memories of people who were there at the time as well as historical articles researched by academics in universities and curators from the Museum. The fact that contributions have come from the Czech Republic, France, Germany and Israel, as well as from Britain, gives it a truly international stamp.

The Museum is pleased and proud to have partnered Royal Holloway, London over this important new contribution to our understanding of the history of Belsen camp.

R.W.K. Crawford CBE
Director-General
Imperial War Museum
London
September 2006

Acknowledgements

This volume grew out of a sixtieth anniversary commemorative seminar on the liberation of Bergen-Belsen organised by the Research Centre for the Holocaust and Twentieth-Century History at Royal Holloway, University of London, in collaboration with the Imperial War Museum and held at the Museum on 15 April 2005. Only a part of what was said on this moving occasion has made it onto the pages of this collection. The organisers would like to thank The Rt. Hon. Ivor Caplin MP, Minister for Veterans' Affairs, and Mr Robert Crawford, Director-General of the Imperial War Museum, who introduced the seminar, and Professor Peter Longerich, Royal Holloway, who chaired the opening session. The event would not have been possible without extensive support and assistance. The editors wish to thank The Big Lottery Fund and the Imperial War Museum's Their Past Your Future team for their financial support of the seminar; Naomi Blum, Catherine Gresty and the Imperial War Museum Events Office for their part in organising it. Many people contributed in a number of different ways to the making of this book. The editors express their thanks to Beth Cook and Jessica Mani of the Holocaust Exhibition Project Office for unstinting effort on copyediting and for coordinating the illustrations and other aspects of the book; Liz Bowers and Gemma Maclagan of the Museum's Publications Office, and Barbara Levy for liaison with the publishers; Frank Cass, Mark Anstee and colleagues at Vallentine Mitchell for their patience and informed interest in this project; and Dr Tom Lawson and Dr James Jordan, co-editors of the *Holocaust Studies: A Journal of Culture and History*, published by Vallentine Mitchell, who helped to guide the project into a special issue of the journal.

Suzanne Bardgett
David Cesarani
September 2006

Introduction

DAVID CESARANI

Sixty years after British troops entered Bergen-Belsen the camp has assumed iconic status in British official memory of the Second World War and the genocide waged against Europe's Jews. This significance was amply demonstrated by the role it played in the Holocaust Memorial Day national ceremony held in Westminster Hall in London on 27 January 2005 which was largely structured around the story of the camp and its liberation.

The ceremony featured a specially made BBC film that recounted the return to Belsen of Susan Pollock, a survivor of the 437,000 Jews deported from Hungary to Auschwitz in 1944.[1] While most were immediately killed, Pollock was selected for work and sent on to other camps. She ended up in Belsen where she was liberated. The film showed her in the present day memorial park meeting Major Dick Williams who, as a captain responsible for supply and transport in the HQ of British VIII Corps, had been amongst the first soldiers to enter the camp.

The first testimony at the ceremony was delivered by Hannah Pick who, as Hanneli Goslar, had been a childhood friend of Anne Frank in Amsterdam. Goslar was amongst the 'privileged' Dutch Jews held in the camp and was amongst the last people to have contact with Anne after she arrived there, in a terrible state, from Auschwitz. Anne Frank died in Belsen and the audience in Westminster Hall and watching on television heard a specially composed oratorio by James Whitbourn that recalled her fate.[2]

The ceremony closed with words from Paul Oppenheimer, a German-born Jew who was deported from the Netherlands to Belsen, where his parents perished, and Helen Bamber, who as a young nurse had participated in the relief operation.[3] To underline the connection between Britain and Belsen, the war and the liberation, the last segment of the film showed Susan Pollock kindling a flame of remembrance in Belsen while a piper of the Royal Scots Dragoon Guards played a lament. The flame, encased in a lantern, was filmed in transit to London where it was carried into the hall by two guardsmen. They stood in attendance as Susan Pollock and Dick Williams used the flame to light memorial candles.

Belsen has thus become almost symbolic of Britain's war effort. Yet at the same time as it becomes ever more important in British history and memory, new research reveals complexities about its evolution and liberation that defy any single narrative. For example, before Jews were immured in Belsen it was a camp for captured Russian prisoners of war, thousands of whom died in terrible conditions during 1941–42. In this respect, the history of the camp is a fragment of the story of Nazi Germany's racial, ideological and genocidal war against the Soviet Union.

Many of the Jews who were held there, like the 'privileged' Dutch Jews, were kept as hostages by the Nazis who hoped to ransom or exchange them. Looked at from this angle, fraught with awkward questions and prone to controversy, Belsen offers a perspective on how the world reacted to the extermination of Europe's Jews.[4] Indeed as time passes, and scholars are able to assess the historical record more objectively, even the British relief operation, while ultimately a magnificent humanitarian achievement, appears somewhat open to question.

Although much has been broadcast and published about Belsen, the essays presented here bring together research and viewpoints that have been made possible only by the passage of time, the benefits of new documentation, and a rigorous scholarly approach.[5] They offer an original, and at times controversial, reassessment of the camp, its liberation, and the shape it has taken in public memory in Britain and Germany. But throughout the collection we hear the voices of those who were there: survivors, liberators, relief workers.

The essays and much of the testimony from eyewitnesses are drawn from the proceedings of a commemorative seminar organised by Suzanne Bardgett of the Imperial War Museum and the Research Centre for the Holocaust and Twentieth-Century History at Royal Holloway, University of London, and held at the

INTRODUCTION 3

Imperial War Museum London on 15 April 2005. The intention of the event was to combine historical expertise in a variety of fields with the recollections of those who participated, unwillingly, in those terrible events. The resulting collection makes no claim to be comprehensive, still less definitive. On the contrary, the essays are all to a greater or lesser extent self-reflective and conscious of the limits of representing the past in descriptive prose, historical narrative, sound recordings or images.

The collection opens with a brief history of Bergen-Belsen by David Cesarani that surveys the many incarnations of the camp and the unpredictable twists and turns in its career. Belsen was not typical of the labour camps, concentration camps or death camps run by the Nazis, but it nevertheless represented in microcosm several characteristics and phases of Nazi expansionism and racial policy between 1940 and 1945. The consequences of Nazi policy as refracted through Belsen can be assessed from the selection of survivor and liberator testimony. Dick Williams, an officer responsible for supply and transport, set down his recollections of the first day, his jarring impressions of what he saw and the desperate efforts to get help to the camp. Anita Lasker-Wallfisch gives voice to the survivors, reminding us that they had personal histories which were initially obscure to the military, medical and relief personnel who saw only 'walking skeletons' and 'human animals'. These vivid eyewitness reports form a bridge to the contribution by Ben Shephard exploring key questions about the medical relief effort.

It is well known that 14,000 people died in the camp after the liberation and that at least 2,000 died because they were given the wrong type of food by well-meaning British soldiers who intended merely to alleviate their starvation. Ben Shephard notes that these terrible facts have given rise to harsh criticism, but he stands back from either celebration or condemnation and instead interrogates the historical material to discover why the dying continued at such an appalling rate. He concludes that the flaws in the initial relief effort were not due to indifference, ignorance or lack of planning.

Rather, the British forces and the Allies in general had simply not anticipated such a humanitarian disaster. The civilian relief agencies were weak; the army tended to see refugees and displaced persons as an obstacle to the business of war fighting. Both anticipated famine conditions, but fears had centred on that portion of the Netherlands still under German occupation in April 1945. Some elements of British military intelligence knew about the camp and probably had a clear notion of how bad things were, but the transmission of information was patchy.

Consequently, Belsen came as a horrendous surprise. The units that were sent in to start the relief work did not have enough personnel for the tasks they faced. Because the burial parties could not dispose of the thousands of corpses piled up or scattered around the camp and keep up with the rate at which people kept on dying, cadavers continued to litter the open areas and the huts in Camp 1 for over a week. Brigadier Glyn Hughes came up with a sound plan to evacuate the living from the 'horror camp' to a hospital set up in the nearby Panzer Training School, but a confused chain of command meant that for days few people were actually moved.

It was not until substantial reinforcements arrived, including 96 medical students from Britain and an American officer well-versed in handling typhus epidemics, that the crisis was brought under control. Shephard does not excuse or disguise the mistakes that were made, but he shows that they were mainly due to understandable factors such as lack of preparedness and lack of experience. His measured analysis is complemented by extracts from the accounts of medical personnel. Major Ben Barnett's pencilled notes give a vivid impression of how British officers and soldiers reacted when they encountered the camp and what they found there. Nurse Molly Silva Jones, one of the first nurses to enter the camps, recorded the early medical operations and the almost incredulous gratitude of the survivors. One of the medical students, Gerald Raperport, noted with an acute eye both the physical and mental degradation of the inmates. Readers can draw their own conclusions from these remarkable documents.

The initial weakness of the relief effort is further dissected by Dieter Steinert who traces back the training of the civilian workers. COBSRA, the British umbrella organisation for relief agencies, had provided basic organisational, medical and psychological training

INTRODUCTION 5

since post-war planning began in 1942, but it was very basic. In any case, the army was not keen to have teams of civilians roaming around in rear areas. During the first days after liberation five six-man Red Cross teams and one Quaker team were thrown into the relief effort. But thanks to the prevailing sexism the army refused to allow women into the camp, depriving the effort of essential skilled personnel.

The inadequacy of the training afforded to the Red Cross teams can be seen in the negative perception of the survivors. Unable to grasp what the pitiful remnant had endured in Belsen, or in ghettos and camps prior to their arrival, the relief workers were appalled by the apparent displays of greed and selfishness. It took many days and a more patient attitude before they got beyond national or racial stereotypes and realised the scope of the medical and psychological challenge they faced.

The written and graphic testimony by Eva Macourková provides an insight into the thoughts and feelings of one of those who was nursed back to health. Her account of how one trainee doctor, Andrew Matthews, met the challenge reveals the depth of humanity shown by so many of the dedicated medical workers. While doctors, nutritionists, nurses and medical students from a dozen countries fought to save the lives of the liberated prisoners, journalists, broadcasters and film makers struggled to record the spectacle and convey it to the outside world.

British army film crews have been criticised for reducing the victims to anonymity as either corpses or mute objects of sympathy.[6] Their names, religious affiliation, ethnicity and life histories were largely absent from the newsreel record. However, Toby Haggith reveals from previously unused documents that the cameramen frequently engaged with the people they were filming and consciously tried to restore their humanity. The daily 'dope sheets' on which the cameramen recorded notes on the subject of the shoot make it clear that they were aware when the survivors were Jewish and understood what this signified. If their narratives did not make it into the finished film this was not their fault. The constraints of working within time-limited newsreels and editorial pressures in London were more to blame for erasing the identities, voices and the personalities of the survivors.

Journalists who arrived at Belsen intending to report what they found there faced numerous problems. They lacked a context for the camp and had to learn the background of the people who ended up there in order to appreciate the significance of their odyssey from Auschwitz and other places. Yet the camp inmates came from many different countries and even though 60 per cent were Jewish, they spoke a bewildering range of languages. Patrick Gordon Walker was better equipped than most because he spoke German fluently and had worked for the BBC's German Service, in which capacity he had learned much about the course of the war. Nevertheless, even he was stunned by what greeted him in Belsen.

Drawing on his diary and unpublished papers Suzanne Bardgett explains that Gordon Walker saw the failings of the relief effort. But it would have been irresponsible for him to broadcast this to the listeners in Britain while the humanitarian endeavour was in full swing, under arduous, appalling conditions. He did realise that a preponderance of the inmates of the camp were Jewish and worked out that Belsen was part of a wider catastrophe inflicted on the Jews. He sought out and interviewed Jewish survivors who were German, Dutch and Czech. He also recorded the first Sabbath service in Belsen after the liberation, an event that moved him to tears. Even though his extensive recordings, including captured SS personnel, were edited down to a 15-minute broadcast they had a profound effect. Within the limits he was working under, Patrick Gordon Walker gave listeners a powerful insight into the camp and the experiences of its Jewish victims.

A further serious effort to bring home the reality of Belsen was made by Leonard Cottrell, a freelance writer of talks and features for the BBC. In a programme transmitted in April 1946 he focused on the experience of a Channel Islander, Harold Le Druillenec, who had been sent to the camp as punishment for defying the German occupiers. Using a combination of dramatised sequences and documentary, Cottrell succeeded in impressing the horrors of Belsen on a post-war audience, albeit through the lens of a British subject. However eccentric this may seem today, it counters the notion that Belsen was allowed to fade from public consciousness after a short-lived burst of outrage.

Another disturbing claim surrounding the liberation of Belsen

INTRODUCTION

and other camps is that no one was interested in the testimony of the survivors.[7] While there is much evidence to support this contention, Boaz Cohen documents an early effort to collect testimony from child survivors. The pioneering work was undertaken by Helena Wrobel who worked as a teacher in the school that served the DP camp established at Belsen. By late 1946 nearly 900 Jewish children, most of whom had arrived with their families from Poland, were attending this school. Wrobel encouraged them to write about their experiences both as a therapy and in order to collect information.

This early testimony, in Polish and Yiddish, has many striking characteristics. The children are offhand about their experiences in the ghettos and camps, reflecting the degree to which horror had become normalised. The moment at which they lost their families marked a break with their old lives that seemed to have slipped far away and to be of little interest any longer. Their writing often circled around the moral dilemmas of survival and recorded the good or bad deeds they had witnessed, as if they were trying to make sense of what had happened.

Despite Wrobel's best efforts, this precious body of fresh testimony was never published. This was not for lack of interest; but those most concerned with the historical record had other priorities.[8] Early testimony was regarded as a source of basic information and data for war crimes trials. It was not regarded as valuable in and for itself as testimony, and when such records did come into fashion a formidable language barrier impeded their utilisation. Thus the statements languished until Boaz Cohen brought them to light.

Much of the visual record has also been overlooked, though for quite different reasons. Antoine Capet argues that the representations by official war artists, notably Leslie Cole and Doris Zinkeisen, were regarded unfavourably by comparison with photographs. The photograph was (and to a large extent still is) seen as the most convincing form of evidence. As long as it has been felt essential to convince the public of the veracity of the atrocities at Belsen, priority has therefore been given to the photo-image.[9] There were also economic and technical reasons for not reproducing drawings and paintings made in the days following the liberation. Yet, Capet suggests, these representations are more immediate and emotive than the familiar – indeed, banalised – black and white photographs.

The merit of the children's testimonies and the war artists' paintings is that they provide us with less intensely mediated or interpreted representations, less freighted with meanings. For, as Tony Kushner explains, it is now almost impossible to approach Belsen without a host of assumptions. In April 1945 Belsen was projected as an atrocity site, de-ethnicised, deracinated and decontextualised. As such, it acquired initial popular currency. So much so, in fact, that it was possible for some writers in the late 1940s and 1950s to use it as a general purpose term for a scene of destruction. However, by the late 1990s Belsen was overdetermined as a place of Jewish suffering. Using an acute textual analysis, Kushner shows how a late twentieth-century understanding of the war and the genocide against the Jews has been superimposed on the historical record. He warns that just as the early neglect of the Jewish victims was a distortion of reality, this latest warp in the record is no less a perversion of the truth and one with potentially dangerous consequences. Kushner admonishes that Belsen is being instrumentalized and politicised to serve present needs at the cost of a truthful rendering of the past.

The manipulation of Belsen is not unique to Britain, though. Rainer Schulze describes how the site was always vulnerable to momentary exigencies. In the early years of the West German Federal Republic the site of the camp was turned into a carefully landscaped park, 'a place of beauty, and of reverence'.[10] This doubtless sincere goal had the added convenience of erasing any sign of what had been there. Even the mounds marking the mass graves carried anodyne inscriptions. It was not until the late 1960s that a rudimentary documentation centre was established on the initiative of the state of Lower Saxony to provide information for the curious visitor. This facility remained quite rudimentary until 1990 when it was expanded in the wake of the controversy over President Reagan's 1985 visit to Bitburg and Belsen. In 1998, following German unification, a commission recommended a major transformation and improvement of the Belsen *Gedenkstätte* (memorial site).

But what story would it tell? Rainer Schulze has himself taken part in the discussions about how to represent the different, contested memories that attach to Belsen. He explains how the proposed new documentation and visitor centre will be open-ended and inclusive while, at the same time, eschewing further interventions in the landscape of the site itself. Above all, the new exhibition will seek to rehumanise the victims, recording the names of as many as possible, thus restoring their individual identities.

Belsen was so complex, so vast, so appalling, so terrifying and so beyond the comprehension of those who encountered it during those fateful days in April 1945 that no comprehensive narrative may ever be possible. Yet the many voices and points of view that criss-cross the pages that follow are, perhaps, the best memorial that can be attained. We hope that this volume may play some part in preserving the memories of Belsen. If readers in future generations, stimulated by this special issue, continue to ask why, and to argue over what happened, then the lives that intersected and ended there, the awful and the good deeds that were done, will not be forgotten.

NOTES

1. The ceremony was recorded by the BBC. The order of the ceremony may be found in the commemorative brochure.
2. On Anne Frank's friendship with Goslar in Amsterdam and in Belsen, see Carol Ann Lee, *Roses from the Earth. The Biography of Anne Frank* (London: Viking, 1999), pp.27–8, 36–7, 96–7 and 189–90; and also Melissa Müller, *Anne Frank: The Biography*, trans. Rita and Robert Kimber (London: Bloomsbury, 1999), pp.51–4, 356–8, 261.
3. See Paul Oppenheimer, *From Belsen to Buckingham Place* (Laxton: Beth Shalom, 1996); and Neil Belton, *The Good Listener: Helen Bamber: A Life Against Cruelty* (London: Weidenfeld and Nicolson, 1998).
4. Max Paul Friedman, 'The U.S. State Department and the Failure to rescue: New Evidence of the Missed Opportunity at Bergen-Belsen', *Holocaust and Genocide Studies*, Vol.19, No.1 (2005), pp.26–50; Rainer Schulze, 'Keeping very clear of any "Kuh-Handel": The British Foreign Office and the Rescue of Jews from Bergen-Belsen', *Holocaust and Genocide Studies*, Vol.19, No.2 (2005), pp.226–51.
5. John Bridgman, *The End of the Holocaust: The Liberation of the Camps* (London: Batsford, 1990), pp.33–60; Jo Reilly *et al.* (eds.), *Belsen in History and Memory* (London: Frank Cass, 1997); Joanne Reilly, *Belsen: The Liberation of a Concentration Camp* (London: Routledge, 1998); Donald Bloxham *et al.* (eds.),

Remembering Belsen (London: Vallentine Mitchell, 2005).
6. Tony Kushner, *The Holocaust and the Liberal Imagination* (Oxford: Blackwell, 1994), pp.213–16; Janina Struck, *Photographing The Holocaust* (London: I.B. Tauris, 2004), pp.133–4.
7. Tom Segev, *The Seventh Million: The Israelis and the Holocaust*, trans. Haim Watzman (New York: Hill and Wang, 1993), p.185; Kushner, *The Holocaust and the Liberal Imagination*, pp.237–40; Peter Novick, *The Holocaust in American Life* (New York: Houghton Mifflin, 1999), pp.83–4.
8. For an insight into early research and publication projects in Palestine/Israel, see Roni Stauber, *Ideology and Memory: Holocaust and Heroism in Israeli Public Discourse in the 1950s* (London: Vallentine Mitchell, forthcoming 2006).
9. Barbie Zelizer, *Remembering To Forget: Holocaust Memory Through The Camera's Eye* (Chicago: University of Chicago Press, 1998), pp.86–140; Struck, *Photographing The Holocaust*, pp.124–38.
10. See below, p.219.

PART I
THE LIBERATION OF THE CAMP
AND THE MEDICAL RELIEF EFFORT

PART I

A Brief History of Bergen-Belsen

DAVID CESARANI

Bergen-Belsen is often described as a peculiar camp that did not conform to any of the types in the Nazi 'concentration camp universe'.[1] It is certainly true that it had a convoluted history, but this is only because it reflects the contorted development of Nazi racial policy and, pre-eminently, anti-Jewish policy. Bergen-Belsen was a crossroads for many paths taken by the Third Reich.

The area around the twin towns of Bergen and Belsen, situated on the Lüneberg Heath, was the location for barracks and training grounds for German army units between 1935–38. The basic infrastructure for a number of camps was laid down in this period and reflects the expansion of the German army set in motion by Hitler with the ultimate intention of fulfilling his expansionist goals. In May 1943 the Waffen-SS added a barrack complex, of which we will hear more.[2]

Once Hitler had launched Germany into war the area became home to POWs from various nationalities, changing in composition as the Germans extended the scope of their military operations. In 1940, 600 French and Belgian prisoners of war were held in a camp at Bergen-Belsen. After the German invasion of the Soviet Union began on 22 June 1941, POWs from the Red Army began to pour into the facilities that now existed there. The story of the Soviet POWs is a terrible one. About 100,000 of the two million men of the Red Army captured by the Germans during the first months of the invasion were transported to camps on the Lüneberg Heath. The Germans regarded them as barely human and did not observe the obligations to POWs under the Geneva Conventions. The camps had almost no sanitary facilities and food supplies were poor. Some 20,000–30,000 Soviet POWs were sent to Stalag XIC/ 311 at Bergen-Belsen. The lucky ones were transferred to work in labour camps serving German industry or on farms. Conditions for the rest were so appalling that men ate grass to survive and cases of cannibalism were recorded. They died at the rate of 100 per day. Between July 1941 and January 1942 it is estimated that approximately 11–14,000 Red Army men perished due to neglect, disease and malnutrition. In a chilling foretaste of what was to come, Stalag XIC/ 311 had the highest death rate of any POW camp in Germany.[3]

Another chilling portent is that from April 1943 to January 1945; part of the site was used as a hospital camp for sick POWs, including French, Dutch, Italians and Russians.[4] In Belsen, the meaning of healing and convalescence was consistently inverted.

If the pre-history of Belsen concentration camp reflects one aspect of Nazi racism and the wars of aggression waged by the Third Reich in the west and, especially, the east, the origins of the more familiar Jewish camp exemplify key elements of Nazi anti-Jewish policy. Bergen-Belsen is sometimes called the 'exchange camp' and it is fairly well known that, initially, Jews were held there as bargaining counters for Nazi schemes to exchange Jews who were considered to be of value to the Allies for Germans interned in Allied countries, for cash, or for diplomatic advantage.[5]

But where did this idea come from? The peculiar notion that Jews had monetary or political value and could be exchanged on a quid pro quo basis is rooted in Nazi antisemitic thought. The Nazis believed that the Jewish diaspora formed one corporate racial group and that Jews in one part of the world had a special loyalty to Jews in another part just by virtue of the fact that they were Jews. More importantly, they believed that Jews had enormous power and wealth.[6]

The Nazi leadership was convinced that if they threatened the well-being of German Jews, the Jews in Britain and America would respond by directing their governments to appease the Nazis. The fact that in the late 1930s the British and American governments were willing to hold international conferences, such as the meeting at Evian in 1938, to discuss the plight of Jewish refugees seemed proof to the Nazis that the Jews commanded authority. It did not seem to matter that the international discussions such as this, or the Bermuda conference in April 1943, did little good for the Jews.[7]

The German Foreign Ministry saw Jews in a more pragmatic but no less utilitarian light. During the war it took responsibility for bringing back to the Reich Germans who were abroad, including those interned by belligerent countries. Several thousand German nationals were held in internment camps by the British, mainly from amongst the 1,400 German settlers in Palestine. A few hundred were also detained in South Africa. Thousands more were later interned by the USA in North and South America. In 1941 and 1942, the German Foreign Ministry was behind several exchange schemes that succeeded in bringing German women and children to the Reich in return for interned British and American citizens.[8] In one such scheme in November 1942, the Jewish Agency succeeded in persuading the British to allow Palestinian Jews trapped in Poland by the war to be exchanged for German settlers from Palestine. Another scheme in July 1943 led to an exchange of Jews with Palestine connections, held by the Germans at a camp at Vittel, for Germans interned in South Africa.[9]

As the deportation of Jews from all over Europe to the death camps in Poland gathered pace during 1942, the German Foreign Office intervened with Office IVB4 of the Gestapo, under Adolf Eichmann, to hold back Jews with certain nationalities. This step was partly a gesture intended to defend the prerogatives of the Foreign Office against encroachments on its traditional areas of responsibility by Eichmann's office. Eichmann was responsible for carrying out the 'Final Solution' and regarded all Jews as fair game, but the Foreign Office argued that Jews who held the passports of neutral countries should be exempted from deportation for fear of provoking a diplomatic backlash from countries that objected to its citizens being arrested and hauled away. The Foreign Office was also keen to preserve a pool of exchangeable Jews.[10]

Meanwhile, Hitler, Himmler and the SS had their own ideas about the worth of certain Jews. In many speeches, Hitler had spoken of making the Jews under Nazi control pay a price for 'atrocity propaganda' in the democracies or holding them hostage as a guarantee that other powers stay out of Germany's business. Himmler shared this view. In December 1942, Himmler first proposed holding as hostages in a special camp 10,000 Jews from Western Europe who had connections with America. He also saw them as a potential source of foreign exchange because of various proposals from Jews to allow some to escape in return for cash. In early 1943 Eichmann initiated the steps to realise this idea. His office issued instructions detailing which nationalities were to be held back from deportation.[11]

In the course of negotiations between the SS and the German Foreign Office between March and May 1943, their respective plans to withhold certain Jews from deportation to the death camps, albeit for different ends, coalesced.[12] The Foreign Office and the SS leadership may have arrived by different routes at the idea for Bergen-Belsen as a camp for 'exchange Jews', but it could not have come into existence and would have had no rationale had it not been for the decision to embark on genocide against the Jews. They did not bargain for the sometimes obtuse, sometimes confused, and occasionally well-meaning if baffled response of the Allies. Tragically, when they had the opportunity to rescue Jews from Bergen-Belsen by means of these deals, officials in the Allied countries either failed to recognise the danger that Jews were facing or placed a higher priority on maintaining the blockade of Germany and eschewed any negotiations with the enemy. In this respect, Belsen is as much a part of the story of Allied reactions to the genocide waged against the Jews as it is part of that story itself.[13]

Already on 25 April 1943 the first group of concentration camp prisoners from concentration camp KL Natzweiler arrived at Bergen-Belsen to begin construction of the camp. Building progressed under the auspices of the WVHA – the Economic and Administrative Head Office of the SS. Three further groups arrived from Natzweiler and Buchenwald: 250 on 30 April, 150 on 7 May, and 200 on 19 May 1943. These 600 prisoners erected the barracks and were the first inmates of the new camp. They were held in a section called the 'prisoners camp' until they were transferred out in February 1944 to make room for incoming transports. The first commandant was Adolf Haas who was transferred from KL Niederhagen, the camp that initially supervised the building work and provided the core SS personnel. Haas had about 90 SS men under his command, some from Niederhagen and some recruited specially. Many of these were ethnic Germans.[14]

The first transport of Jews arrived in the 'special camp' on 29 April 1943, followed by another in mid-June. They were 2,400 Polish Jews who held papers issued by Central and South American countries. Theirs was a tragic story of false expectations and deception. The Nazis had already decided not to honour these diplomatic papers and most of the Jews were deported to Auschwitz in late 1943 and early 1944. The next influx, beginning in July 1943, was composed of 350 Sephardi Jews, mainly from Salonika, who were citizens of various neutral countries, mainly Spain, but also Turkey, Argentina and Portugal. They were held in a separate section of the special camp, known as the 'neutral camp', where they enjoyed relatively good conditions. In February 1944, after prolonged negotiations with the Spanish, some 365 Jews from the 'neutral camp' bearing authentic papers were despatched to the border of Spain and safety.[15]

Early in 1944, 3,670 'exchange' Jews were sent from the Netherlands and housed in what became known as the 'star camp', a fenced-off area of barracks where the prisoners were allowed to live in family groups, wearing their own clothes bearing the yellow Star of David. Some 200 Jews from North Africa, Belgium, France, Yugoslavia and Albania were also placed in the 'star camp', giving it a strangely cosmopolitan atmosphere. Few were actually ever exchanged, though. In July 1944, 222 Jews with ties to Palestine were allowed to depart for Haifa. In January 1945, 136 Jews with genuine South American papers were permitted to enter Switzerland. The rest endured worsening conditions in the 'star camp'.[16]

Life in the 'star camp' was relatively benign compared to concentration camps and ghettos. But it was still harsh. The inmates subsisted on poor food with little nutritional value, supplemented by occasional food parcels that reached them from the JDC and the Red Cross. They had to perform work tasks, notably dismantling shoes for recycling. And they suffered endless roll calls administered by brutal SS guards.[17] However, they struggled to create some semblance of normality – especially for the 684 children in the camp. Rudimentary schooling was provided in secret, and the significant proportion of Orthodox Jews who had been allowed to bring prayer books and prayer shawls with them maintained an active religious life.[18]

In stark and bewildering contrast to the situation of the 'exchange Jews', in March 1944 1,000 sick and exhausted prisoners from the concentration camp Dora-Mittelbau were sent to Belsen for 'convalescence'. In fact they were dumped in the old 'prisoners camp' with almost no accommodation or facilities. Only 57 survived.[19]

Then, in July 1944 the camp reflected yet another stage in the 'Final Solution' – the deportation of the Hungarian Jews. German forces had occupied Hungary on 19 March 1944 and imposed a collaborationist government that eagerly co-operated with a special SS unit under Eichmann that was charged with organising the ghettoisation, despoliation, and deportation of the 750,000 Jews on Hungarian territory. Between May and June 1944, Jewish leaders in Budapest had tried desperately to make a deal with the Nazis to save Jewish lives. The negotiations took a bizarre and horrifying twist when the Nazis proposed exchanging one million Jews for 10,000 trucks and supplies that the Third Reich urgently needed. While a Jewish envoy from Budapest, Joel Brand, conveyed this 'offer' via Istanbul to the rightly suspicious and dilatory Allies, his colleague Rudolf Kasztner tried to spin out the talks. In the absence of any official Allied response to the barter proposal, Kasztner succeeded in persuading Eichmann to spare one trainload of Jews from deportation as a gesture of 'good faith' intended to encourage the Allies. As a result, in July 1944, 1,684 Jews were dispatched to Belsen and accommodated in a demarcated area known as the 'Hungarian camp'. They would reach Switzerland a few months before the end of the war after further, tortuous negotiations between the Nazis and Jewish representatives.[20]

The extension of the 'Final Solution' to Hungary led to other changes in the camp. In August 1944, 4,000 mainly Hungarian women arrived. They were joined by women from camps and ghettos in Poland and formed a separate 'women's camp'. However, there was no proper accommodation for them and they lived in tents. As more transports arrived, barracks were cleared for them in the 'star camp'.[21] Amongst the new women arrivals from Plaszow and Auschwitz were Margot and Anne Frank whose health quickly deteriorated in the squalid environment.[22]

The camp was now becoming seriously overcrowded and the situation was deteriorating. An outbreak of typhus was quickly approaching epidemic proportions. The camp authorities withdrew most of the privileges enjoyed in the 'special camps' and imposed a regimen common to other concentration camps. Because Bergen-Belsen was under the SS-WVHA and was not a civilian internment camp, there was no fear of intrusions by the Red Cross. However, things were about to get even worse. In December 1944, Josef Kramer, formerly commandant of Auschwitz, replaced Haas. He brought with him new personnel, swelling the SS contingent to 277 men and 12 women guards. Kramer imposed the standard regimen of the concentration camp throughout Belsen, including the *kapo* system which led to the appointment of brutal ex-Auschwitz inmates to run barracks and work parties. Under Kramer, conditions in the camp worsened catastrophically. When he took over, its population numbered about 15,000. Belsen now received thousands of prisoners evacuated from camps in the path of the advancing Red Army, including Auschwitz and Ravensbruck. By March the number of inmates reached 42,000 and in April peaked at 60,000.[23]

At the best of times the camp could barely cope with the numbers it had originally been designed to hold. The 'star camp' possessed one washroom with 12 taps for 4,000 inmates, and the number of prisoners rocketed during early 1945. The 'prisoners camp' had no sanitary facilities at all and no water supply. Due to the dislocation caused to German lines of communication by the Allied advance and sustained bombing, food supplies began to run out – although ample stocks were available at the nearby Panzer Training School if the SS had wanted to take emergency measures to feed the camp. When the water supply for the entire camp was disrupted by nearby bombing, the inmates were forced to drink from contaminated puddles. Despite the earlier establishment of a camp hospital, medical facilities and stocks of medicine were almost non-existent. The typhus epidemic finally ran out of control. In February 1945, 7,000 inmates died of disease, malnutrition and exposure. The fatalities soared to 18,000 in March. Some 9,000 lost their lives in the first part of April and, tragically, 14,000 died after the liberation.[24]

Amidst this chaos, Himmler continued to play out the Nazi fantasies. On 10 March, he issued vain orders to combat the typhus epidemic and so protect his bargaining asset. He still believed that Jews could be used to broker a deal with the Allies and used Red Cross channels to explore the possibilities. Meanwhile, the camp administration attempted to reduce numbers by evacuating 7,000 prisoners to Theresienstadt on 6–11 April. Yet there were tensions between the leadership of the SS head office, the RSHA, that was happy to go on tormenting Jews, and Himmler himself who wanted to appear as their saviour. In early April, Himmler appointed an SS colonel, Kurt Becher, to oversee the concentration camps remaining under German control and ensure the safety of Belsen. But by this time Kramer had realised that the situation was hopeless. With his knowledge, on 12 April German army commanders in the area opened negotiations for the surrender of the camp to the approaching British forces. The liberation of Bergen-Belsen was about to take place.[25]

NOTES

1. Christine Lattek, 'Bergen-Belsen: From "Privileged" Camp to Death Camp', in Jo Reilly *et al.* (eds.), *Belsen in History and Memory* (London: Frank Cass, 1997), p.46; Richard Breitman, 'Himmler and Bergen-Belsen', in ibid., p.72. For a full history of Belsen, see Eberhard Kolb, *Bergen-Belsen: Geschichte des 'Aufenthaltslagers' 1943–1945* (Hannover: Verlag für Literatur und Zeitgeschehen, 1962), revised and reprinted as *Bergen-Belsen 1943 bis 1945* (Göttingen: Vandenhoeck & Ruprecht, 1996). References below are to the most recent version. An English version of the 1985 edition was published as *Bergen-Belsen: From 'Detention Camp' to Concentration Camp, 1943–1945*, trans. Gregory Claeys and Christine Lattek (Göttingen: Vandenhoeck & Ruprecht, 1986 edn.).
2. Alexandra-Eileen Wenk, *Zwischen Menschenhandel und Endlösung* (Paderborn: Schöningh, 2000), pp.94–5.
3. Ibid., pp.95–6, 97–100, 102–6; Lattek, 'Bergen-Belsen', pp.44–5.
4. Wenk, *Zwischen Menschenhandel und Endlösung*, pp.100–2.
5. Gerald Reitlinger, *The Final Solution* (London: Sphere, 1971), first published 1951 and revised 1961, pp.364–5; Jacob Presser, *Ashes in the Wind: The Destruction of Dutch Jewry*, trans. Arnold Pomerans (Detroit: Wayne State University Press, 1988), first published in Dutch in 1965 and in English in 1965, pp.5512–15; Leni Yahil, *The Holocaust: The Fate of European Jewry*, trans. Ina Friedman and Haya Galai (New York: Oxford University Press, 1990), first published 1987, pp.416–17.
6. Breitman, 'Himmler and Bergen-Belsen', pp.72–82. For a recent, exhaustive discussion, see Shlomo Aronson, *Hitler, the Allies, and the Jews* (Cambridge: Cambridge University Press, 2004).
7. Wenk, *Zwischen Menschenhandel und Endlösung*, pp.38–44.
8. Kolb, *Bergen-Belsen 1943 bis 1945*, pp.21–4; Kolb, *Bergen-Belsen: From 'Detention Camp' to Concentration Camp*, pp.20–2; Wenk, *Zwischen Menschenhandel und Endlösung*, pp. 57–67.
9. Dina Porat, *The Blue and the Yellow Stars of David* (Cambridge, MA: Harvard University Press, 1990), pp.144–8.
10. David Cesarani, *Eichmann: His Life and Crimes* (London: Heinemann, 2004), pp.123–4.
11. Kolb, *Bergen-Belsen: From 'Detention Camp' to Concentration Camp*, p.23 and facsimile of entry in Himmler's *Vortragsnotizen*, 10 December 1943, noting a discussion with Hitler at which a special camp for Jews with connections to America was raised; Wenk, *Zwischen Menschenhandel und Endlösung*, pp.82–4.

12. Wenk, *Zwischen Menschenhandel und Endlösung*, pp.84–93.
13. Max Paul Freidman, 'The U.S. State Department and the Failure to Rescue: New Evidence of the Missed Opportunity at Bergen-Belsen', *Holocaust and Genocide Studies*, Vol.19, No.1 (2005), pp.26–50; Rainer Schulze, 'Keeping very clear of any "Kuh-Handel": The British Foreign Office and the Rescue of Jews from Bergen-Belsen', *Holocaust and Genocide Studies*, Vol.19, No.2 (2005), pp.226–51. Compare to Kolb, *Bergen-Belsen: From 'Detention Camp' to Concentration Camp*, p.27.
14. Wenk, *Zwischen Menschenhandel und Endlösung*, pp.116–18.
15. Kolb, *Bergen-Belsen 1943 bis 1945*, pp.27–9; Kolb, *Bergen-Belsen: From 'Detention Camp' to Concentration Camp*, pp.24–7.
16. Lattek, 'Bergen-Belsen', pp.44–6.
17. Ibid., pp.46–52.
18. See Thomas Rahe, 'Jewish Religious Life in the Concentration Camp Bergen-Belsen', in Reilly *et al.* (eds.), *Belsen*, pp.85–121.
19. Lattek, 'Bergen-Belsen', pp.52–4.
20. This tangled episode is explained in Yehuda Bauer, *Jews for Sale? Nazi–Jewish Negotiations, 1933–1945* (New Haven, CT: Yale University Press, 1994), pp.145–221.
21. Lattek, 'Bergen-Belsen', p.54.
22. For the experiences of Anne Frank and her family in Belsen in these last months, see Carol Ann Lee, *Roses From the Earth: The Biography of Anne Frank* (London: Viking, 1999), pp.179–84, 189–91, 194–8.
23. Kolb, *Bergen-Belsen 1943 bis 1945*, pp.35–41; Lattek, 'Bergen-Belsen', pp.55–9.
24. Kolb, *Bergen-Belsen 1943 bis 1945*, pp.42–61; Lattek, 'Bergen-Belsen', pp.55–9.
25. Breitman, 'Himmler and Bergen-Belsen', pp.78–81. On Kramer's selective misgivings, see John Bridgman, *The End of the Holocaust: The Liberation of the Camps* (London: Batsford, 1990), pp.40–7.

A Survivor's Memories of Liberation

ANITA LASKER-WALLFISCH

I will give you a brief account of my background and how I came to be an inmate of Belsen. I was born in Germany, in a town called Breslau. In July 2005, this will have been 80 years ago. Now Breslau is in Poland, and it is called Wroclaw. My father was a lawyer. My mother was a very fine violinist. I had two sisters, we all learned to play musical instruments. On Sundays we had to speak French, which I thought was completely stupid, but my father maintained that a person has as many souls as he has languages, and today I know that he was right. I'm looking back at a very happy childhood where being Jewish did not seem to be a particular problem.

The clouds gathered in the thirties with all the implications, which I don't have to go into here. All efforts at emigration failed dismally. Partly because they were started too late, but mainly because of the difficulties made by governments of countries that might have saved my parents, along with many, many others, from their ultimate fate. The inevitable happened, my parents were deported and on the 9th April 1942, 63 years ago, they were sent to a place called Isbica, near Lublin. I never saw them again. I was 16 years old.

My sister and I had been conscripted to work in a paper factory, making toilet rolls. We were arrested by the Gestapo in the same year, and sent to prison, because we had been caught forging papers for French POWs and had tried to escape ourselves, posing as French factory workers. After over a year in prison I was sent to Auschwitz and after a year in Auschwitz I was sent to Belsen. In Auschwitz I had the great good fortune to be a member of the camp orchestra, or *Lagerkapelle* as it was called, which gave me at least a temporary chance of survival.

We have seen a great deal of Auschwitz-Birkenau this year, 2005, as we commemorated the liberation of this infamous place, and there will be few people who have not at least a tiny inkling of the horror that reigned there. When in May/June 1944 thousands upon thousands of Hungarian Jews poured into the camp, the death machinery could no longer cope. The crematoria worked around the clock, gassing, burning, murdering and those that could not fit into the gas chambers were thrown into the flames alive. We had no information about events outside the camp. We existed from day to day, always wondering how long this would last.

And then one day, at the end of October, the dreaded moment came. We had to line up – Jews to one side, Aryans to the other, and this could only mean one thing – the gas chamber. But a miracle happened – the Russian front had advanced, and believe it or not we were going to be sent to another camp. To actually put a distance between oneself and the murder factory of Auschwitz seemed nothing short of a miracle. Of course, we didn't know what was awaiting us on our arrival at the new destination. We were issued with some really atrocious outfits, certainly most inadequate for the temperature of the time of the year. But I managed, with great cunning, to retain my red jumper which I had been wearing day and night in Auschwitz. I kept wearing it day and night until the liberation some six months later. You can see it now, resting in a glass case in the Discovery section of the Holocaust Exhibition at the Imperial War Museum.

We were loaded into cattle trucks and began our journey westwards. Rumours circulated that we were going to a convalescent camp, and that it was called Bergen-Belsen. Nobody had ever heard of it. Although we were no longer an orchestra we were a group of people who had already survived against impossible odds and it was obvious from the beginning that we were going to stick together, come what may. We kept ourselves going through these freezing nights by singing our respective orchestral parts and trying to create some warmth for ourselves by huddling together. One day the train stopped, in the middle of nowhere, and then came the usual shouts – *'Raus, schnell, schnell'*. We had to group ourselves in rows of five and started marching. There was not a living soul about. It was freezing cold and the road seemed endless.

Eventually we reached the entrance of the camp. Belsen did not look then what you have come to know now. The mountains of corpses were not there yet – that was yet to come. We just stood there and saw some creatures milling about. They were pretty dishevelled-looking. We observed someone with a Kapo armband scraping out an obviously empty soup vat, and my sister remarked drily: 'If a Kapo needs to do that things must be pretty bad here'. She was right – things were pretty bad, but not as bad as they were to become.

There were some 3,000 people on our transport, and there were simply no barracks there for us. We were herded into vast tents, completely exhausted, and just flopped down on the bare ground. It needs a great deal of imagination to appreciate what this meant in reality. We were completely exhausted and just sat there and waited for God knows what. And then came the famous storm, the tents collapsed on top of us, in the middle of the night. How we survived that night I shall never understand. Somehow we managed to scramble free and just stood there in the pouring rain and howling storm. The next morning we were led to a shoe-bunker and remained there for some days. There was hardly any room to move but we were glad to have a roof over our heads. And then suddenly, and inexplicably, there were barracks available for us. We shall never know how this was achieved, but we had our suspicions.

After some weeks of sitting around and doing nothing, we were put to work in what was called the *Weberei*. We had to plait strips of cellophane into a sort of *ersatz* rope. The dying had started. I remember the first body in our block, the first body. With the advancing Allied troops the brave Germany shrunk in size and camps were being emptied in an attempt to cover any trace of them ever having existed. Thousands upon thousands of prisoners were made to march – the famous Death Marches had begun. The sight of these poor people arriving in Belsen, some of them on their knees, defies description. Thousands had perished on the way.

Conditions deteriorated more and more, bodies became so commonplace that one just simply ignored them. The watery so-called soup we got became irregular and eventually stopped all together. Typhus raged and people dropped dead like flies. The mountains of corpses grew higher and higher, and those of us who were still able to walk were given some string. We had to tie the arms of the dead together and drag them along the *Lager Strasse* to a big ditch, but this operation was soon abandoned as futile. There were too many corpses and we were too weak.

By now it was April, and very hot, and the bodies started to decompose. The stench must have been horrendous. We didn't notice it. We saw fewer and fewer guards and somehow felt that the end must be near. For days we had heard rumbling noises of heavy artillery, but we didn't know who was firing. We had no idea what was happening and suddenly, it was about midday, the noise came closer and then a voice through a loudhailer, first in English, then in German. At first we were too confused to take it in, but the announcement kept being repeated again and again, and at last we understood. British troops stood before the camp gate.

'Please keep calm. You are liberated'.

We were also told – this was no news to us – that there was typhus in the camp and that we should wait for the troops to come in. We should be patient. Medical help was on the way. It took a while for the significance of these announcements to sink in. When the first jeep finally rolled into the camp, we looked at our liberators in silence. We were so suspicious.

The date was Sunday April 15th 1945, and the time of the liberation was approximately 5 o'clock. A date no one would ever forget. The nightmare had come to an end. After years of living for the moment, and if you were lucky, for the next day, there was suddenly space in front of us. It was very hard to believe. I was 19 years old, and I felt like 90. I doubt that anything could ever match the feeling of relief, incredulity and gratitude that began to seep into our consciousness as we slowly dared to acknowledge that it was true. We were alive, and the soldiers walking about the camp were not our enemies.

I recently learnt that when Richard Dimbleby reported what he found when he went to Belsen, the BBC had to send someone to check that he was not exaggerating. Well, he wasn't. The period that followed the liberation is a long story in itself. What the British Army had to cope with was simply mind-boggling. Thousands of corpses and thousands of starved and half-dead people, with no identity, displaced persons. The catastrophe was without precedent. After the tremendous elation of having survived came the sobering realisation that one had lost everything – family, home, everything. And then one had to realise that one had to start over again.

And that was not all. We had to find a country that would allow us to do that. Believe me, this was not exactly easy. Endless difficulties were put in our way. And it took me over a year before I finally achieved my dream and I began a new life in this country. I think everyone who was liberated in Belsen will join me in a very, very big thank you not only to our liberators but equally to all the people, here at the Imperial War Museum who created, with such unstinting devotion, a lasting memorial to these terrible things. Thank you.

The First Day in the Camp

MAJOR DICK WILLIAMS

17 April 1945 was just another day. That was, until midday. I was a Staff Captain in the Supplies and Transport branch of Headquarters 8th Corps. I got the message to go and report to Brigadier Glyn Hughes, who was our Chief Medical Officer of 8th Corps. It seems a senior German officer had come to our front line under a white flag and wanted to see our Corps Commander. He told the Corps Commander that there was a camp in the direct line that our troops were advancing and he wanted to make arrangements so that fighting could bypass that camp and that they would withdraw.

The Corps Commander agreed, and he sent his second in command back with that German officer to work out the military details. At the same time he instructed Brigadier Glyn Hughes to go forward and find out exactly what this camp comprised of, and the conditions there. Brigadier Glyn Hughes then called for a representative from our side of the Royal Army Service Corps to accompany him and check on food and water.

Our major role in life was the carriage of ammunition, petrol and rations, in support of our fighting Divisions, so I suppose that we were probably the right people to send a representative. I was picked to be that one. In addition there was to be a member from the Royal Engineers, an officer from the Military Government and there was a Jewish padre, Leslie Hardman.

We went forward under white flags and followed the instructions to find the camp, which was something like 14 km up the Bergen road from Celle, which at that time was the front line.

When we arrived at that particular point on the road it was just dense woods on each side. There was a small cutting into the wood on the left hand side. There was nothing visible on the main road at all, no signs, absolutely nothing, just the road going through the middle of the forest. We went down that small cutting, and as we went round the bend in it, there we saw – the first sign was a German sentry box – one of these horrible red, black and white striped things – a barrier which had been put across the road, red and white, was in the lifted position. Behind that was a huge wall of barbed wire. Luckily the gates were open and we went straight through.

Inside and obviously waiting for us, with all the SS on parade there, were Commandant Kramer and Irma Grese, the head of the women's side – obviously expecting us.

My role was food and water. Two armed SS were detailed off to show me the way through the camp to where the cookhouses were to be found. We had to actually be very careful as we went on, because covering the ground, throughout the camp, were just piles of this horrible striped uniform, the emaciated faces and shaven heads, sunken eyes. Just everywhere, some hanging on the barbed wire, some lying, some trying to stand. As we went through, two tried to come forward to speak to me, but the SS bashed them on one side.

As you know, there was absolutely no food or water in that camp. I went through all the five cookhouses that were there to supply the camp, and all I found was about 50lb of rotten turnips – that was the total food inside the camp. I went back to report to Brigadier Glyn Hughes and told him what I'd found. He said to me - he'd obviously been into the camp himself by that time, it must have been possibly an hour later - his two priorities would be to 'bury the dead and to get the living out of there'. He told me to go back to Corps Headquarters, see my Colonel, and arrange to bring fresh water and rations as quickly as possible, if not sooner. I went out, after that meeting with him, and told my Colonel what I had found there, and the thousands and thousands we had to feed, and the thousands and thousands that lay dead and had to be buried. He organised immediately to have water tankers provided to tow behind our normal vehicles, and the next day I was able to take in the first food and fresh water into the camp.

We had enormous trouble moving the vehicles down to the cookhouses and getting things started, but very luckily the Engineers who had come in with me in the first party also had support and they were able to get the water supply reconnected and the electricity. Without that particular help our job would have been more impossible than it was at the time.

We realised that people had just put up with the pains of

THE FIRST DAY IN THE CAMP

starvation, and it was starvation and dehydration that had killed all the people who were left lying throughout the camp. Apart from those who had already died and were piled up into stacks - maybe 8 feet high and about 30 feet long. The bodies were just being piled one on top of each other, naked and rotting, with no human benevolence at all.

We started to break open the army rations, which was the only food we had. We broke open the composite ration boxes, and made bulk supplies available of tea. So we got the kettles going and started – our first idea was to get as much hot tea as we could available for those who could come and take it. We realised also that we had to tell them not to drink too much, because with their shrunken stomachs it could probably have been worse than not having anything at all. The same with the food stuffs. We watered that down to make it as close as we could into something like soup. We realised that solid food was absolutely a non-starter, because of the condition of the people, and we didn't want to further injure those who had already suffered starvation.

Anita Lasker-Wallfisch has eloquently described the conditions of the camp and what they had had to put up with. I would like to tell you a little bit as to how the Army faced and overcame the problems that confronted them as liberators of that particular camp.

As I've explained to you, my role was the beginning of the food supply, but the biggest problem was for the Royal Army Medical people. Their first job was to sort out the living from the dead, and that must have been a terrible decision for them to make, because two lying side by side, it was very difficult to tell one from the other at that particular time, so their medical skills came into play straight away making that first big decision. It was their initial tender care of those who they decided were alive, to fan the small sparks of life, and bring a glow for their eventual liberation.

They made huge efforts to bring some life back to these people, introducing the 'human laundry' which was actually one of the biggest innovations that they ever started and that exactly fitted the circumstances that faced them. The other arms of the Army played their part – it was the Engineers who miraculously got the water and the electricity connected very, very quickly. So it must have been in the capability of the SS to keep those supplies going if they'd wanted to. Other Engineers provided the bulldozers which dug the mass graves and later on were used to move some of the decomposing bodies from these huge stacks into their final resting places in those trenches. I met one of those bulldozer operators ten years ago at Belsen. He could not stay away from Belsen, he had to go back every year. The sights and the duties he had to perform at that time were still with him.

The Artillery also played a key role. An Anti-Tank Regiment came and were put in charge of the SS. The SS were given the task of collecting all the dead bodies left lying about from all over the camp, loading them onto trailers and taking them through to the mass burial trenches which the bulldozers had dug. Some of the SS decided that they would make a break for it; they were shot down, and their colleagues were sent after them, and I'm afraid they went into the pits as well.

Also, we must make note of the corps of chaplains who came forward. Not only was Rabbi Leslie Hardman there, but later more chaplains came, and brought comfort to the living and blessing to the dead.

I think of all the acts which took place in the war, nothing could have been more cruel than the inhuman act of depriving human beings of food and water, when it was well within their capability to keep supplies going. Because just outside the main concentration camp itself there was an army tank barracks. A couple of days after I had been there, I went exploring and in that barracks there was a fully working bakery and a lot of foodstuffs which would have been ideal to meet the conditions inside the camp. I asked why had they not been used, and I was told the answer, that the SS were just not interested.

So although events, by the piling up of more and more people into that confined area, obviously aggravated the whole situation, I make no excuse for the SS at all in this. It must have compounded what was getting completely out of hand. We had seen the very worst of what the SS was able to do to innocent people. To all the survivors, many of them are here now who were children at the time, and all those who died, I say to them 'Please God, never again'.

The Medical Relief Effort at Belsen

BEN SHEPHARD

This essay will address the two main questions which the story of the medical relief of Bergen-Belsen in 1945 poses in the mind of the modern reader. They are, firstly, why were the British not medically prepared for what they found at Belsen? And, secondly, why did so many people – nearly 14,000 – die *after* the British entered the camp? It should be stressed that only broad answers to those questions can be given here: readers looking for more detailed explanations should turn elsewhere.[1]

Firstly, why were the British not prepared for Belsen? One possible answer to that question was given recently by Rabbi Irving Greenberg, formerly Chair of the United States Holocaust Memorial Council. 'The Holocaust did not end on VE Day', Rabbi Greenberg told a conference in 2000:

> The organised mass killing stopped but the dying went on. Out of tragic lack of understanding of the condition of survivors, prisoners in such camps as Dachau were fed food too rich for starvation-reduced stomachs and died. This mishandling reflected Allied ignorance and failure to plan, which in turn mirrored the democracies' lack of concern for the fate of the Jews. Even in Bergen–Belsen, the Holocaust claimed 14,000 additional victims during the two months after the liberation.[2]

Greenberg's argument is threefold: the Allies, he says, were indifferent to the fate of the Jews; therefore they did not plan to help them; and, as a result, people died unnecessarily. It also conflates two issues which have hitherto been kept separate and are generally known as *rescue* and *relief*. The *rescue* of the Jews – should the Allies have bombed Auschwitz, and so on – has generated an enormous literature over the past decades; I shall not add to it here. But much less has been written about *relief* – what could have been done to help the survivors of the camps. It is the question of relief which will be addressed in this essay.³

Rabbi Greenberg's statement that there was a failure to plan, born of the now well-documented indifference of the Allies to the fate of the Jews, is an oversimplification. There was, in fact, a good deal of planning in 1943–45: the aftermath of Hitler's downfall was as elaborately prepared for as the aftermath of the removal of Saddam Hussein was not. It was just that the planning was not specifically targeted at the needs of concentration camp survivors.

There are two aspects to this: how the problem was conceptualised; and how it was prepared for – the organisational steps that were taken.

First, the concept. In the early years of the war, between 1940 and 1943, a torrent of books and publications appeared in Britain and the United States foretelling what the end of the war would be like: *Relief and Reconstruction in Europe*; *Medical Relief in Europe*; *Children in Bondage*; *Starvation in Europe*; *When Hostilities Cease*, and so on. The British contributors fell into two main categories. On the one hand, such great and good people as Leonard Woolf, Julian Huxley, Harold Laski and Gilbert Murray, all agreed that the Nazis would bequeath to Europe an apocalypse: its worst crisis since the 30 Years War in the seventeenth century, worse than the aftermath of the Great War; an apocalypse attended by the usual horsemen – famine, epidemics of diseases like typhus, and millions of refugees; a humanitarian catastrophe which would require new, international mechanisms of aid and reconstruction to address. At the same time, doctors and relief workers who had worked on the aftermath of war a generation before offered more specialised assessments of the challenges to come and the technical measures to be taken.⁴

Why then was this expertise not brought to bear at Belsen? In many ways it was – but by a rather indirect route.

The intellectual pressure in the early wartime years produced the dominant concept in planning for post-war relief, that of the 'Displaced Person' or DP. Throughout 1945, even as late as 1950, Allied soldiers and relief workers referred to Jewish camp survivors as 'Displaced Persons' – the 'Holocaust survivor' is of course a 1970s construct.⁵

Was this wrong? It is true, as Bernard Wasserstein, Louise London, and other historians have shown, that British policymakers

THE MEDICAL RELIEF EFFORT AT BELSEN

systematically and deliberately played down the specifically anti-Jewish nature of Nazi genocide. On the other hand, millions of people had indeed been displaced all over Europe. The genocide of the Jews was contained within a larger cataclysm.[6]

On the organisational side, the Allies recognised that new mechanisms would be needed to address the likely aftermath of the war and to deal with the problems of the Displaced Persons, and so they created a new international organisation, the United Nations Relief and Rehabilitation Administration (UNRRA) in late 1943. Unfortunately, however, UNRRA proved ineffectual – for several reasons. It was poorly led by the former Governor of New York State, Herbert Lehman; it failed, in the middle of the war, to attract properly qualified staff; and it did not win the respect of the military. In early 1945 UNRRA was supposed to put 450 relief teams in the field with the Allied armies; it managed only eight.[7]

And so, in practice, the problem of the Displaced Person fell mainly to the military. They saw DPs primarily as obstacles – refugees who would get in their way, as fleeing civilians had hampered the British in France in 1940; and their plans, accordingly, were mainly designed to round up DPs in assembly centres, sort them by nationality, and then send them home. The military took on some high-level civilian advisers (such as the British nutritionist, Sir Jack Drummond), but their operational procedures did not draw on medical expertise with civilians after the First World War. An American soldier, hastily redeployed to an Army DP team in April 1945, was given minimal training and sent to minister to DPs with only 'a personal bottle of aspirin and a tube of penicillin eye-ointment by way of medical supplies'.[8]

There was, though, one important exception to this. A *national* medical relief agency, the United States Typhus Commission, created by President Roosevelt in 1940, did collaborate successfully with the military. It had also seen the potential of the insecticide DDT as a weapon against typhus and developed the technology for spraying it. As Paul Weindling has pointed out, the breakthrough came when Fred Soper of the Rockefeller Institute 'invented a DDT spraying gun suitable for spraying clothed persons, overcoming the difficulty of persuading Muslim women to remove their clothing. This device to improve civilian compliance was hailed as a quick and easy method of tackling reservoirs of infection when the Allies organised trial DDT-dusting programmes in Morocco, Tunis, and Sicily'. This technology also proved highly effective in fighting typhus in Naples in 1943 and, building on this experience, the Commission had assembled huge supplies of DDT and anti-typhus vaccine prior to the Allied arrival in Germany.[9]

Two other general points should be borne in mind. Firstly, Jewish groups failed significantly to influence the Allied relief agenda. For reasons which historians have not adequately explored, the well-funded, long-established, well-respected American Joint Jewish Distribution Committee was kept out of the German camps by the US military until June 1945; while in Britain, the newly founded Jewish Committee for Relief Abroad was not among the aid organisations which banded together, under the Red Cross banner, to assist the military in relief work in Europe.[10]

Secondly, other issues preoccupied the British agencies – most notably, the consequences of the British policy of economic blockade. The Oxford Committee for Famine Relief, Oxfam, was established in 1942, specifically to lobby the British government to mitigate the effects of the blockade, arguing that while 'economic warfare' did little damage to the Germans themselves, it inflicted needless suffering on millions of people in German-occupied Europe. The campaign had some effect – the blockade was slightly relaxed in the case of Greece, after some 200,000 Greeks had died of starvation in 1941–42 – but otherwise Churchill and his ministers remained adamant. Even after the invasion of North-West Europe, the threat of starvation remained: the crisis preoccupying Allied relief workers in early 1945 was not Belsen but the prospect of starvation in northern Holland.[11]

What Did the British Know About Belsen?

The Foreign Office and Colonial Office knew about Bergen-Belsen camp because it was from there that many of the prominent Zionists who were exchanged for Germans in Palestine in July 1944 came. British consular officials in Lisbon and Istanbul were instructed to get information on the place; in the early months of 1945, languid efforts were made to get the Germans to allow international inspections. And then, mystifyingly, in March 1945, a security officer in Liverpool interviewed a certain Dr Levy, a Belsen prisoner holding Turkish nationality, who had recently been released from the camp and was in passage by ship from Stockholm to Istanbul, on behalf of the Prisoners of War departments of the Foreign and War Office.[12] There *may* be a connection between this event and the fact that the first British troops to enter Belsen were from the SAS: they went in and removed a member of their unit, a man called Jenkinson. How did they know he was there? How did they extract him so quickly? It is not clear. It seems bizarre that, because of the fetish of official secrecy which cloaks the deeds of the SAS, we still have to rely on anecdotal accounts of this episode by elderly veterans. The British Ministry of Defence should long ago have released all surviving information.[13]

But whatever contacts there may have between the War Office and the SAS, there is no evidence that the regular British units which had to confront this problem – 11th Armoured Division, VIII Corps, Second Army – had any foreknowledge; except in the sense that they had already come across camps which, if nothing like as frightful as Belsen, had contained starving prisoners of war and slave labourers.[14]

We come now to the 'but surely' argument. 'But surely', a German television producer said to me, 'the British must have been expecting something like Belsen, because the Russians had liberated Auschwitz in January 1945 and the Americans had gone into Buchenwald two days earlier. They must have known'. When, however, you look at what actually happened – rather than make assumptions from chronology, the premises underlying that statement disappear. Firstly, 'for reasons that are not completely clear, the Soviet government did not give the publicity to the liberation of Auschwitz that it lavished on the liberation of Majdanek [in July 1944]; indeed, it seemed determined to prevent the world from finding out anything about Auschwitz and what happened there'.[15] It took two months for the Russians to respond to Foreign Office enquiries, the only English-language account of the camp appeared in an obscure Polish journal, and when the Russians did finally publish an account of the liberation of Auschwitz – on 7 May 1945 – it 'was buried in the news of the unconditional surrender of Germany. The general public took almost no notice of the story'. Secondly, although, by contrast, the entry of elements of the United States First Army into Buchenwald on 11 April, generated enormous publicity (for many reasons), the time interval between that event and the British arrival at Belsen was too short, in the state of communications then existing, for its significance to have filtered through to front-line units of the British Army.[16]

Why Did So Many Die? The Medical Relief Effort

On 12 April 1945, two *Wehrmacht* officers approached elements of 11th Armoured Division, offering a truce in the area around Belsen because typhus had broken out in the camp. Three days later, on 15 April, the Deputy Director of Medical Services (DDMS) of British Second Army, Brigadier H.L. Glyn Hughes, reached the camp. The following day he carried out an inspection and made a plan.[17]

Hughes found in the region of 60,000–65,000 people divided between two sites. 'Belsen' proper, the original camp, contained between 40,000 and 45,000 prisoners crowded into some 90 huts apportioned between five separate camps. Conditions here were dreadful, with typhus, starvation and dysentery widespread. Hughes estimated that 70 per cent of the inmates would need to be hospitalised. There were also many thousands of unburied bodies. About a mile and a half away, a further 15,000-plus prisoners were crammed into part of a *Wehrmacht* Panzer Training School. These inmates, mainly men, had only recently arrived from other camps and were in better health; there was starvation and dysentery but no typhus.[18]

Hughes's plan involved simple triage – to evacuate the 'fit' and those of the sick thought capable of surviving to a hospital to be improvised in the Panzer Training School, while leaving the doomed to die. His problem was that, with the war still going on and the whole British army committed, transport was stretched to the limit, and many of the Rhine bridges were still unusable. Consequently, there were few resources immediately available. The British force which began the medical relief effort on 18 April consisted of two Field Hygiene Units, a Casualty Clearing Station (a mobile hospital with 8 doctors, 8 nurses and back-up) and a Light Field Ambulance, plus garrison and Military Government troops. The commander of 32 CCS, Lt Colonel James Johnston, who became the senior medical officer at Belsen, while Glyn Hughes remained with Second Army, later recalled thinking that he could have done with 12 General British Hospitals, each capable of treating 1,200 patients; instead he had about 300 men.[19]

So far as is known, neither Hughes nor Johnston was involved in the first initiative the British took – to rush supplies of food and water to the camp. On the evening of 16 April, after a day of frantic activity, a convoy of water tankers and lorries carrying rations arrived at Belsen and, after an abortive attempt to provide them with hot stew, the inmates were issued with Army 'compo rations'. British commanders expressed quiet satisfaction with their efforts, but the effect of giving greasy pork in tins to people whose digestive systems had been weakened by years of starvation was disastrous. Nor was it possible to control the amount eaten. Some prisoners were able to handle the food, but many succumbed at once to diarrhoea. It was later estimated that some 2,000 people perished because of being given inappropriate food. After this harsh initiation into the basics of disaster medicine, the British would spend the next month struggling to get the diet right and bringing nutritional expertise to bear.[20]

The first, acute, phase of the British medical relief effort at Belsen falls into four rough phases, each of about a week, marked by the progress reports which Johnston produced on 18 April, 23 April, 2 May, 10 May and about 20 May.[21]

The First Week, 18–23 April 1945

During the first week, the British tried to implement the original plan. They made a start on burying the mountains of dead in Camp 1, using German personnel to move the corpses into pits. Then on 21 April, after various delays, they began to evacuate the sick from Camp 1 to an improvised hospital which they were simultaneously creating in the Panzer Training School, taking them by ambulance via the so-called 'human laundry', a converted stable building in which prisoners were washed and sprayed with DDT and given clean clothing. (The work was done by German nurses from the nearby military hospital.) The British also began to uncover sources of food in the Panzer Training School and the surrounding countryside and to get food sent in from Britain.

But, overall, progress seemed to be very slow. A central part of the plan was immediately to evacuate 'fit' inmates from the 'horror camp' to the Panzer Training School, so that they could be removed from the typhus. Yet that did not happen at all during the first week. Also, the plan to spray all the inmates with DDT – and thus to contain the typhus – could only be partially implemented. And all efforts to clear the mountains of bodies were frustrated by the fact that inmates were continuing to die in terrible numbers – some 7,000 in the first week.[22]

At the time, observers such as Derrick Sington, Rabbi Leslie Hardman, and the journalist Patrick Gordon Walker – people who at once realised the moral enormity of Belsen and the special value of its survivors' lives – felt that the British Army was too slow; circling round the problem and not engaging with it properly. All were, of course, members of what today are called 'the chattering classes', with neither medical nor military experience to draw on.[23]

Contemporary records present a complex picture. Of course, the resources available were totally inadequate, but there was also a divided chain of command, with responsibility awkwardly split between army medical units, Military Government, and garrison troops, and a considerable turnover in personnel. Lack of experience in dealing with such situations made it difficult to establish priorities. According to the garrison commander's report, 'owing to the lack of man power it was impossible to deal with all the extremely urgent problems at once and therefore the two main problems of water supply and food supply overshadowed everything else'. This report prints a long list of tasks – 26 in all – and then adds, tartly, 'the solutions varied according to the relative urgency of the different points and the availability of means to cope with them'. The military government officers blamed the garrison commander for the week-long delay in getting the Germans out of the buildings in the Panzer Training School earmarked for 'fit' evacuees from Belsen, while 'coordination between the Mil Gov Det and the medical staff' needed, a visiting relief worker noted, to be improved. There was also an inherent tension in the plan – an uncertainty whether to concentrate resources in the old 'horror camp' or in the new hospital that had to be created, and, not unnaturally, a tendency to prefer to work in Camp 2.[24]

But one can also detect something else – a war-weariness among British soldiers and officers, a feeling of disbelief that this crowning horror should be added to all the others they had seen in the war. 'All of us were in a state of utter shock – young soldiers as well as senior officers', a British officer has recently recalled. 'What SHOULD you do when faced by 60,000 dead, sick and dying people? We were in a war to fight a war and beat an enemy. What we were suddenly thrust into was beyond anyone's comprehension, let alone a situation which could have been organised and effectively planned for'. We perhaps get some insight into the psychology of the British at Belsen from an American doctor's account of going into Dachau a couple of weeks later. Marcus Smith recalled that his primary feelings were a wish not to catch any of the diseases in the camp, a disbelief that such a thing could have happened, and resentment that he had been chosen for the job.[25]

The Second Week, 23 April–2 May 1945

Conditions at Belsen began to improve in the second week. For one thing, thanks to the dedicated work of the 113th Light Anti-Aircraft Regiment in supervising burials, the backlog of dead bodies was cleared on 28 April. In addition, 'fit' inmates finally began to be evacuated to the married quarters buildings in the Panzer Training School (which became known as Camp 2), and the first prisoners from the Panzer Training School (who had not been exposed to typhus) began to leave – about 2,300 French, Belgian and Dutch. The first hopeful moment in the grim film record of the liberation shows a lorryload of departing Frenchmen, two of whom are belting out the *Marseillaise* on a trumpet and accordion, while British Tommies dance.[26]

Medical reinforcements also reached Belsen, both expert and amateur. The amateurs were a consignment of British aid workers under the Red Cross umbrella who had been working in Holland and were rushed to Germany, across the rickety Rhine bridges, in response to Glyn Hughes's appeal. The men were at once put to work as ambulance drivers and dogsbodies in Camp 1 – where two Quakers made a useful contribution to the problem of getting a clean water supply. The women, only four of whom were medically qualified, helped out at the hospital which the doctors and nurses of 32 CCS were creating in the Panzer Training School. Their letters and diaries vividly convey the challenges and frustrations of trying to nurse starving inmates without adequate resources. They also suggest that the arrival of women raised morale.[27]

Much more important, however, was the bringing of medical expertise to bear. Captain Davis, adviser in typhus to 21 Army Group, was followed by a widely experienced British Army physician, Lt Col Martin Lipscomb, and two dietary experts, Dr Arnold Meiklejohn of

UNRRA and (briefly) Sir Jack Drummond, the adviser to the Ministry of Food. However, a contrast soon emerged. In tackling the typhus epidemic, the Allies were able to draw on tried-and-tested procedures, appropriate and well-resourced technology, and – in the person of Captain Davis – on an experienced, competent and enthusiastic expert, who had learned his trade in the 1943 Naples epidemic. Everyone agreed that Davis was 'cracking', not the least of his qualities being that he had learned in Italy to involve the patient population and was able to sidestep the reluctance of British soldiers to work in the huts in Camp 1 by promoting them to supervisory positions, while getting Hungarians and Poles to do the spraying. By 30 April, some 30,000 people had been powdered in Camp 1, so that, barring relapses, they would be free of typhus by 21 May.[28]

However, when it came to the other main medical issues – the effects of starvation, the treatment of diarrhoea, tuberculosis – there was nothing like the same level of competence or, indeed, agreement. 'Although in our lifetimes, millions have died from starvation in India, Russia and elsewhere', Sir Jack Drummond admitted in 1946, 'it is not possible to find clear-cut advice on how to resuscitate people who are near death from this cause. That fact is, I think, a terrible reflection on our lack of concern for the human race as a whole'. There were evidently arguments about how to proceed – 'a dietician is here – if not several – and they give conflicting advice', a British relief worker wrote in late April. It took some time to devise different levels of diet for Belsen's diverse population – and longer to apply them in practice. The natural response to the early disaster of overfeeding was to ration the intake of food very severely, which then produced immediate howls of protest from prisoners who were able to eat anything. A group of Russians in Camp 2 demanded British Army rations and made unpleasant threats until they were forthcoming.[29]

Of course, the British were not strangers to famine. Their colonial empire had given them considerable experience of it – most recently, when some 3–4 million people had died in the famine of 1943–44 in the Indian province of Bengal. In responding to that emergency, new feeding techniques had been developed which, it was thought, might now be applicable to famine in war-torn Europe. A cheap dietary supplement known as Bengal Famine Mixture had been devised, and a team of doctors in Calcutta had developed a procedure which

THE MEDICAL RELIEF EFFORT AT BELSEN   41

involved administering protein hydrolysates by intravenous injection or nasal drip which, they claimed, had saved the lives of many moribund patients. Early in 1945, in response to the threat of starvation in Holland, the Medical Research Council in London had persuaded British drug companies to manufacture supplies of hydrolysates and had put together a medical team and 100 volunteers from London medical schools to carry out trials. Steps were now taken to divert these materials to Belsen.[30]

Reviewing the situation on 2 May, Colonel Johnston expressed both hopes and fears. By then, some 7,000 sick inmates had been admitted to the improvised hospital in the Panzer Training School, where the staff of 32 CCS, helped by Red Cross volunteers, were struggling to create some sort of order and sanitation while continuing to convert barrack squares into new wards ('12,000 sets of pyjamas, nightdresses, or any form of covering' were most urgently required, Johnston wrote). But there were still another 10,000 people in Camp 1 needing to be hospitalised. And a further problem was now looming. Johnston and Hughes's assumption that the medical care of sick patients evacuated to the newly created hospital could be left to the odd 150 doctors and nurses among their fellow inmates was proving unfounded: most were too weak, mentally disturbed, or preoccupied by their own survival to function as carers (some male nurses simply went from one canteen to another, eating continuously). Johnston had therefore asked for more British medical personnel, but had recently learnt that he would be sent German doctors and nurses instead.[31]

Johnston's greatest worry, however, was the situation in Camp 1. 'The death rate in this camp is still extremely high', he wrote, 'and starvation is the main cause. The failure lies in the distribution of food. Fit internees are interested only in their own feeding and will make no attempt to feed the thousands who are prostrated from weakness or disease. The result therefore, is that the fit get the rations of the unfit as well as their own and diarrhoea ensues; the unfit die of starvation'. He hoped that the impending arrival of 100 British medical students would rectify this problem.

The Third Week, 3–10 May 1945

The 96 medical students who came to Belsen early in May were all men from the London hospitals, who had done some clinical medicine and, in some cases, worked with air-raid casualties. They had volunteered in February to work on trials of new experimental feeding techniques in Holland, only then to be asked, in late April, if they would mind going to Belsen instead. At least five of them kept daily diaries and over a dozen published accounts of their work later in the year.[32]

The students were the first people to work systematically in the huts in Camp 1. Assisted throughout by Hungarian soldiers, they managed gradually to ensure that food was more equally distributed and were able to do a little basic medicine, though for the first fortnight the medications available were limited – only aspirin and opium. One group, under the leadership of a Czech-born RAMC officer, Captain Gluck (who had belatedly been appointed the Medical Officer in Camp 1 late in April), turned some of the huts in Camp 1 into makeshift 'hospitals'.

The students' journals make it possible to recover what was happening day by day inside a single hut. They remind us, too, of the diversity of the Belsen population: three of the diarists, Peter Horsey, Alex Paton and Alan MacAuslan, worked with Polish and Russian, not Jewish, inmates. At one level, these accounts are moving narratives of medical triumph. In early May, when the students first entered the huts, the death rate in the camp was about 500–600 a day. But then, as the effects of their work are felt, it started to fall and within a week had come down to about 100 a day. On 12 May, one student was able to record that 'nobody died today' in his hut. By then several of the students were ill, others were finding that they had less to do. By 14 May most of the students had been moved to the new hospital established in the Panzer Training School.[33]

At another level, however, the diarists record failure: it quickly became apparent that the experimental feeding techniques developed in India were not working at Belsen. The Bengal Famine Mixture – a thick gruel of sugar, dried milk, flour, salt and water – was pretty generally rejected by the inmates as too sweet for their Eastern European palates, causing some British incredulity that starving people could be so fussy about their diet. Some students then tried, with varying success, to adapt the Mixture, but most simply gave up on it.[34]

High hopes rested, too, on the hydrolysates, but they too quickly proved ineffective. All attempts to use needles or nasal feeding tubes met with violent physical resistance from the inmates – who had seen the Germans inject dying prisoners with petrol to make their bodies burn more easily. The preparation was also foul-tasting and therefore difficult to give by mouth; and even when successfully administered had no beneficial effects on patients. Janet Vaughan and Rosalind Pitt-Rivers of the Medical Research Council team quickly conceded that the hydrolysates did not work, but trials continued until the end of May, possibly in the hope that findings applicable to British POWs in the Far East might emerge.[35]

The medical students' work at Belsen is one of the epics of British medicine. The impact they made on the mood in the camp by their arrival, coming fresh from London, and the effectiveness of their work was acknowledged at the time. But there were other reasons why the death rate had begun to fall, notably the DDT spraying programme initiated by Captain Davis. 'When we got there', one student reflected a year later, 'things were getting more or less under control...as most of the worst cases had already died before we arrived, it would be accurate to say that the average case was nearer to the reasonably fit people than the shattered expiring scarecrows which were almost exclusively shown in the Belsen films'.[36]

Meanwhile, another drama had been taking place in the new hospital. German doctors and nurses had begun to arrive – the doctors from prisoner of war cages; the nurses from Hamburg and around – often to a violently hostile reception from the patients. A British Red Cross sister witnessed a group of German nurses being stripped bare, clawed and scratched by inmates before order could be restored. But within a few days the Germans' presence was accepted and, in the view of most British observers, they worked harder than anyone. The hospital was starting to function.[37]

Johnston's third report, dated 10 May, divided Belsen's survivor population into three main groups. Some 7,300 'sick' people were now housed in the new hospital in the Panzer Training School, about 8,000 'fit' inmates were in the German married quarters, and some 5,000 were still in the huts of the 'horror camp' being ministered to by the students, making a total of some 20,300 people. With the war finally over, reinforcements were beginning to reach Belsen, including most of a British General Hospital – badly needed if a further 3,000 medical beds were to be created. Indeed, Johnston asked in addition for a further 75 German doctors and 625 nurses.[38]

However, alongside this note of progress, Johnston also noted a tragic setback. Many of the 8,000 who had been evacuated as 'fit' people – because they passed the 'Belsen standard of fitness', being able to walk and get their own food – were now coming down with typhus. Johnston was forced to change his plan, and to give priority to these new cases, so that the evacuation of the sick from Camp 1 had reluctantly to be suspended. At least, though, these inmates were now receiving decent care from the medical students.

The Fourth Week, 11–21 May 1945

This relapse further delayed implementation of the British plan. It was not until the end of the fourth 'week', on 20 May 1945, just over a month after the relief effort had begun, that Johnston was finally able to report 'completion of the major task, that of hospitalization'. The Panzer Training School had by then been turned into the largest hospital in Europe, with 13,500 beds spread over four sites, though only 11,801 of the beds were occupied, because of the large numbers who had 'evacuated themselves from all camps and were now "leading a gypsy existence" in the surrounding country', preferring to 'organise' food themselves rather than rely on the British rations.[39]

By this time, hospital routines had more or less been established and the feeding problem sorted out, with three different diets being provided. The patients fell into two crude categories – those whose health had been completely destroyed or who had developed tuberculosis and those 'who had merely been starved and degraded but who responded immediately to treatment, diet and mental liberation'. For the lighter cases, medical help was now at hand. For example, trials with captured German drugs had established that a daily combination of nicotinic acid and sulphathiazole brought diarrhoea under control in about four days. With blood transfusions and post-mortems now possible, further refinements of procedure quickly evolved, but the absence of penicillin contributed to some further deaths.[40]

'The general improvement in the condition of patients since admission is marked and satisfying', Johnston wrote. He noted also that, contrary to his worst fears, their mental states seemed to be returning to normal: 'It is not considered that psychosis will, as was first thought, prove to be much of a problem in future. Providing rehabilitation is carried out energetically, the majority of patients should be mentally stable, in my opinion, within a month'. Colonel Lipscomb, who had more experience of psychiatry, agreed: 'Return to normal behaviour as bodily health improved was often surprisingly rapid, leaving only a feeling akin to that of having experienced a bad dream', he wrote later in the year, while cautioning that 'the resumption of normal manners was not always accompanied by return of willpower and initiative'.[41]

Johnston's report of 20 May was the last he wrote from Belsen. In it, he recommended that his unit, 32 CCS, be relieved, after over a month's intense work in the camp. The following day, he joined Glyn Hughes and other officers at the ceremony to mark the burning of the last hut in Camp 1 and in the evening, got thunderously drunk.[42]

Conclusion

The medical operation at Belsen did not end on 21 May; indeed, for some inmates, it never ended. There is a substantial, and very moving, literature on the later phases of the doctors' work and on the complex task of psychological rehabilitation. But by 21 May the bulk of the recorded deaths had taken place and it is therefore this acute phase which needs to be examined when judging the work of the British.[43]

Can a judgment be made? Even at the time there were those who were profoundly grateful to the British – 'it is thanks to you I am in life', a Dutch girl wrote to one of the aid workers later that year – and those who felt resentment that so many had died, like some of those interviewed by David Boder in 1946 and many of the French. It is easy enough now to point to the 'mistakes' the British made, many of which were acknowledged by Glyn Hughes in a talk in London in June 1945. But, as one of the medical students has recently pointed out, such hindsight is not very useful. In judging this kind of operation, the historian has, I believe, to give much more credit for what was done than discredit for what was not done; one has only to look at the handling of such modern disasters as the Asian tsunami of 2004 and the Kashmir earthquake of 2005 to see how difficult emergency relief work can be.[44]

But simply to assess the effectiveness of the medical relief operation at Belsen is to leave out half the tale. One also needs to understand why this subject has always been so highly charged. It is partly because the sheer scale of the Holocaust – and the fact that many of the very few survivors ended up in Belsen – means that enormous weight attaches to *any* lives which *might* have been saved there and to any measures which might have saved more of them. But this subject is also highly charged because it soon became entangled in wider Anglo-Jewish relations. As early as May 1945, the medical problem of Belsen was becoming subsumed in the political question of Belsen, as relations rapidly soured between the British Army and Jewish survivors of the camp – who did not want to return to Eastern Europe, wished to be treated as Jews not Poles, and hoped to go to Palestine. By September 1945, the British military hierarchy was accusing the survivors (and their supporters in the British Jewish community) of ingratitude. When Lady Reading complained about the Army's treatment of Jewish Displaced Persons, General Templer, the Director of Civil Affairs and Military Government angrily replied that the British had done 'prodigious' things at Belsen, and deserved more credit than they had received. Soon afterwards, and probably at his instigation, the *British Zone Review* published a lengthy and detailed account of the army's work at Belsen.[45]

The bitter and dirty political battle between the British and the Belsen DPs quickly restored the natural antisemitism of British officialdom, briefly suspended by the specific human problem of Belsen. The British were further annoyed when the Americans took up the cause of Jewish survivors and argued that they should receive special treatment – the last straw for them was the presence in Germany of numerous representatives of American Jewish organisations, each claiming to speak exclusively on behalf of survivors. By 1946, as the battle over Palestine was intensifying, some British generals in Germany were privately using antisemitic language.[46]

In recent years, judgments on the British relief operation have been overshadowed by the related, but separate, issue of whether camp inmates could have been rescued. The well-catalogued indifference of the British Foreign Office to the fate of Europe's Jews under the Nazis has coloured the argument about Belsen – as can be seen in Rabbi Greenberg's statement at the head of this essay. It is now widely believed in survivor circles that 'British antisemitism led to these deaths' and that had Jewish relief units been allowed in from the start, many more lives would have been saved, a claim which the performance of the Joint and JCRA teams later in the year does not entirely bear out.[47]

All in all, this is a subject which can never really be laid to rest. In discussing the historiography of Soviet Russia and the Eastern bloc, the French post-structuralist writer, Jean-François Lyotard, made a distinction between 'master narratives' and 'local narratives' in historical writing; between the overall, official, version 'imposed and sanctified by the state' and the 'individual stories told by prisoners, students, peasants and deviants of various kinds, impossible to incorporate into the state's version and thus directly subversive of it'. In the case of Belsen, too, there will always be many narratives, each equally valid.

NOTES

1. B. Shephard, *After Daybreak: The Liberation of Belsen, 1945* (London: Jonathan Cape, 2005); J. Reilly, *Belsen: The Liberation of a Concentration Camp* (London: Routledge, 1998); J. Reilly et al. (eds.) *Belsen in History and Memory* (London: Frank Cass, 1997); H. Lavksy, *New Beginnings: Holocaust Survivors in Bergen-Belsen and the British Zone in Germany 1945– 1950* (Detroit: Wayne State University Press, 2002). E. Trepman, 'Rescue of the remnants. The British emergency medical relief operation in Belsen camp, 1945', *Journal of the Royal Army Medical Corps*, Vol.147 (2001), pp.281–93, is an authoritative survey of the medical evidence.
2. I. Greenberg, 'Preface', in M.Z. Rosensaft (ed.), *Life Reborn: Jewish Displaced Persons 1935–1951* (Washington, DC: United States Holocaust Memorial Museum, 2001).
3. R. Breitman, *Official Secrets: What the Nazis Planned, What the British and Americans Knew* (London: Penguin, 1998); and W.D. Rubinstein, *The Myth of Rescue: Why the Democracies Could Not Have Saved More Jews from the Nazis* (London: Routledge, 1997). Two important recent articles argue that more Jews could have been rescued from Belsen itself had the Allies conducted exchange negotiations with the Germans with greater urgency: M.P. Friedman, 'The U.S. State Department and the Failure to Rescue: New Evidence on the Missed Opportunity at Bergen-Belsen', *Holocaust and Genocide Studies*, Vol.19, No.1 (2005), pp.26–50; R. Schulze, 'Keeping very clear of any "Kuh-Handel": The British Foreign Office and the Rescue of Jews from Bergen-Belsen', *Holocaust and Genocide Studies*, Vol.19, No.2 (2005), pp.226–51.
4. *Relief and Reconstruction in Europe – the First Steps: Report by a Chatham House Study Group* (London: Royal Institute for International Affairs, 1942); M.D. Mackenzie, *Medical Relief in Europe: Questions for Immediate Study* (London: Royal Institute for International Affairs, 1942); Save the Children Fund, *Children in Bondage: A Survey of Child Life in the Occupied Countries of Europe and in Finland* (London: Longman, Green, 1942); G.H. Bourne, *Starvation in Europe* (London: Allen and Unwin, 1943); J. Huxley et al., *When Hostilities Cease: Papers on Relief and Reconstruction prepared for the Fabian Society* (London: Gollancz, 1943); F. Wilson, *In the Margins of Chaos: Recollections of Relief Work in and between Three Wars* (London: John Murray, 1944); National Planning Association, *Relief for Europe*

(Washington, DC: 1943); Z. Warhaftig, *Relief and Rehabilitation: Implications of the UNRRA Programme for Jewish Needs* (New York: Institute of Jewish Affairs in the American Jewish Congress and World Jewish Congress, 1944).
5. British soldiers referred to Belsen inmates as 'DPs'. Imperial War Museum Department of Documents (IWM, D). Some psychiatrists used the term till the end of the decade. E. Streba, 'Emotional problems of displaced children', *Journal of Social Casework*, Vol.30 (1949), pp.175-81. At a Pittsburgh hospital in the 1950s, a social worker later recalled, 'the staff called people "displaced persons" then. They were not "Holocaust survivors". We had no sense of the Holocaust as we know it now, with a capital H': Ethel Landerman, quoted in B.S. Burstin, *After the Holocaust* (Pittsburgh: University of Pittsburgh Press, 1989), p.112, P. Novick, *The Holocaust in American Life* (Boston: Houghton Mifflin, 1999).
6. B. Wasserstein, *Britain and the Jews of Europe*, 2nd edn. (Leicester: Leicester University Press, 1999); L. London, *Whitehall and the Jews, 1933-1948* (Cambridge: Cambridge University Press, 2000). On dislocation, see A. Dallin, *German Rule in Russia*, 2nd edn. (London: Macmillan, 1981); and U. Herbert, *Hitler's Foreign Workers* (Cambridge: Cambridge University Press, 1997).
7. G. Woodbridge, *UNRRA* (New York: Columbia University Press, 1950); M. Proudfoot, *European Refugees 1939-52: A Study in Forced Population Movement* (London: Faber, 1957); F.S.V. Donnison, *Civil Affairs and Military Government North-West Europe 1944-1946* (London: HMSO, 1961), p.345. Lehman's decency and integrity were generally respected, but not his administrative gifts. 'The simplest executive task was beyond him', Dean Acheson later wrote: See D. Acheson, *Present at the Creation* (London: Hamish Hamilton, 1970), p.43. A British diplomat considered him 'entirely without common sense or guts', The National Archives (TNA) FO 371/ 51346.
8. M.J. Smith, *Dachau: The Harrowing of Hell* (Albany, NY: State University of New York Press, 1995), pp.92-3.
9. E.C. Hoff, *Medical Department, United States Army. Preventive Medicine in World War II. Volume VII Communicable Diseases. Anthropod-borne Diseases Other then Malaria* (Washington, DC: Office of the Surgeon General, Dept. of the Army, 1964), pp.232-49; P. Weindling, *Epidemics and Genocide in Eastern Europe, 1890-1945* (Oxford: Oxford University Press, 2000), pp.373-4.
10. Warhaftig, *Relief and Rehabilitation*; Y. Bauer, *Out of the Ashes: The Impact of American Jews on Post-Holocaust European Jewry* (Oxford: Pergamom, 1989), pp.41-2; Reilly, *Belsen*, pp.118-44.
11. Some half a million Greeks, out of a population of seven million, died of starvation during the war. M. Mazower, *Inside Hitler's Greece* (New Haven, CT: Yale University Press, 1995); M. Black, *A Cause for our Times. Oxfam. The First 50 Years* (Oxford; Oxford University Press, 1992), pp.1-21; W.N. Medlicott, *The Economic Blockade. Vol.2* (London: HMSO, 1959), pp.254-81; Z. Stein et al., *Famine and Human Development: The Dutch Hunger Winter of 1944-1945* (New York: Oxford University Press, 1975); G.C.E. Burger et al. (eds.), *Malnutrition and Starvation in Western Netherlands: September 1944-July 1945* (The Hague: Kingdom of the Netherlands, 1948).
12. Shephard, *Daybreak*, pp.30-2; A.N. Oppenheim, *The Chosen People: The Story of the '222' Transport from Belsen to Palestine* (London: Vallentine Mitchell, 1996); TNA: FO 916/ 847; FO 916/1163.
13. Shephard, *Daybreak*, p.217; M.R.D. Foot, 'British Prisoners in Belsen', in Reilly et al., *Belsen in History and Memory*.
14. TNA: WO 171/4184; WO 177/343.
15. J. Bridgman, *The End of the Holocaust: The Liberation of the Camps* (London: Batsford, 1990), pp.26-7.
16. Ibid.

THE MEDICAL RELIEF EFFORT AT BELSEN 49

17. Shephard, *Daybreak*, pp.7–8, 44–53; E. Kolb, *Bergen-Belsen: Geschichte des 'Aufenthaltslagers' 1943–1945* (Hannover: Verlag Fur Literatur und Zeitgeoschehen, 1962); A.-E. Wenck, *Zwischen Menschenhandel und 'Endlösung: Das Konzentrationslager Bergen-Belsen* (Paderborn: Schöningh, 2000).
18. TNA: WO 235/19; R. Phillips (ed.), *Trial of Josef Kramer and Forty-Four Others (The Belsen Trial)* (Edinburgh: Hodge, 1949), pp.30–44.
19. Shephard, *Daybreak*, pp.43–53.
20. Ibid., pp.40–2. The management of severe malnutrition continues to be difficult and the mortality rate high. A 1996 World Health Organisation report singles out 'failing to differentiate that the acute illness should be managed before any attempts to correct weight loss' as one of the four major errors of management commonly made. Alan A. Jackson, 'Severe malnutrition', in *Oxford Textbook of Medicine* (Oxford: Oxford University Press, 2003), Vol.I, p.1054.
21. Johnston's reports: TNA WO 177/669; J.A.D. Johnston, 'The relief of Belsen concentration camp: Recollections and reflections of a British Army doctor' (n.d., c.1981), Rosensaft Papers, United States Holocaust Memorial Museum, Washington, DC.
22. Shephard, *Daybreak*, pp.54–67.
23. D. Sington, *Belsen Uncovered*; (London: Duckworth, 1946) L. H. Hardman and C. Goodman, *The Survivors: The Story of the Belsen Remnant* (London: Vallentine Mitchell, 1958); R. Pearce (ed.), *Patrick Gordon Walker: Political Diaries 1932–1971* (London: The Historians' Press, 1991).
24. 10 Garrison report on work at Belsen. TNA: WO 219/3944A.
25. Colonel Leonard Berney, 'The liberation of Belsen Concentration Camp', BBC World War Two Peoples' War website, www.bbc.co.uk/uk/dna/ww2/A2722501 [n.d.]. One of the first British officers into the camp, Berney later played an important role in helping inmates to recover. Derrick Sington plays tribute to his work.
26. IWM. Film A 700/311/5.
27. 'Reports on Team 100 at Belsen Camp', in J. Sutters (ed.), *Archives of the Holocaust, Volume 12: American Friends Service Committee, Philadelphia* (New York: Garland, 1990), pp.550–64; Molly Silva Jones, 'From a diary written in Belsen', in Jean McFarlane papers, IWM (D) 99/86/1.
28. Wellcome: RAMC 792/3/3 Lipscomb papers; J. Drummond, 'Notes on Feeding Problems concerning liberated prisoners at Belsen concentration camp', TNA: FD1/142; W. Davis, 'Typhus at Belsen', *American Journal of Hygiene*, Vol.46 (1947), pp.66–83; A. Paton, 'Belsen, April–May 1945' (in possession of Dr Paton). In a forthcoming article, P. Weindling, '"Belsenitis": Liberating Belsen, its hospitals, UNRRA, and selection for re-emigration, 1945–1948', *Science in Context*, Vol.19 (2006, in press), Paul Weindling argues that the British did not at first appreciate the full extent of the typhus problem at Belsen. Glyn Hughes, who had been a medical officer in the First World War, 'adopted a traditional sanitary approach' and did not appreciate how the development of 'flying squads' spraying with DDT had transformed treatment of the disease. He also suggests that the second peak in the death rate at Belsen, at the end of April, was caused by the failure of the British immediately to carry out delousing and by the greater mobility within Camp 1 after liberation. My thanks to Professor Weindling for letting me see this important article.
29. J. Drummond, 'Famine conditions and malnutrition in Western Europe', *Journal of the Royal Society of Arts*, Vol.94 (1946), pp.470–7; Drummond, 'Notes on feeding problems...'; Johnston, 'Relief'. For a magisterial review of the enormous literature on wartime starvation and malnutrition, see P. Helweg-Larsen *et al.*, 'Famine disease in German concentration camps: Complications and sequels', *Acta Medica Scandinavica*, Supplement 274 (1952).

30. Shephard, *Daybreak*, pp.97–9; TNA: FD1/6346.
31. TNA: WO 177/669.
32. Shephard, *Daybreak*, pp.90–104; Trepman, 'Rescue'.
33. Paton, 'Belsen'; M. Hargrave, 'Diary of a medical student at Belsen', IWM (D) 76/74/1; P.J. Horsey, 'Record of our time in Germany', IWM (D), con shelf; D. Bradford, 'Expedition to Belsen', IWM (D) 86/7/1; A. MacAuslan, 'A month in Germany', IWM (D) 95/2/1 are the most detailed accounts. Trepman, 'Rescue', lists the articles published by the students.
34. Shephard, *Daybreak*, pp 99–101.
35. Ibid.
36. Horsey, 'Record of our time'. Fine accounts include G. Raperport, 'Expedition to Belsen', *Middlesex Hospital Journal*, Vol.45 (1945), pp.21–4; and A. MacAuslan, 'Belsen, May 1945', *St Thomas's Hospital Gazette*, Vol.43 (1945), pp.103–7.
37. Shephard, *Daybreak*, pp.112–13.
38. TNA: WO 177/669.
39. Ibid.
40. Shephard, *Daybreak*, pp.126–8.
41. TNA: WO 177/669; F.M. Lipscomb, 'Medical aspects of Belsen concentration camp', *Lancet* (1945), ii, pp.313–15.
42. Shephard, *Daybreak*, pp.123–6.
43. Sington, *Belsen Uncovered*; R. Collis and H. Hogerzeil, *Straight On* (London: Methuen, 1947); H. Nerson, 'Report on the situation at the Bergen-Belsen camp', in OSE, *Report on the Situation of the Jews in Germany, October–December 1945* (Geneva: Union Oeuvre de Secours aux Enfants, 1946); H. Stern, 'The aftermath of Belsen', in H.B.M. Murphy (ed.), *Flight and Resettlement* (Lucerne: UNESCO, 1955), pp.64–75.
44. Shephard, *Daybreak*, p.177; D.P. Boder, *I Did Not Interview the Dead* (Urbana, IL: University of Illinois Press, 1949); A. Wieviorka, 'French internees and British liberators', in Reilly *et al.* (eds.), *Belsen in History and Memory*, pp.; TNA; WO 222/201 (Hughes's talk on Belsen as published in Sir H.L. Tidy (ed.), *Inter-Allied Conferences on War Medicine* (London: Staples Press, 1947) omits some of his franker remarks); A. Paton, Review of Shephard, *Daybreak*, *British Medical Journal* (2005), i, p.1030.
45. TNA: FO 1030/301; FO 1030/300; FO 1049/81. Templer had been closely involved with the Belsen relief effort, see J. Cloake, *Templer of Malaya* (London: Harrap, 1995), p.153.
46. E-mail to the author from daughter of a Belsen survivor; Meeting at Imperial War Museum 15 April 2005. See also S. Milton and F.D. Bogin (eds.), *Archives of the Holocaust, Volume 10: American Jewish Joint Distribution Committee, New York* (New York: Garland, 1995); E. Somers and R. Kok (eds.), *Jewish Displaced Persons in Camp Bergen-Belsen, 1945–1959* (Amsterdam: NIOD, 2003); N. Belton, *The Good Listener: Helen Bamber, a Life Against Cruelty* (London: Weidenfeld, 1998); K.S. Pinson, 'Jewish life in liberated Germany: A study of the Jewish DPs', *Jewish Social Studies*, Vol.9 (1947), pp.101–26. Sir Frederick Morgan, 'UNRRA Diary' (IWM Department of Documents).
47. R. Evans *In Defence of History* (London: Granta, 1997), p.88.

The Medical Relief Effort: Eyewitness Accounts

SOLDIER MAJOR BEN BARNETT, NURSE MOLLY SILVA JONES AND MEDICAL STUDENT GERALD RAPERPORT

The Soldier: Major Ben Barnett

Major B.G. Barnett, commanding 249th Battery (Oxford Yeomanry), was one of the first British officers to enter Belsen. His contemporary pencil notes provide interesting details on the liberation, conveying some of the feelings of a British officer.

> Arrived Sunday 15th
> <u>1. Initial negotiations and subsequent agreement and arrangements for taking over</u>
>
> Own dispositions – 11 A[rmoured] D[ivision] & 15 Scottish [Division]
> German deputation over [ALLER to 11AD – BGS & Oberst Harries] Comdt of BERGEN-BELSEN
> Hungarians (1000/3000) Wehrmacht (300/800) SS Guards & admin personnel- telephones us to give authority to Hungarian and German guards 33 +25 girls. Wehrmacht not allowed with 200x of Camps
> My [Bty] + Broadcast van + interpreter + 1 [HPR/T set] and 1 sec PRO – German internees political and criminal
>
> <u>2. Entry of 1st Tps and dealings with Wehrmacht</u>
>
> L[iaison] O[fficer] on ahead to lay on meeting with Harries – shown 1/4s etc – discussion; nos of Wehrmacht & SS & Hungarian – food situation – condition in camps – told of 2

camps – no escapes – arrival of Phantom & SAS off[ice]r. Reports of shooting in Camp I

3. Conditions in Camp

Meeting with Kramer about 1900 hours. disarming of SS. Nos of SS – no records of internees nos of internees – (Arrival of Brig Hughes DDMS 2 Army) – Reports of rioting in cookhouses all food for tomorrow gone – so we decide to go into the inner camp (and I will now try & describe what I saw during this the first evening & during the subsequent 6 days –).

The things I saw completely defy description. There are no words in the English language which can give a true impression of the ghastly horror of this camp. I find it hard even now to get into focus all these horrors, my mind is really quite incapable of taking in everything I saw because it was all so completely foreign to anything I had previously believed or thought possible. I will nevertheless try & give an accurate description of all I saw & at the end I will include some of the stories told me by various internees.

Firstly then I will take events as they unfolded themselves: the smell – the people and their clothes – the wounded and the dead by the gates – the potato clumps – the kitchens – the spirit of the people – the condition of the people – their clothing – no food for 4 days or water for 5 days except in stinking pit – cookhouses garbage heaps – a mass of fires cooking – Plea from people to stay there and not leave them – 1 Tp arrived – Kramer made to carry wounded – DDMS message to Army Comdr-Kramer under close arrest – riot in food stores – official visit next morning with Harries, Schmidt and Kramer – the latter not ashamed of all the horrors, the former definitely so – 1st to crematorium then to mass open graves size 30 ft deep x 30x long x 10x wide others of same size obviously filled in – several hundred corpses in same compound some very bad, women's hut also there. Broadcasting van told people what we were trying to do.

From here on I can only give you a rather jumbled impression – Firstly, the huts, there must have been about 120 all told capable of holding 50 or at most 100 people some with 500 or 700 people in them (About 40x X 8x) incl dead and dying some beds and rags for blankets etc – Latrines NIL – 1 open trench for women no seats – Hospitals Typhus – dead – excreta from dysentery patients – operating room – Corpses – living walking or piles of dead – besides heap by grave mass pile by childrens huts and naked – cannibalism – food [illegible] & "broth" – water – old concrete tank Mortuary – Internees class of person, nationality, from Hanover and Brunswick. Children – between 500 and 1000 – 2/3 women, old clothes and books – Dying persons walking to die over 200 every day – Cooks – SS arrested on Monday evening & pt in cells men and women and made to work and feed same as internees – Jewellery etc: Gallows and cells.

1st meal on Monday night by blocks & laagers – water carts – breakfast bread and hot sweet milk – people lost all sense of civilization – thieving – spare compo boxes untouched – Distributing food – Clothing stores – Food stores. Living took no notice of dead.

Why did Germans do this? I say it was deliberate policy of extermination by starvation.

I was told of – living tied to dead – of petrol or air injections beatings up –

Hangings – shootings and lined into huts – women made to stand up. Wearing old clothes …

5. cookhouses – CO's maid

Camp II conditions not too bad but no food – starvation
Sack of meal burst picking up flakes of meal. Picking up odd bits of food.

Fires on the first evening.

What I expected to see – huts and compounds with tolerable living conditions – latrines etc.

Barnett's unit left Belsen on 21 April 1945. In a letter thanking Barnett's Commanding Officer, Lt Col Taylor, for his 'colossal work' at Belsen, Brigadier E. P. Sewell of Main Headquarters, 8th Corps wrote, 'It should have been a Corps "Q" party, but we simply could not spare the officers – nor did we have the men – to cope'.

[Papers of Major B. G. Barnett. Efforts have been made to contact the copyright holder, but as contact has not been possible, the extract appears with the permission of the Trustees of the Liddell Hart Centre for Military Archives, King's College, London.]

The Nurse: Molly Silva Jones

Born in 1904, Beatrice Mary (Molly) Silva Jones was one of four medically qualified nurses in the Red Cross party which arrived at Belsen on 20 April 1945, after being sent from Holland. Assigned to work in the new hospital being created out of the Panzer Training School, Molly Silva Jones 'took command'; thanks to her leadership, all but three of her unqualified colleagues 'rushed willingly into work in that typhus-ridden hospital and stuck it nobly throughout our stay there'.[1] Silva Jones was later awarded the MBE. Nothing is known of her later life. This diary survives among the papers of her colleague, Jean McFarlane.

> 19 April 1945
> Who could imagine that a Concentration Camp could be hidden in such country? It seemed fantastic, the peace of the pine woods became somber and sinister. On the left we caught the first glimpse of barbed wire through which people peered at us, strange figures clad in blue striped pyjamas. Increasing gradually was an indescribable stench that pervaded everything – a stench of filth, rags, excreta and the dead, as we later discovered.

Molly watched some of the first women patients evacuated from the 'horror camp' being bathed and DDT-ed in the 'human laundry' before being admitted to the Hospital area.

> Going into that place, we could forget it? Living corpses, skeletons covered with parchment like skin, discoloured by filth and neglected sores lay on the bath tables. Mostly they lay inert, occasionally they lay moaning as they were touched by the nurses. They lay with open eyes sunk deep into hollow sockets, eyes which registered little, save fear and apprehension, mainly they were expressionless. Many had to have their heads shaved.

Possibly none of us had ever been so stirred – with pity – shame – remorse – yes, because even in 1934 we had heard of these camps and had not realised, not wanted to realise, that such things could happen. And lastly but not least we were stirred with a cold anger against those primarily responsible, the Germans, an anger which grew daily at Belsen. Stirred also an increased desire to help; nothing we could do was enough to attempt to restore these sub-humans to some measure of mental and physical health. We went back to the road without speaking. We knew the uselessness of words, not for the last time at Belsen.

After a day spent settling in, Silva Jones and her colleagues reported for work at the new hospital. They found that none of the British Army nurses there could spare the time to 'show them the ropes' and went to Square 1 'to attempt to cope with the first 600 patients admitted the previous day'.

21 April
There were no pillows, very few BP's [bed pans] (augmented by dog bowls), no washing bowls, few towels, not enough cups, [and] these had to be washed once or twice during every meal. The food consisted of coffee without milk or sugar, soup and black bread. These people had[,] because of starvation, illness, weakness, apathy, and the lack of sanitation in Camp 1[,] become used to defecating and urinating where they lay, probably a few yards off if they could get so far. So in the wards, they defecated and urinated where they lay or struggled to the floor beside their beds. They could not grasp that someone would come if they called. Then in the next twenty-four hours we all experienced the same difficulty, trying to get the Internee Staff to empty the BPs (proper and improvised) regularly. It was almost as difficult to get the blankets changed and the patients washed. Brown paper took the place of macintosh sheeting. Most of the patients suffered from acute diarrh[oea] and the internee doctors considered that both water and milk, even in the smallest quantities were very bad for them. They wanted

them to have strong coffee only, and as this was ersatz, the nutriment value was nil. There was no sulphaguanadine [the standard British drug for diarrhoea] only Tanalbin, a German preparation which appeared to be of little value.

The day following admission was never so difficult as the succeeding days when the patients would be less apathetic, less apprehensive and as soon as any meal appeared in the wards, the clamour for food would start. Those cries of the hungry will haunt the ears of those who heard them for a long time to come. Several who succeeded in obtaining more food than prescribed, died... The Internee staff were most disgruntled with the food in the beginning, they were limited as they too could only take small quantities. Some said that they wished they had stayed in camp 1 where they had far more to eat.

The following day, the medical commander at Belsen, Lt Col. James Johnston, took Silva Jones and her colleague Myrtle Beardwell into Camp 1 at Belsen.

22 April
The work of clearing up had been going on for five days. Still the dead lay in heaps, bodies lay horribly contorted and the living dragged themselves around the dead. The living were in filthy rags, striped pyjamas. There were a few girls, decently clad, walking about, laughing and chatting. These must have been those kept for the use of the Germans, 14 'clients' per day and two days off per week, such is the Germanic order. Children amused themselves by throwing stones at the dead. People sat and ate leaning against stinking corpses. A woman covered in only one dirty torn garment, defecated a few yards away, her hip bone showing through taut yellowish grey skin. An army lorry was drawn up outside a hut. SS men were bringing out the dead, grotesque, naked inhuman forms caught up by the arms and legs and flung into the truck or carried out a-dangling form with head lolling against a German face ...

THE MEDICAL RELIEF EFFORT: EYEWITNESS ACCOUNTS

27 April
The water and light failed in the camp for a few hours. There were rumours of sabotage. A call was sent out for water carts and the RAF brought a German one to the rescue. On two succeeding days the water failed again for long periods. These were the hardest days of all to keep going. Some who had not seen Camp 1 questioned whether it would not have been better to have left the people in the Horror Camp rather than to have brought them out with so few available supplies, personnel or equipment, for their use. The thought of the early days came back, when we felt – at least we can help them to die in peace. The enormity of the task was overwhelming at times and as each new square was opened and filled with patients the difficulties of staffing seemed insurmountable. Approximately to every 600 patients there were two trained sisters, one English and one Swiss. Close supervision was impossible during the day and there was none at night. The best of the internee nurses had come out of Camp 1 in the early days and the latter ones were nothing like as good. They were untrained, mostly about 16 or 17 years and an increasing number of the total strength were daily becoming ill themselves. It was at this stage that the decision was made to employ German doctors and nurses, psychological[ly] a detrimental move, but a practical necessity. A few were very good but many were hard and callous ...

Silva Jones describes problems in getting prisoners the right food and early efforts to keep hospital records. By the middle of May, with the war over and army medical units arriving at Belsen, the worst was over. Silva Jones concludes with a reflection:

It was the job that mattered every time – not the person, the position – for the time one lived in an atmosphere of a task that was bigger than the individual, in which first things came first. Dull possibly in detail, inspiring in experience. The hour produces the man; Col Johnston was that man.

[From the diary of nurse Molly Silva Jones, Department of Documents, Imperial War Museum (McFarlane Papers, 99/86/1).]

The Medical Student: Gerald Raperport

Ninety-six students from the London medical schools worked at Belsen in May 1945. Several kept diaries and many published articles, often of great literary distinction, in student journals on their return. Gerald Raperport studied medicine at Cambridge and the Middlesex Hospital and later became a GP in Portsmouth.

> We felt a little apprehensive as we bumped and bounced in our transport along the shell scarred road from Camp 2 to Camp 1 on the morning after our arrival. About a quarter of a mile from the camp the stench that we were to know so well became obvious. Smells such as this are indescribable, but in it were compounded the stinks of faeces, decaying flesh, burning rags and the warm, sour, acid scent of human sweat. Then we saw the camp for the first time. Half a square mile in area, it held 28,000 persons. They lived in wooden huts which were much the same size as EMS hospital huts. They were all dilapidated and falling apart, roofs holed, windows broken, floorboards collapsed, and drains stopped up. No light. No water. In many huts no beds or bedding of any kind. And under these conditions lived not forty people, as in an EMS hut, but some 600! It was impossible for anyone to lie down at full length. Instead they had to stand or huddle up on top of one another on the floor, the sick, the starved, the dying and the dead – all one huge, wretched, seething mass of disease-riddled, vermin-infested, stinking humanity. The stench in the huts was almost more than we medical students, brought up though we are to meet bad smells unflinchingly, could bear, for universally the floors were carpeted – literally – with a thick glutinous mass of weeks' old excreta. In the majority of cases people had become too apathetic to care or else too weak to move, and remained where they were, saturated time and time again with their own excretions (nearly all suffered from a fulminating diarrhoea) unconcerned, unashamed.
>
> The lack of shame, this apathy, this regression to sheer animality was evident on all sides. Men and women would walk around the camp stark naked, cold as it was, and think nothing of it; they would sit side by side on the latrines and gaze on passers-by unblushingly, expressionlessly. Before long we ceased

to marvel at the sight of emaciated figures crawling out of their huts with eating bowls in their hands which they had first used as bedpans, emptying them down the nearest latrine, wiping them on the filthy rags that served as clothing, and then returning to the huts to take their meals from these self-same bowls. And when the food was brought, those that were strong enough would fall upon it and fight for every morsel they could obtain, thinking only of themselves and caring nothing for those who could not move and who consequently went without, all gibbering unintelligently in high-pitched tones the while like a swarm of angry monkeys. Death was meaningless for them and corpses reviled them not a bit: we would do 'corpse-rounds' each morning to pick out the dead in much the same way as a nurse would do a [ward] round here in England and with the identical atmosphere of routine normality.

Only intense and prolonged suffering could have produced the extreme mental, moral and physical degradation that we witnessed. These people were utterly broken, spiritless, amoral. The world had offered them only misery: why then should they care about the world?

Physically the most startling sight was the degree of emaciation to which they had been reduced. 'Skin and Bone' here was a literal description. Their heads were no more than parchment-covered skulls, their thighs could be circled by finger and thumb, and it was easy to grip the bones of their vertebrae through their anterior abdominal walls. Their muscles were mere fibrous strands and the women's breasts just wrinkled flags of skin. Famine oedema of the ankles and sacral region was widespread and in occasional cases ascites due to starvation were found. Bedsores and ulcers, some deep enough to expose bone, were to be seen everywhere, and nutritional, post-typhus and thrombotic gangrene of the extremities was not uncommon. Few if any definite vitamin deficiency syndromes were diagnosed – there were several doubtful cases of beri-beri, pellagra and scurvy, and the diarrhoea may in part have been due to nicotinic acid deficiency, though intensive therapy with nicotinic acid had no remarkable effect on it. Chest troubles were legion, a very large percentage of them being almost certainly tuberculous (one could not be certain in the absence of facilities for sputam examination, radiography, etc.)...

That, in brief, was the general medical picture which lay before us, set against a background of unreproducible squalor. No attempt could be made to take accurate histories because of the language difficulties and often it was impossible to examine cases because it would have meant kneeling on two or three people beside them. Immediate action was imperative and we delayed to act not a moment.

The biggest problem was that of improving living conditions. A team of 10 student volunteers set to work on this on our second day at Belsen. We had to start from scratch. First the huts had to be scrubbed out with cresol, then dusted with DDT powder: beds (2 tier bunks) found, scrubbed, and dusted, palliasses and blankets obtained, patients brought in and passed through the 'human laundry', nursing staff organised from the fit internees, feeding utensils, bedpans, drugs and instruments secured and a multitude of other small details attended to. By the end of the first afternoon we had bedded down some hundred patients and by the end of the twelfth day our hospital area comprised twelve huts containing about eleven hundred patients.

Our hospital established, medical work was begun in earnest. Perhaps the most striking and worthwhile result that we achieved was the change in the people's outlook. Apathy had gone from them. They no longer stared or grimaced in terror when approached by a man in uniform. They thanked us now for what we did for them and were anxious to talk to us and hear news of the outside world. Their sense of shame and decency had come back. Hope was rekindled within them.

So came the end. Two RAMC hospitals and 150 Belgian medical students took over from us on May 26 and after we had shown them the ropes on May 28 we boarded the plane for home.

This is our story, or part of it. We shall remember Belsen for many a day, not only for its vileness, but also for the many lessons it had to teach us; for the comradeship and team spirit we found among all with whom we came into contact; for the hardest and most worthwhile month's work of our lives. It was an invaluable experience and none of us regrets the time spent there.

We regret but the cause.

[G. Raperport, 'Expedition to Belsen', *The Middlesex Hospital Journal*, Vol.45 (1945), pp.21–4.]

NOTE

1. M. Beardwell, *Aftermath* (Ilfracombe: Arthur H. Stockwell, 1953), p.42.

British Relief Teams in Belsen Concentration Camp: Emergency Relief and the Perception of Survivors

JOHANNES-DIETER STEINERT

When British troops entered Bergen-Belsen concentration camp on 15 April 1945 it was obvious that the liberators had no idea about what was to confront them.[1] During the following days a number of specialised military units as well as the first relief teams provided by the British Red Cross and the Society of Friends were called to take care of the 60,000 dying, sick, hungry and exhausted people encountered at the camp. Whether or not the advancing troops could have been better prepared for what they found, is a question that raises the far more fundamental issue about the extent of detailed knowledge the Allies had concerning the Holocaust and other German war crimes. It is well known that the Allied Governments issued a joint declaration as early as December 1942, condemning the mass murder of Jews in Europe. During the years that followed, a number of reports on this subject appeared in the media, but obviously all this failed to influence military planning, and likewise, there is no evidence to suggest that the widespread Soviet reporting of their liberation of Majdanek in July 1944 had any effect on the Western Allies.[2] Nobody, it seems, expected to come across high numbers of survivors of the German mass murder in Western Europe.

This essay is based on a research project examining British humanitarian assistance in Germany, which is generously supported by the British Academy.[3] In the first part, the main objectives of British wartime planning will be analysed. Secondly, I will turn to the training of relief workers. Finally, the essay will address the actual deployment of the first relief teams, and their perception of the survivors.

Wartime Preparations

International humanitarian assistance was a prominent theme in twentieth-century history, and it appears to remain a solid part of the twenty-first century agenda too. However, what we take for granted today is the result of a long learning process, in which the two world wars played a significant role. Official documents demonstrate that the planning of international humanitarian assistance during the Second World War was strongly influenced by the experience gained in the First World War and its aftermath, whose consequences were reflected at both national and international level: nationally, by the creation of the Council of British Societies for Relief Abroad (COBSRA) in 1942; internationally, by the foundation of the United Nations Relief and Rehabilitation Administration (UNRRA) in 1943.

COBSRA did not have any executive function. It was chiefly concerned with facilitating an exchange of information and opinions, as well as advising and co-ordinating the NGOs, both among themselves and with State authorities and international institutions. A total of 40 British NGOs joined the Council, and 11 of these eventually sent their own teams to continental Europe: the British Red Cross (BRC) Society and Order of St. John of Jerusalem, the Friends Relief Service (FRS), the Friends Ambulance Unit (FAU), the Young Women's Christian Association, the Save the Children Fund, the Salvation Army, the Catholic Committee for Relief Abroad, the Jewish Committee for Relief Abroad (JCRA), the International Voluntary Service for Peace, the Boy Scouts Association, and the Guide International Service.

In 1942 efforts began to prepare relief workers as thoroughly as possible for overseas deployment. Three interconnecting phases of humanitarian aid were identified, that would follow each other: 1) 'medical work with the forces', 2) 'emergency relief' and finally 3) 'longer-term work of rehabilitation and reconciliation'.[4] Most of the NGOs involved considered their work to fall within phases two and three; while an extensive knowledge of field medical services was demanded from the members of the British Red Cross teams and the FAU.[5]

The training did not focus on technical matters, but also included knowledge about the target countries, behaviour patterns and psychological schooling. During a training course for the BRC and St John's Ambulance, in January 1943, Lady Falmouth urged the importance of professional training:

> If there is one thing that is more shocking than another, it is the thought of untrained eager enthusiastic English men and women setting out and settling down in an unfortunate country, trying to do relief work in it ... We must have a knowledge of the work that we are going to do. If we do not, quite apart from the fact that we may do real physical harm and we may kill more than we cure, we shall do an enormous amount to destroy the confidence and good relationship we want to establish in the countries we go to.[6]

The practical training involved a good basic knowledge of first aid and nursing, hygiene, how to recognise and treat contagious illnesses and diseases, nutritional issues and the care of large numbers of people, the construction, equipping and administration of camps, child and youth welfare, economic, social and cultural aspects of the individual countries and rudimentary language acquisition. The Society of Friends published and warmly recommended to their teams a 50-page extensive *Relief Worker's Vocabulary*, containing the most important terms and phrases in English, French and German.[7] Jewish Relief Units expected a basic knowledge of Yiddish from their members, to enable communication with Eastern European Jewish survivors. They were supplied with an 88-page *Yiddish Phrase Book*, compiled by Solomon A. Birnbaum, lecturer in Yiddish Studies at the University of London.[8]

Furthermore, the relief workers were given a more or less concrete view of the conditions they could expect to find. The Salvation Army's first *European Relief Study Paper* presented a vivid picture: Hunger and homelessness were prevalent in many European countries. Burnt fields, slaughtered animals, plundered property, destruction of factories, streets and methods of transport. Millions of people were far away from their homes, among them prisoners of war, concentration camp inmates, forced labourers, and people who fled from war, crime and hunger. Danger and disease lurked everywhere. After the fighting, chaos and disorder would prevail in many countries. The helpers should prepare themselves for a hard life, full of privations, under conditions similar to those following a heavy air raid. The emotional and spiritual torment of the victims, their suffering and fear, so the Paper said, demand a type of welfare that extends beyond material and physical aid.[9]

At a training conference of the JCRA on 2 May 1943, Dr Emmanuel Miller presented *The Psychological Aspect of Relief Work*. He warned participants to be prepared for the fact that people who have suffered for a long time, were likely to be completely apathetic. Some would refuse to accept any offers of help, even from Jews. He called for every unit to include a member trained in psychology.[10]

Most relief workers undertook an extended training course lasting several weeks or months. During these, their theoretical knowledge and practical abilities were improved through practical exercises such as building a field kitchen or cooking in the open air, as well as visits to large canteen kitchens, disinfection firms, hospitals and welfare establishments.[11]

Relief Work in Belsen

The initial period following the liberation was marked by ad hoc measures, improvisations, attempts to get an overview of the situation, and some emergency relief activities. This had two aims: firstly, to provide help for the 60,000 victims as soon as possible, and secondly, to prevent the spread of typhoid. In 1945, antibiotics were not yet available, and while it was possible to immunise people by a vaccination, this was not practicable at Belsen or other camps due to the sheer numbers of people needing treatment. This meant that the intensive use of DDT against lice, the main transmitter of the disease, and strict quarantines remained the only options.[12]

This, as well as the ignorance about the situation within the camp, is often used to explain why the first British units allowed the German and Hungarian guards to remain at their posts. Only after reinforcements had arrived, were the camp guards disarmed and taken into custody. Up to that point, the 63rd Anti-Tank Regiment had been largely left to its own devices, only supported by the 76th Field Hygiene Section that had immediately begun to deal with the sanitation facilities.[13] On 17 April 1945 the period of waiting, taking stock and planning was over, and many prisoners got to see their liberators for the very first time, as the 224th Military Government Detachment rolled in followed by the 11th Field Ambulance, the 32nd Casualty Clearing Station (CCS), the 30th Field Hygiene Section and the 7th Mobile Bacteriological Laboratory. Further units followed in the next days and weeks.[14]

There were also six British relief teams involved in the provision of humanitarian assistance: five from the BRC and a team from the FRS. They arrived almost a week after the camp had been liberated, and none of them had been especially equipped or trained for work in a former concentration camp – they had simply been in operation on the continent.[15] Each team consisted of 12 male and female members, each one of whom was qualified to undertake a different task, including four trained nurses and some nursing auxiliaries. Among the other members, there were, for example, drivers, cooks, quartermasters, secretaries and general welfare workers. The teams were given standard equipment to allow a degree of self-sufficiency including cooking and washing facilities, two ambulances, two lorries and a three-ton truck.[16] Their arrival coincided with the first phase of humanitarian aid, in which survivors were given emergency care, a hospital area was established and initial evacuations were begun. Improvisation was still the order of the day and routine slow to emerge.

The military were not entirely pleased at the arrival of the relief teams. 'There was a moan of disgust and at least two more bottles than usual were drunk that night', Lieutenant Colonel Gonin (11th Light Field Ambulance) remembered:

> You see it was, as we thought, just some more people to show round, more helpless folk who would have to be looked after. They'll want everything there isn't: bedpans, sheets, blankets, nightdresses, they write home saying how awful the conditions are here and why isn't more being done about it. No, there was despair and despondency in the ranks that night. We felt that they would be just a damn nuisance.[17]

The next day, however, his attitude changed:

> I was detailed to meet them and to show them where they were to live with the very definite instructions that as they'd come

they would have to look after themselves. The first one I saw was a lady dressed in the grey uniform of the Society of Friends. She looked pretty fierce to me but I asked if there was anything I could do and had they found their accommodation? 'Yes', she said, 'we're all right, come and have a gin'.

The authorities decided that women should be spared the most horrific sights, and Molly Silva Jones and M. F. Beardwell were among a very few British women to be allowed entry into the concentration camp during the first few days. Both were qualified nurses, belonging to the BRC teams. They were taken inside the camp the day after their arrival, by Colonel Johnston of the 32nd CCS:

> The smell was terrible – the sickly smell of death mingled with the stench of excreta and burning boots, shoes, and rags of clothing ... The few broken-down arid derelict looking wooden huts were full of people – the dead lying on the living and the living on the dead; corpses were hanging out of the windows – heaps of dead thrown in grotesque masses – skeleton arms intertwined with skeleton legs and great vacant eyes staring up through the morass of sprawling dead. The majority of the living inmates looked more like animals than human beings. They were clad in filthy rags – and were crawling and grovelling in the earth for bits of food. They took no notice of us or anyone – they vomited and stooled where they stood or sat – lavatories just did not exist – large square holes about ten feet square had been dug with a crude pole around, but most of the inmates were beyond getting to that pole.[18]

It appears that a whole week after the liberation conditions in the camp had hardly changed. The improvements that had been made went unnoticed by the women; the horror and incomprehensibility dominated everything. In their view, the relief teams' accommodation appeared to be sheer luxury. They had been allocated 'well built houses among the trees' on the grounds of a former military training area. A boiler that they had brought with them provided continuous hot water, which could be used to fill thermos flasks or carried into their rooms in buckets, thus sparing them from having to wash in a basin full of cold water. In addition, there was a bathhouse, with 24 bathtubs and hot running water: 'that just makes all the difference to comfort at the end of a long and gruelling day in those grim surroundings'.[19] The *Wehrmacht* had only just vacated the quarters a few days earlier, and, once all the Hitler portraits had been taken down, they were quickly cleaned, tidied and made comfortable.[20]

Detailed accounts, however, taken from individual letters, diaries and contemporary reports, remain the exception: there was not a lot of time left over for anything other than work. Lilian Impey, the leader of the FRS team gives us a picture of a team in operation on 25 April 1945: Work began at 7am and continued until 8 or 9pm. The male members of her team worked in the former concentration camp: Bill Broughton and Bill Rankin helped in the reconstruction of the sanitation facilities and water supply, Michael Hinton worked in a First Aid Station, Hugh Jenkins transported foodstuffs and colleagues, Eryl Hall Williams helped with the evacuation of patients. All the female members had taken over duties in the hospital area: Lilian Smith was responsible for patients in five different buildings, Jane Leverson was responsible for patients in two, Kit Broughton took over one of the kitchens, Beth Clarkson ran a canteen, Joyce Parkinson managed the nursing duties, and Margery Ashberg ran the children's department.[21]

Lilian Impey's short report records an instant in time: the duties were continually changing. Special diets had to be prepared under canvas. Heavy trucks plied the camp all day, delivering dirty bed linen and clothes to the laundries. The professional challenges were immense. One of the team members, who in civilian life had worked in the special diet kitchen of a hospital, was temporarily given overall control of all the hospital food, of Red Cross cooks, and the Hungarian, Russian and Polish assistants. The few qualified nurses supervised the masses of voluntary but completely untrained assistants.[22]

Before the arrival of the first British General Hospital, the authorities had to improvise. Each army nurse took responsibility for a block that consisted of four hastily patched up and minimally equipped barrack huts. In the course of the day 600 patients would be admitted into these from the so-called 'human laundry'. After one day's handover the army nurse then delegated care of that hut's patients to a colleague from the relief teams, who in turn supervised the voluntary helpers drawn from among the former camp prisoners.[23] Evelyn Bark (BRC) later wrote:

> I particularly remember how quickly and willingly Jean McFarlane, who was an excellent driver, a good linguist, a capable secretary and a sweet soprano, but who simply hated nursing, donned the dungarees, army boots, gaiters and triangular head-square, which was the nursing outfit we improvised to give the maximum protection from the virulent attacks of lice.[24]

Perceptions

Doing their work, the female members of the relief teams became particularly close to the survivors of Belsen. 'We could do little for them physically, but they needed a feeling of security far more than anything else', Muriel Blackman (BRC) remembered.[25] In the written sources available, one sees a mixture of disgust at the German crimes, curiosity and an unwavering will to help the situation. Jane Leverson, the first Jewish relief worker and a member of the Quaker team, praised the British helpers' spirit in her report, dated 5 May, but warned of a possible change:

> In the early days of the liberation of the camp, the British workers were amazed at the horrors which they saw, and could not do enough to help the internees; they lived on half-rations for a fortnight, to feed the camp. They gave enormous presents of cigarettes and sweets. English sergeants blew the noses of invalid children, and 'potted' them. No job was too much, no hours were too long. The situation was more stimulating than the worst of London's blitzes. However, many of the British workers are tired now; as the internees gain strength, and as it dawns upon them that 'liberation' will not prevent them from catching typhus, nor give them immediate happiness and freedom, they become more difficult and less grateful, and this re-acts most unfavourably on the British workers. So far I have not heard anti-Semitic remarks on this account ... I await them, however ...[26]

These remarks reflect not only the dilemma facing British helpers in Belsen but the whole Allied liberation of concentration camps in general. Not only were there deficiencies in the advance material planning; it was also clear within the first few days even, that the psychological training of team members had not been intensive enough. As quoted above, in January 1943 Lady Falmouth (BRC) had appealed: 'We must have a knowledge of the work that we are going to do', otherwise there was the possibility of doing more harm than good. There was no shortage of relevant knowledge; the problem obviously lay in its practical application. In view of their inadequate psychological training, many liberators greeted the attitudes of those liberated with shock, bewilderment and a lack of understanding. Often they interpreted it as ingratitude. In addition to this there were also massive difficulties with language.

In an early letter Jane Leverson described the very positive attitude of the newly liberated prisoners: 'We can do practically nothing, but they are so glad to have us here'. She even asked for 20,000 Magen David and Mezuzoth to be sent across from London:

> A large number of them are Jews, and you can't imagine how thrilled they are (nurses and patients) at seeing my 'Magen David', they can hardly believe that I am a Jewess from London. I feel horribly inadequate, but they don't seem to mind at all that I can't speak Yiddish! When they ask me, I just say 'Nein, ich bin Meshugener' and they love it.[27]

A short while later, however, there was already a degree of misunderstanding and criticism evident in her observations, when she wrote: 'Everyone steals some things; some steal everything. It makes life a little bit difficult'. In a different context, she also noted that it appeared as though the people were waking up from a bad dream and now remembering their earlier lives:

> They are very often not grateful for that which is done for them. They are extremely fussy about the clothes with which they are issued. They grumble about their food; they complain if they are asked to eat their meat and vegetable course from their soup plates. They will not take 'no' for an answer, and will beg in an irritatingly 'whiney' voice, for preferential treatment; they will

bribe one in a most pathetic way ... If they are like this now, so soon after liberation, one wonders how they will re-act when once again they are really free.

Many of the former prisoners criticised the British from top to bottom, and rarely offered any praise, despite the fact that they 'have brought a remarkable amount of order into this area of chaos'.[28]

Such observations were by no means exceptions. One clearly senses the irritation and lack of understanding felt when the liberated failed to respond as the liberators had wished or expected. Many had survived months or even years in the most extreme conditions, and had adopted modes of behaviour and survival strategies that could not be shaken off simply within a matter of days. Primo Levi captured this phenomenon in a simple sentence:

> However, it took several months, before I lost the habit of fixing my gaze to the ground whilst I went about, as though I was continually searching for something edible or something I could swiftly put in my pocket and swap for bread.[29]

Before liberation, possession of a piece of bread or other foodstuff could mean the difference between life and death. Eating not only satisfied a moment of hunger, it also prevented starvation, for a certain length of time at least. That was why patients lying in bed, sometimes weeks later, would still loudly draw attention to themselves when the food was being distributed: 'When they began to carry round the bowls of soup a horrible animal-like clamour broke out', reported a British journalist. 'Skinny arms were held out, blankets fell back, and naked, scarecrow figures flung themselves forward in their beds. They were not really hungry, but craved food'.[30] Those who did not need to be served food in bed, often refused to eat in the hastily furnished dining rooms set up directly next to the kitchens in the hospital area. They preferred to take their food back to their rooms, where they could eat half of it and hide the rest. Much to the annoyance and bafflement of the helpers, a lot of this food then rotted under mattresses or pillows and behind lockers: 'Camp commanders and care workers fought a hopeless battle to stop this practice and to persuade their charges that food was no longer in short supply and that keeping it in bedrooms constituted a health hazard'.[31]

Written sources frequently contain comparisons with 'animal' or 'inhuman' behaviour: 'Children attack their food like wolves',[32] 'people who were ill gained super-human powers as soon as any food appeared', the liberated prisoners 'are hardly reminiscent of human beings',[33] they 'were abnormal mentally'.[34] 'The internees of Camp I had been reduced by starvation and the lack of facilities for normal human life, to the state of animals', HQ 10 Garrison reported: 'Their minds were completely dulled and their first reaction to the arrival of British troops was one of apathy'.[35] Occasionally there are also indications of more extreme behaviour; such instances were presented as early as in the summer of 1945 at a medical conference and were interpreted within the context of the level of prior suffering:

> Loss of normal moral standards and sense of responsibility for the welfare of others was widespread; in severe cases interest in others did not extend beyond child or parent; eventually the instinct to survive alone remained even to the extent of eating human flesh. These psychological changes were proportional to the degree of starvation.[36]

As in the case of food, there was also a great demand for clothing and this too involved safety issues. Many of the prisoners had been found naked, whilst others wore clothes that offered no protection against the weather. The living had taken the shoes and clothes from the dead, in order to survive. Appropriate or not, the clothing department that the relief teams ran at Belsen was nicknamed 'Harrods'. To begin with, it had been necessary for the team members to search the freshly dressed former internees before they left the department, but just a short while later it proved difficult to satisfy the camp residents with these mainly donated or requisitioned garments.[37] On the other hand there were some survivors who insisted on wearing their old prison uniforms even after they had received the fresh clothing, and some who continued to go about the camp naked.[38]

Very much sought-after was a consignment of lipsticks that arrived shortly after the relief teams: 'I believe nothing did more for those internees than the lipstick', Lieutenant Colonel Gonin remembered:

> Women lay in bed with no sheets and no nightie but with scarlet lips, you saw them wandering about with nothing but a blanket over their shoulders, but with scarlet lips ... At least someone had done something to make them individuals again; they were someone, no longer merely the number tattooed on the arm. At least they could take an interest in their appearance. That lipstick started to give them back their humanity.[39]

Survival strategies learned in the camps were not easily discarded. Some ill patients continued to be up and about, even though it would have been 'better' for them to lie down in bed; but it had been their past experience that those who lay around in bed were soon taken to the gas chamber.[40] Even months later patients refused to be treated by German doctors out of sheer terror.[41] Patients also refused to wear British Red Cross pyjamas out of fear that it was just another German deception, using the red emblem to reassure the patients before sending them to the gas chambers after all.[42] Fearing this to be the case, patients also refused to get into the Red Cross ambulances that were due to take them to a ship bound for Sweden.[43]

'Psychological Warfare teams could have made a big difference', a military report commented: 'Unfortunately only one team was available and that had to be withdrawn for operational reasons at the time that the evacuation from Camp I started'.[44] There were few indeed, among the military or civilian helpers, who were adequately prepared for what they found. According to Michael Marrus, the military kept the liberated prisoners at a distance, were annoyed by their needs, and misunderstood their curses.[45] Criticism of the British, as already recorded by Jane Leverson, could easily lead to the point where the former prisoners themselves, and especially the Jews among them, were viewed solely as a nuisance.[46] Frank Stern quoted a British officer, who had become involved in an argument with a Jewish survivor: 'There was a great barrier between us'. During a tour of one of the camps the survivor had stood on a mound of white ashes and asked the officer if he knew what it was he was standing on. Before the former prisoner could even finish the sentence: 'I am standing on the bodies of ...' the officer screamed at him to get down off the mound. According to Frank Stern 'This great barrier between the liberators and the liberated, ... who had differing experiences and perceptions of the horror of everyday death', only intensified the problems between the two groups in the time that followed.[47] 'You must realise that we and our liberators saw the camp with different eyes', Anita Lasker-Wallfisch later wrote:

> We had lived surrounded by filth and death for so long that we scarcely noticed it. The mountains of corpses in their varying degrees of decay were part of the landscape and we had even got used to the dreadful stench. It would be wrong to assume that everything was instantly transformed the moment the first tank entered Belsen. What the British Army found was far removed from anything it had ever had to deal with, even in wartime.[48]

The tense relationship continued. Survivors like Josef Rosensaft complained that during the early months the liberators had viewed them as nothing more than pitiful objects:

> They had forgotten that we were not brought up in Belsen, Auschwitz and other concentration camps, but had, once upon a time home and a background and motherly love and kindness; that before the calamity we, too, had our schools and universities and Yeshivot.[49]

With this, Josef Rosensaft raised important questions concerning human dignity and self-determination even under the most pitiful conditions. It was in connection to this that Henri Stern spoke about the dependence of an 'outcast and frustrated population ... on the paternal benevolence of the relief bodies'.[50]

Not all relief workers were capable of providing mental support and psychological help. Helen Bamber was just such a person, and she reported that:

> there was a need to tell you *everything*, over and over and over again. And this was the most significant thing for me, realising that you had to take it all. They would need to hold onto you, and many of them still had very thin arms, especially the ones who had come from or gone back to the East and then dragged themselves to Belsen, hands almost like claws, and they would hold you, and it was important that you held them, and often

you had to rock, there was a rocking, bowing movement, as you sat on the floor – there was very little to sit on – and you would hold onto them and they would tell you their story. Sometimes it was Yiddish, and although I had learned some, it was as though you didn't really need a language. It took me a long time to realise that you couldn't really do anything but that you just had to hang onto them and that you had to listen and to *receive* this, as if it belonged partly to you, and in that act of taking and showing that you were available you were playing some useful role. There wasn't much crying at that time, it was much later that they began really to grieve; some people had got far beyond that and they might never again have been able to weep; it wasn't so much grief as a pouring out of some ghastly vomit like a kind of horror, it just came out in all directions.[51]

One survivor gave Eva Kahn-Minden a lock of hair, and in so doing, the survivor 'unburdened [herself] for the first time about the worst period of [her] life'. Senta Hirtz wrote about 'hungry people ... not only hungry for physical food but also hungry for love, hungry for life'.[52] Others, with the best of intentions, avoided all confrontations with the past. Ruth Abrahams wrote in her 1945 essay, 'Children of Belsen',

It is difficult to say how far these children will be permanently affected by their experiences in the concentration camps. We obviously did not discuss horrors with them and all our efforts were concentrated on driving out of their minds the memories of these terrible things. They certainly look happy, are not shy or nervous when you speak to them and one can only hope that kind treatment, good food and decent living conditions may have succeeded in clearing these terrors from their thoughts.[53]

With this approach, Ruth Abrahams came very close to the contemporary view, that was later mockingly referred to as 'Wiener Wald- und Wiesenpsychoanalyse' by Ruth Klüger, which had it that the experience of the concentration camps would be of 'no lasting significance' for those under six years old.[54]

Indeed, nobody was thinking about the lifelong consequences of the recent trauma. To begin with, it was just a matter of providing 'relief', although it was also clear that 'rehabilitation' would have to follow. But this again was geared far more towards material needs, to improving the chances for a new start in life, and made little allowance for the emotional needs. Colonel F. M. Lipscomb, who was temporarily assigned to the 32nd CCS as medical adviser to the Senior Medical Officer, reassured that as the liberated prisoners' physical recovery progressed, 'normal behaviour' would also resume accordingly – 'leaving only a feeling akin to that of having had a bad dream'.[55]

NOTES

1. J. Reilly, *Belsen: The Liberation of a Concentration Camp* (London: Routledge, 1998), p.28; B. Shephard, *After Daybreak: The Liberation of Belsen, 1945* (London: Jonathan Cape, 2005), pp.31–2.
2. B. Wasserstein, *Vanishing Diaspora: The Jews in Europe since 1945* (London: Hamish Hamilton, 1996), p.1.
3. J. D. Steinert, *Nach Holocaust und Zwangsarbeit: Beobachtungen und humanitäre Hilfe in Deutschland nach dem Zweiten Weltkrieg* (Osnabrück: Secolo Veslag, forthcoming). See also J. D. Steinert, 'British NGOs in Belsen Concentration Camp: Emergency Relief and the Perception of Survivors', in J. D. Steinert and I. Weber-Newth (eds.), *Beyond Camps and Forced Labour: Current International Research on Survivors of Nazi Persecution. Proceedings of the first international multidisciplinary conference at the Imperial War Museum, London, 29–31 January 2003* (Osnabrück: Secolo Verlag, 2005), pp.44–57.
4. Friends Library, London (FL) FRS/1992/Box 8, Friends War Relief Service. Service Bulletin, 30 July 1943.
5. FL FAU/1947/3/4, FAU. Mediterranean Section to Assistant Chief of Staff, G-5, 20 September 1944.
6. Falmouth (Viscountess), 'Discussion and Closing Speech', in War Organisation of the British Red Cross Society and Order of St. John of Jerusalem (ed.), *Training Course of Pre-Armistice Civilian Relief Overseas. Report of Lectures. January 1943* (London, 1943), p.94.
7. V. Underwood, D. Scott and R. Ullmann, *A Relief Worker's Vocabulary. French–English–German*, ed. by Friends War Relief Service (London, Society of Friends, 1945).
8. S. A. Birnbaum, *Yiddish Phrase Book* (London: Linguaphone Institute, 1945).
9. Salvation Army Archive, London (SA) Relief Work: European Post 2nd World War, European Relief Study Paper No. 1. The Salvation Army European Relief Correspondence Training Course. Relief Conditions and Service (undated).
10. Wiener Library (WL) Henriques Archive 3/5, Executive Committee for European Relief. Conference on Volunteers, 2 May 1943.
11. Jewish Committee for Relief Abroad (ed.), *Dialogue on Relief* (London: Jewish Committee for Relief Abroad, 1944).
12. P. Kemp, 'The Liberation of Bergen-Belsen Concentration Camp in April 1945: The Testimony of Those Involved', *Imperial War Museum Review*, Vol.5 (1990), p.40.
13. F.S.V. Donnison, *Civil Affairs and Military Government North-West Europe 1944–1946* (London: HMSO, 1961), p.219.

EMERGENCY RELIEF AND THE PERCEPTION OF SURVIVORS

14. Ibid., p.221;, Imperial War Museum (ed.), *The Relief of Belsen, April 1945: Eyewitness Accounts* (London: IWM, 1991), p.31.
15. FL FRS/1992/Box 8, Friends War Relief Service. Digest of Overseas Reports No. 3, Week ending 5 May 1945.
16. IWM 99/86/1 (Miss J. McFarlane), Talk given to CAD; M.C. Carey, 'Progress at Belsen Camp', *British Red Cross Quarterly Review*, Vol.7 (1945), p.103.
17. IWM 85/38/1 (Lieutenant Colonel M. W. Gonin), The RAMC at Belsen Concentration Camp.
18. M.F. Beardwell, *Aftermath* (Ilfracombe: Arthur H. Stockwell, 1953), p.40.
19. Carey, 'Progress at Belsen Camp', p.104.
20. British Red Cross Archive (BRC) Acc 96/29, Belsen Letters. Letters sent from Miss Margaret Wyndham Ward MBE to her mother Sarah Langlands Ward from 24 February 1945–14 August 1945, here: 23 April 1945.
21. FL FRS/1992/Box 8, Friends War Relief Service. Digest of Overseas Reports No. 3, Week ending 5 May 1945.
22. Carey, 'Progress at Belsen Camp', p.103.
23. Ibid., Beardwell, *Aftermath*, p.42.
24. E. Bark, *No Time to Kill* (London: Hale, 1960), p.51.
25. IWM 01/19/1 (Miss M. J. Blackman), In Retrospect.
26. WL Henriques Archive 3/13, Jane Leverson: Bergen-Belsen Concentration Camp, 6 May 1945.
27. Ibid., [undated, April 1945].
28. Ibid., 6 May 1945.
29. P. Levi, *Die Atempause* (Munich: DTV, 1994), p.245.
30. 'Red Cross in Belsen. Battle Against Death', *The Times*, 16 May 1945.
31. E. Kolinsky, 'Jewish Holocaust Survivors between Liberation and Resettlement', in J. D. Steinert and I. Weber-Newth (eds.), *European Immigrants in Britain 1933–1950* (Munich: Saur, 2003), p.123.
32. M. Wyman, *DPs: Europe's Displaced Persons, 1945–1951* (Ithaca, NY: Cornell University Press, 1989), pp.96–7.
33. 'Report of Myrtle Beardwell-Wielzynska, on her work as a nurse in the liberated concentration camp Bergen-Belsen', in Niedersächsische Landeszentrale für Politische Bildung und Gedenkstätte Bergen-Belsen (ed.), *Konzentrationslager Bergen-Belsen* (Hannover: Niedersächsische Landeszentrale für politische Bildung und Gedenkstätte Bergen-Belsen, 1995), p.202.
34. IWM 85/38/1 (Lieutenant Colonel M. W. Gonin), The RAMC at Belsen Concentration Camp.
35. IWM Misc 104 (1650), Belsen. Report by HQ 10 Garrison on period 18–30 April 1945.
36. F. M. Lipscomb, 'German Concentration Camps: Diseases Encountered at Belsen', in Sir H. Letheby (ed.), *Inter-Allied Conferences on War Medicine, 1942–1945* (London: Staples Press, 1947), p.464.
37. Beardwell, *Aftermath*, pp.54–5.
38. M.R. Marrus, *The Unwanted: European Refugees in the Twentieth Century* (Oxford: Oxford University Press, 1985), p.332; A. Königseder and J. Wetzel, *Lebensmut im Wartesaal: Die jüdischen DPs [Displaced Persons] im Nachkriegsdeutschland* (Frankfurt a. Main: Fischer, 1994), p.27.
39. IWM 85/38/1 (Lieutenant Colonel M. W. Gonin), The RAMC at Belsen Concentration Camp.
40. B. McBryde, *A Nurse's War* (Saffron Walden: Cakebreads, 1993), p.168.
41. 'Work of the Jewish Relief Unit', *British Zone Review*, 29 March 1947, p.17.
42. McBryde, *A Nurse's War*, p.92.

43. Wyman, *DPs*, p.133.
44. IWM Misc 104 (1650), Belsen. Report by HQ 10 Garrison on period 18–30 April 1945.
45. Marrus, *The Unwanted*, p.308.
46. Ibid.
47. F. Stern, *Im Anfang war Auschwitz. Antisemitismus und Philosemitismus im deutschen Nachkrieg* (Gerlingen: Bleicher, 1991), p.61.
48. A. Lasker-Wallfisch, *Inherit the Truth, 1939–1945: The Documented Experiences of a Survivor of Auschwitz and Belsen* (London: Giles de la Mare, 1996), p.96.
49. J. Rosensaft, 'Our Belsen', in Irgun Sheerit Hapleita Me'haezor Habriti (ed.), *Belsen* (Tel Aviv: Irgun Sheerit Hapleita Me'haezor Habriti, 1957), pp.25–6.
50. H. Stern, 'The Aftermath of Belsen', in H.B.M. Murphy (ed.), *Flight and Resettlement* (Paris: UNESCO, 1955), p.71.
51. N. Belton, *The Good Listener. Helen Bamber: A Life against Cruelty* (London: Weidenfeld and Nicolson, 1998), p.109.
52. Ibid., p.111.
53. R. Abrahams, 'Children of Belsen', *The World's Children*, Vol.11 (1945), p.176.
54. R. Klüger, *Weiter leben: Eine Jugend*, 10th edn. (Munich; DTV, 2001), p.240.
55. Lipscomb, 'German Concentration Camps', p.464.

Andrew Matthews and the Two Sachselová Sisters

RAINER SCHULZE

Andrew Matthews was 20 years old and in his final year of medical school at St. Mary's Hospital London when, in late March/early April 1945, notices went up in the London teaching hospitals asking for student volunteers to help with the famine relief work in the Netherlands. Matthews was one of the 12 medical students selected from St. Mary's.[1] On 28 April all student volunteers were summoned to assemble at the headquarters of the British Red Cross, and were told that their destination would not be Holland, but, instead, the recently liberated concentration camp at Bergen-Belsen, where assistance with nursing, feeding and cleaning the survivors was desperately needed. They departed immediately for Cirencester, from where they were to be transported by air to Celle, but due to unseasonal bad weather the flights were delayed by up to three days, and the group from St. Mary's only arrived at Bergen-Belsen in the evening of 2 May 1945.[2]

Matthews was put in charge of one of the huts in the former women's camp. His first impression upon entering the hut stayed with him for the rest of his life, but he – as so many others – found it all but impossible to put into words what he saw, smelt and felt:

> No picture could capture the stench and even words could hardly do it justice. Add the cries and moans to the drone of insects for a cocktail of sound and smell which will never be forgotten by anyone who entered those huts. It symbolised the hopelessness and cruelty of this ghastly place ... I was helpless, I could not communicate or comfort. I felt sick ... Dead bodies roused little emotion. It was the 'living dead' that haunted me, human animals half-naked and dying, bereft of all hope and common dignity. I could not visualise them in the context of

Figure 1: The twelve medical students from St Mary's Hospital medical school who participated in the relief work at Bergen-Belsen; Andrew Matthews is in the rear row, third from the right. HU59499 (©IWM)

normal living yet they were still alive and breathing the same foul air as myself.[3]

When all the survivors of the concentration camp had been relocated to the former *Wehrmacht* barracks nearby, which British troops transformed into a huge emergency hospital and transit camp, Matthews was also posted there and allocated a women's ward with 60 beds which had been set up in a former canteen. It was here that he met Hana and Eva Sachselová, 19 and 14 years old at the time, 'two young sisters from Czechoslovakia who were very special to everyone'.[4]

Hana and Eva came from a middle-class Czech Jewish family. Their father Alfred Sachsel, a businessman, was arrested by the Germans on 1 September 1939. He was first incarcerated in Bory Prison in Pilsen and then transferred to Buchenwald concentration camp and later to Auschwitz where he perished in November 1942. His wife Růžena Sachselová and their two daughters were deported to Theresienstadt (Terezín) in January 1942. From there they were moved to Auschwitz and then to Christianstadt, a sub-camp of Groß-

Rosen. With the approach of the Red Army, the camp was hurriedly cleared in the first days of February 1945, and the prisoners were made to march on to Cheb (Eger), on a tortuous route of several hundred miles which took them via Bautzen, Pirna, Teplice-Šanov, Most, Karlovy Vary (Karlsbad), and Mariánské lázně (Marienbad). During the Allied air raid on Dresden on 13–15 February 1945, they were locked into a barn near the town, unaware of what would be happening to them. Those who survived this 'death march' were transported by train from Cheb to Bergen-Belsen. They eventually arrived at Bergen-Belsen, 781 Jewish women in all, on 15 March 1945. Eva and Hana had managed to stay together with their mother until the very end, but tragically Růžena died on 25 April 1945, ten days after the liberation of Bergen-Belsen by British troops.[5]

Matthews befriended the two orphaned sisters. After the horror and despair which he had felt earlier, they seemed to him almost like a symbol of 'the immortality of youth and hope. Throughout their long ordeal they had managed to retain their femininity. Quietly dignified and uncomplaining, they smiled their beautiful smiles whenever anyone came to help'.[6] The morning when Hana started her first period after almost three years was a particularly poignant experience as he saw this as the dawn of a new beginning after the horror of the concentration camps. The other pre-menopausal women on the ward soon followed. No one had menstruated since entering the camps, and everyone celebrated this event like a miracle: 'It was a marvellous time!'[7]

Before he returned to Britain at the end of May 1945 after 'a lifetime of almost a month' at the former concentration camp,[8] Eva gave him a little album with eight drawings depicting scenes from their life on the women's ward. Matthews was convinced that the two sisters had not survived their ordeal and had died of typhus at the Bergen-Belsen hospital after he left. He, therefore, treasured Eva's drawings even more.

Even though Matthews later said that the experience of Bergen-Belsen had not influenced his career or that of any of his peers, it can be argued that there is a link with his professional work. He became a consultant obstetrician and gynaecologist and acted as chairman of the Medical Committee of the British Amateur Athletic Board and as an honorary consultant of the Women's Amateur Athletic

Association. As such, he took a particular interest in women athletes whose periods stopped under the stress of an upcoming important competition. The impact of Bergen-Belsen is even more visible in his personal life. The memory of Hana and Eva stayed with him, and he passed their story on to his daughters, Joanna and Sally, for whom the little booklet with the eight drawings became an integral part of their childhood experience.

Matthews returned to Bergen-Belsen, but found it difficult to retrace his steps. In 1949 he was in Germany as a member of the RAF, and when he ordered a car to take him to Belsen,

> the young German girl [in the transport office] looked puzzled, 'There's no such place of that name, do you mean Hohner, sir?' She was right, as the only evidence of its existence in the lush parklands were the many grass covered mounds, each with a stark notice proclaiming, 'Approximately so many thousands of bodies buried here.'[9]

How deeply he was affected by his experience showed again in 1995, on the fiftieth anniversary of the liberation of Bergen-Belsen. Matthews visited not only the recently established documentation and information centre at the *Gedenkstätte* (memorial) but also wanted to see the former DP camp and hospital ward where he had worked in May 1945, which is again serving as military barracks, now for NATO troops.[10]

It was only after Andrew Matthews' death in 1997 that the *Gedenkstätte* learnt that Hana and Eva were both alive and well. They had returned to their native Pilsen in late June 1945, and were now living in Prague. The news was related to Matthews' two daughters who established contact with them. After more than 55 years the story had come full circle. The remarkable drawings, the result of a chance encounter of a British medical student 'willingly plucked from his sheltered life in an English country town'[11] and two young Jewish concentration camp survivors from Czechoslovakia in the aftermath of the Holocaust, now represent more than ever the immortality of hope which Matthews already detected in the faces of the two sisters when he met them in the women's ward of the *Wehrmacht* barracks next to the former concentration camp of Bergen-Belsen.

1 'The Whole Day'. HU 59502A © Eva Macourková. Reproduced by kind permission of Mrs Joanna James and Mrs Sally Harris

2 'The beds are made, the patients are washed and now come the English-men'. HU 59502B © Eva Macourková. Reproduced by kind permission of Mrs Joanna James and Mrs Sally Harris

3 'After the breakfast, patients want to hear radio. But it doesn't play!' HU 59502C © Eva Macourková. Reproduced by kind permission of Mrs Joanna James and Mrs Sally Harris

4 'Then comes the English doktor wit the Swiss-sister'. HU 59502D © Eva Macourková. Reproduced by kind permission of Mrs Joanna James and Mrs Sally Harris

5 'Dinner!' HU 59502E © Eva Macourková. Reproduced by kind permission of Mrs Joanna James and Mrs Sally Harris

6 'In the afternoon the sister takes the temperature'. HU 59502F © Eva Macourková. Reproduced by kind permission of Mrs Joanna James and Mrs Sally Harris

7 'And then comes supper!' HU 59502G © Eva Macourková. Reproduced by kind permission of Mrs Joanna James and Mrs Sally Harris

8 'Goodnight'. HU 59502H © Eva Macourková. Reproduced by kind permission of Mrs Joanna James and Mrs Sally Harris

NOTES

1. Information on Andrew Matthews was kindly provided by his daughter Joanna James, Sunbury on Thames. Matthews started medical school early at the age of 16.
2. For more detail on the work of the group from St Mary's, see J. Hankinson, 'Belsen', *St Mary's Hospital Gazette*, Vol.51 (1945), pp.74–8; and A. Matthews, 'The Belsen Experience', *St Mary's Hospital Gazette*, Vol.97 (1991), pp.18–21. For an overview of the work of the British medical student in Bergen-Belsen in general, see E. Trepman, 'Rescue of the Remnants: The British Emergency Medical Relief Operation in Belsen Camp, 1945', *Journal of the Royal Army Medical Corps*, Vol.147 (2001), esp. pp.288–90.
3. A. Matthews, 'Belsen – 1945', typescript, undated, pp.16–17 (in possession of his daughter Joanna James).
4. Ibid., p.40.
5. Most of this information was kindly provided by Eva Macourková (née Sachselová) Prague. See also *Book of Remembrance: Prisoners in the Bergen-Belsen Concentration Camp* (Bergen-Belsen: Stiftung Niedersächsische Gedenkstätten – Gedenkstätte Bergen-Belsen, 2005), Vol.2, p.894; data files on prisoners of Bergen-Belsen concentration camp held at the Gedenkstätte; Archive of the Gedenkstätte Bergen-Belsen (hereafter GBB), list of transports arriving at the women's camps of Bergen-Belsen concentration camp, compiled by Bernhard Strebel, October 2005.
6. Matthews, 'Belsen – 1945', p.40.
7. GBB, BC 43: Audio-Interview with Dr Andrew Matthews, 25 April 1995.
8. Matthews, 'The Belsen Experience', p.18.
9. Ibid., p.21. Hohne was the name the British gave to the DP camp set up in the former *Wehrmacht* barracks which existed until the summer of 1950. Matthews quotes it here incorrectly as 'Hohner'.
10. GBB, BC 43: Audio-Interview with Dr Andrew Matthews, 25 April 1995.
11. Matthews, 'Belsen – 1945', p.14.

A Few Words to Explain the Origin of My Drawings

EVA MACOURKOVÁ

In the middle of April 1945 the Bergen-Belsen concentration camp was liberated by British soldiers. For some short time they were not allowed to enter the camp until they could procure the equipment necessary to protect them against the dangerous lice that were spreading typhus. The Germans fled and the camp was completely deserted. My mother, my sister Hana and I were lying helpless, weakened by fever, hunger and thirst, surrounded by heaps of excrement and by the dead bodies of those who did not survive.

Some British soldier, wishing to help us, threw us a tin of lard over the wired fence. We eagerly devoured it which, as we realised later on, was very bad for our weakened bodies, especially for mother. She had practically not eaten at all, trying to share with us every piece of bread we got. Though only aged 45 in 1945, in my last memories of her she is a very old, ill and wrinkly woman.

Then the British soldiers returned, all of them dressed in special hermetical suits, and started transferring us into the deserted German *Wehrmacht* hospitals. Hana and I were in the same ward but mother was taken somewhere else. After some time I recovered and so was able to communicate with the Swiss Red Cross sister and the British medical staff. Then – probably due to her extremely high fever – my sister lost her hearing and did not react to the doctors' words. They thought she was in agony and wanted to bring her to some place where patients expected to die were assembled. I was lying in a bed next to hers and, being able to put together a few English sentences, I started convincing the medical personnel that I was her sister, that she would certainly recover, and that I would take care of her. My sister often says that in this way I probably saved her life because, finally, she was left in our ward.

Thereafter we both started recovering under the kind care of a young British doctor whose name was Andrew Matthews. After the almost three and a half years we had spent in various German concentration camps, we felt as if we were in heaven. He was the first one to treat us as human beings. My sister and I shall never forget him, his thoughtful and tender care, kindness and sense of humour. Upon our request and under his guidance the Swiss nurse tried to find our mother. Having found out that she died in another ward, she did not tell us until we recovered and were strong enough to cope with the loss. Moreover, doctor Matthews used all then available means to help us in many ways. To give an example: he instructed the hospital nurse to apply camphor in order to relieve our pains caused by bedsores. I also remember that, knowing I was an orphan, he suggested the possibility of adopting and taking me to England but, although I admired and respected him very much, I preferred to return to Czechoslovakia. However, the recollection of his kindness has accompanied my sister and me throughout the whole of our lives. In gratitude for the way he helped us return to life after the horrors of Auschwitz and of typhus I made him these drawings which describe one day in the hospital ward after our liberation in April 1945. They express my thanks for having survived, for beginning a new life after more than three years of deprivation, for the miracle of the doctor's and nurse's kind and soothing words, the clean bed, the regular meals after the never-ending and gnawing pains of hunger.

Our parents had been aware that we should learn foreign languages. That is why, even before the war, my sister and I had taken English lessons which enabled me in the Bergen-Belsen ward to accompany my drawings with the funny little English texts (with a lot of mistakes). But I remember being very proud of them. Unfortunately, our parents did not live to witness how prudent they had been when insisting upon our learning languages. Father perished in the gas chambers in Auschwitz and mother lies in a mass grave in Bergen-Belsen.

I was 14 when I produced the drawings. In 2003, having almost forgotten them, I was extremely touched to get a letter from doctor Matthew's daughter, Mrs Joanna James. She wrote that her father, who had died some years ago, gave her the little booklet with the drawings I had made for him. For 58 years my sister and I did not know anything about the fortunes of doctor Matthews and, when getting the letter from Mrs James (who had established contact with us through Dr Thomas Rahe from the Bergen-Belsen Memorial), we were happy and proud to hear how he had cherished the little booklet drawn for him and how the determination and bravery of the women he had to look after in Bergen-Belsen were the crucial motives for his decision to become a gynaecologist.

What happened to us after Belsen? We returned to our native Pilsen in Czechoslovakia and my sister Hana (who was 19 in 1945) took over the role of our deceased mother. She could not study because she had to earn money for both of us. Luckily she soon married a very kind man with whom she created a home for me. Later on she completed her education and was employed as a clerk. She has two daughters, six grandchildren and four great-grandchildren. When returning from Bergen-Belsen, I was happy to be allowed to go to school again. After finishing my university studies in Prague, I worked as a translator until 1994. I have one daughter and two grandchildren.

Despite the cruel experience of 1942–45 we lived a happy life, being able to appreciate even small and seemingly unimportant things and events which we were missing so much in the concentration camps and which are taken for granted by other people who did not share our fate.

PART II
COMPILING THE RECORD

The Filming of the Liberation of Bergen-Belsen and its Impact on the Understanding of the Holocaust

TOBY HAGGITH

The 33 rolls of film and more than 200 photographs taken of Bergen-Belsen by members of the British Army's Film and Photographic Unit (AFPU) is arguably the most influential of any record or artefact documenting the Nazi concentration camps.[1] Not only have these images ensured that the story of this particular concentration camp will never be forgotten, but they have been so widely used in film and television programmes that they have become an icon not of just the Holocaust, but of the evils of the Nazi regime as a whole.[2] Indeed, this iconic status was controversially exploited at the time of the discovery of a 'modern' day equivalent of a Nazi concentration camp, filmed by a camera crew in Trnopolje, Bosnia in August 1992.[3]

Among the images of concentration camps most familiar to the general public, those taken at Belsen are some of the most grotesque and disturbing. Ronald Tritton, Director of Public Relations at the War Office, recorded in his war diary, 'The Belsen pictures came in this evening – 103 of them. They are so awful that words cannot describe them. I was almost physically sickened, and felt shaky and very upset'.[4]

Other factors set the film shot at Belsen apart from other records. Firstly, no other camp was filmed so comprehensively and over such a long period. The film is not just a record of the 'liberation', but also documents the efforts of the British army to stabilise the conditions in the camp, to save lives and return the survivors to health. Secondly, the Belsen footage was the first to be admitted as evidence to a war crimes trial, when it was screened in the courtroom at Lüneburg during the Belsen trial between 17 September and 17 November 1945. Thirdly, because of Belsen's function as an 'exchange camp' and as the main destination for prisoners moved from the camps in the east (notably Auschwitz-Birkenau) as the Red Army approached in early 1945, it had a particularly high proportion of Jewish inmates, and has thus become closely associated with the Holocaust.

All the footage shot by British Army cameramen at Bergen-Belsen in the spring and summer of 1945 has been preserved in the archives of the Imperial War Museum. It is supported by contemporaneous documentation, notably the cameramen's dope sheets or 'Secret Caption Sheets' in which they detailed the scenes they had filmed, bundling these together with the exposed rolls of films sent back to the AFPU base in Pinewood for developing. The Museum also holds recordings of sound interviews with the cameramen, recalling their experiences at Belsen.[5]

Existing Historical Examinations of the Belsen Film

Surprisingly, until recently there was little examination of the work of the AFPU cameramen, despite most scholars acknowledging that their images have been crucial in publicising the horrors of the Nazi concentration camps.[6] For example, in the book arising out of a conference to mark the 50th anniversary of the camp's liberation, there is only a brief account of the role of the cameramen after the liberation and their recollections were not included among a wide range of other reminiscences by survivors and liberators printed as appendices.[7] Even in Joanne Reilly's study of the period after the liberation of the camp, there is slight attention to the work of the cameramen, with an acknowledgement of the challenges they faced, but no real analysis.[8] It is particularly surprising that film and cultural historians have paid so little attention to this resource. For example, the leading Holocaust film scholar Annette Insdorf makes only a passing reference to the unedited film of the camps, which she inaccurately describes as 'newsreel'.[9] She does not explore how it was shot, who the cameramen were or the context of the filming, but focuses instead on well-known filmmakers – the directors or editors such as Alain Resnais and Erwin Leiser – and how their works treated the archive footage – often reshaping it dramatically. Therefore,

Insdorf and others have shown much more interest in the *Memory of the Camps* (1945, 1985), the unfinished British film about the concentration camps, a large proportion of which is based on the rolls shot at Belsen. Not only does *Memory of the Camps* present the unedited footage in a far more accessible package (a narrative structure with a voice-over commentary), it is also closely associated with prominent figures from British cinema – Sidney Bernstein (the producer) and Alfred Hitchcock (treatment adviser).

When one turns to the photographic record of the liberation of the camps, a similar pattern emerges. Thus while there are plenty of published studies on the work of independent war photographers such as Lee Miller (who photographed Dachau for *Vogue*), Margaret Bourke-White (Buchenwald) and George Rodger and Bert Hardy who both covered Belsen (for the Magnum agency and *Picture Post* respectively), very little is known about official military photographers such as Sergeant Harry Oakes, one of the Army photographers at Belsen.[10] This reflects a general scholarly neglect of military photography, possibly stemming from suspicion that such work is propagandist and cannot be relied upon to provide a truthful record of war.

Ignorance of the unedited footage covering the liberation of Belsen, combined with the ubiquity of certain sequences that have been seared on the minds of the general public, has led to confusion about the film and the history of the camp itself. Tony Kushner observes that the repeated use of the famous sequence of the bulldozer pushing corpses into a mass grave has been insensitive to the memory of the dead, the dignity of the individual lost in the heaps of anonymous bodies.[11] This is a valid observation, but Kushner wrongly assumes that these scenes were first used in the newsreels released in the spring of 1945. In fact many of the most shocking scenes from Belsen, including the bulldozer sequences, were not released to the newsreels at the time. (The bulldozer sequences do not even feature in the special newsreels and longer films which German audiences were compelled to view.) But Kushner is not alone in making this error: many people who saw the newsreels covering the liberation of the concentration camps have vivid recollections of watching these scenes. Even the silent cinema expert Kevin Brownlow was prompted by a festival screening of *Memory of the*

Camps to recount the first time he had watched these scenes as a child:

> In 1945 when I was six, I was taken by my mother to a children's matinee of a Russian fairy tale called *The Little Hump-Backed Donkey* at the Cameo-Poly in Regent Street. The newsreels did not require censorship, and no one knew what was going to be in them. The newsreel came on and we were treated to the horrors of Belsen - the shots of the bodies being bulldozed were even more grotesque than the ones in MEMORIES. We children didn't understand what was going on - but the mothers were hysterical, and this terrified us. Oddly enough, all my fear was transferred to the Soviet fairy tale and I was horrified by scenes in that rather than by the newsreel.[12]

In actual fact the first public exposure of this footage was probably not until it was incorporated into Alain Resnais' film *Night and Fog*, ten years after the liberation of the concentration camps. Even so, Resnais was himself wrongly accused, by those who watched his film in 1955, of 'suppressing' the most terrible images of the liberation they had seen in 1945.[13] Historian Christian Delage's explanation for this phenomenon is that in the intervening years, people's memory of these events had been darkened, 'by the thousands of written testimonies published since as well as the exhibitions and reconstructions'.[14]

More worrying is the confusion about the purpose of Bergen-Belsen and its place within the history of the concentration camps, created by the indiscriminate use of the most horrific imagery to illustrate numerous television and film documentaries. Film scholar Joshua Hirsch believed for many years that the bulldozer sequence in *Night and Fog* (1955) showed a *Nazi* soldier driving the vehicle, in other words, that the film was actually documenting a scene in one of the death camps.[15] This understandable error arose partly because elsewhere in *Night and Fog*, Alain Resnais could not resist the temptation to use the footage covering the efforts of the British Army to bury the thousands of corpses at Belsen, to stand for everyday life in the camps. This sleight of hand has been repeated again and again. In *The Angel of Bergen-Belsen* (1998), a documentary for television celebrating the efforts of Luba Trysanska to preserve the lives of a group of 50 children who arrived at Bergen-Belsen, her experiences as a prisoner at Auschwitz were illustrated with footage from Belsen shot after liberation.[16]

Ironically, given the common misattribution of Belsen footage for scenes in extermination camps, there is the danger that without properly contextualising this film it is not clear to the viewer that the majority of the dead and survivors found at Belsen were Jewish, a problem compounded by the fact that the 1945 coverage of the liberation tended to universalise the suffering and downplay the high number of Jews in the camp.[17] The anonymous nature of the corpses seen in the Belsen footage has even led Holocaust deniers to claim that these were in fact the victims of Allied bombing![18]

A more insidious criticism of the screening of the Belsen footage is that it demeans and dehumanises Holocaust survivors, reinforcing a common perception that they did not resist their fate.[19] There is also a danger that the viewer becomes brutalised by the endless views of naked, emaciated corpses, the anonymity of the bodies distancing us from what the Holocaust meant in human terms.[20] Inevitably, the cameramen have been blamed for contributing to these distortions, by concentrating on images of the dead and losing sight of the individual in the urge to prove the grotesque scale of the suffering.[21] There is also an implied criticism that they acted callously when filming the helpless inmates, transgressing taboos about the portrayal of the dead and the human body and showing little respect for their subjects. For these reasons, many have qualms about the screening of the Belsen footage, some arguing that it so distorts our understanding of the Holocaust that it should never be shown.[22]

Recent research by Hannah Caven and this author has led to a much more sympathetic assessment of the efforts of the AFPU's cameramen at Belsen.[23] Moreover, analysis, particularly by Caven, of press and newsreel coverage of the liberation of the camps, has shifted the blame for the distortions in accounts of Belsen from the cameramen to the wartime media.[24] Anna Reading's work on gender and the representation of the Holocaust led to a similar conclusion, when she suggested that *Memory of the Camps* had not been released, because the cameramen had decided not to self-censor the scenes in front of the camera, notably by recording images of men and women's naked bodies, whether as corpses or survivors.[25] This essay will build on this earlier reassessment of the work of the AFPU, and explore through a detailed analysis of the work of the cameramen and a typological survey of the film, its great historical and cultural value.

The Filming at Bergen-Belsen

On the evening of 15 April 1945, members of the AFPU accompanying other elements of the 11th Armoured Division entered the camp of Bergen-Belsen. The cameramen remained deeply troubled by what they saw that first evening. In an interview in 1979, Harry Oakes recalled the awful moment when he was shown into a marquee in the women's camp, where he expected to find people who had been beaten up as they had previously found at Celle, and instead there was a heap of corpses, 5-6 feet deep.[26] As it was the evening, and perhaps reflecting the casual air with which the cameramen approached the camp, Oakes and his comrades had left their cameras in the vehicles and so no photography and filming took place during that first visit. After leaving the camp the Unit went to look for a billet in a nearby village, appropriately enough settling on a small cinema. After eating and the usual soldierly banter about matters unrelated to the camp, they tried to sleep. But the cameramen had found their brief 'recce' of the camp disquieting and a brooding silence descended. Oakes found that, 'When my head was on that pillow I thought it would explode. I just couldn't unwind for hours and hours'.[27] Sergeant William Lawrie was also disturbed:

> I remember that night trying to sleep and being completely unable to sleep. And there was no – you couldn't say it was fear, you couldn't say it was discomfort, because we were comparatively comfortable, we were under a shelter...There was a kind of terrible horror. I can't explain it ... I didn't disturb anybody else. And everybody else that was there was the same – drivers and cameramen. Everybody pretended to be asleep and nobody was sleeping for some reason or another.[28]

The next morning Sergeants Haywood, Lawrie, Lewis and Oakes (photography), under the command of Lieutenant Martin Wilson, began to film and photograph the camp. Cine-cameramen Lewis and

Lawrie stayed until 26 April, compiling most of the moving images taken at Belsen during the crucial phase when the British army struggled to stabilise the horrendous situation in the camp.[29] As a unit the AFPU continued to cover activity at the camp up until 9 June 1945, including the ceremonial burning of the camp huts from 19–21 May.[30]

AFPU policy of recruiting from the ranks meant that the cameramen who went into Belsen were tough and battle-hardened, but this had not prepared them for the mounds of naked corpses, and the vast scale of suffering and death. Moreover, the dead bodies they had previously encountered, men in uniform, were an expected consequence of battle. As Oakes recalled, 'we couldn't understand it. We had seen corpses, we had seen our own casualties, but these bloodless bodies ... they were so young some of them as well, men and women'.[31]

In common with British civilians, these soldiers and military cameramen had been sceptical of previous press reports of German atrocities.[32] Dick Williams, who was with the Royal Army Service Corps and one of the first to enter the camp, confided to a friend, 'I

Figure 2: Sergeant Oakes and Sergeant Lawrie with their cameras next to a jeep, no date. BU 8368 (©IWM)

never believed all the fantastic stories we've heard, read about, and the atrocities committed by the SS men and women, but after being here four days, boy some experience'.[33] Even for Sergeant Lewis, who was Jewish, the discovery of Belsen was a tremendous shock:

> The terrible discovery came to me, a sort of revelation, a flash of lightning because it penetrated these terrible scenes, to make me think. All the stories I'd heard about the persecution of people from my mother and father, here they were true.[34]

Before April 1945, the Allied armies' direct contact with the German camp system had revealed that the regime included torture and mistreatment but the evidence had not suggested mass murder.[35] Once the British Army moved into Germany, however, more camps were discovered and now they contained inmates who bore witness to their treatment. The discovery on 12 April of Stalag XIB at Celle, a town only 13 miles from Belsen, provided a foretaste of what would come later. Here the shocked cameramen recorded scenes of a dead inmate and various other brutalised and emaciated prisoners of the camp.[36] But as Sergeant Lawrie recalled, although this was terrible, '... as we found later, this was actually a Sunday school picnic as to what was really happening once we got further up the road'.[37] One should stress that the British army was totally ignorant as to what was really happening in Belsen. Indeed the cameramen were fairly blasé about the prospect of going into the camp and accepted the German description of it as containing political and criminal prisoners. For the British the most interesting aspect of Belsen was the unique opportunity, created by the neutral zone, to observe and film the *Wehrmacht* and SS close-up and fully armed, in their natural habitat. Sergeant Grant noted that 'One shot shows German officers greeting each other with the Nazi salute'.[38]

AFPU training was designed to equip men with 'a sound basic knowledge for battle photography', not how to cover civilian situations.[39] Surprisingly there were no official guidelines on filming military dead, let alone the kind of scenes found in concentration camps. Instead, AFPU cameramen imposed their own strict but straightforward set of guidelines: enemy dead were filmed; badly wounded or dead Allied servicemen were not. This self-censorship was also extended to the corpses of civilians or those in distress.

These guidelines arose out of a strong sense of comradeship with the men who served alongside the cameramen. But it was also a practical response to the sensibilities of British newsreel editors, who had produced a sanitised account of the war – initially newsreel company heads had even been reluctant to use film of the concentration camps.[40]

Although members of the AFPU were encouraged to produce footage suitable for the commercial newsreels, their primary role was to compile a historical record of Britain's armed forces. If the AFPU decided something was important, they would cover it. The fact that so many units of the Army became involved with Belsen and that the camp was under Army jurisdiction for so long, was justification enough.[41] Moreover, a precedent for this kind of filming had already been set by the advancing Red Army: Soviet-filmed scenes of German atrocities had even appeared in British newsreels.[42] AFPU cameramen had long understood the importance of filming camp liberations: the propaganda derived by the Soviets from footage of German atrocities, along with scenes of British soldiers helping civilians, were among the examples given in the instructors' notes at Pinewood to instil 'news sense' in the trainees.[43]

Figure 3: A dead German officer filmed at Arnhem, probably by Sergeant 'Jock' Walker, 14 September 1944. FLM 3727 (© IWM)

Figure 4: A camp inmate grasps the hand of Lieutenant Martin Wilson (AFPU), 16 April 1945. MH 2436 (© IWM)

Colonel Hugh Stewart, who commanded No. 5 Section of the AFPU and entered Belsen on the first day, immediately realised that this discovery 'was so much one of the things that the war was about'.[44] Therefore he instructed Lieutenant Wilson and the sergeants to stay in Belsen for a couple of weeks to get total coverage. The cameramen shared Stewart's conviction that Belsen deserved special coverage, despite the great emotional and psychological strain involved. Years later Lawrie recalled simply, 'This had to be recorded somehow'.[45] Paul Wyand 'willingly accepted' the job, 'as we feel it is the duty of everybody to see it, as it is the most revolting proof of what we are fighting for'.[46]

It is possible that they, and Stewart in particular, may have been aware of the wider value of this footage, and specifically for a SHAEF (Supreme Headquarters Allied Expeditionary Force) project to make a documentary about German atrocities. As early as February 1945, Sidney Bernstein, head of film in the Psychological Warfare department of SHAEF, was investigating the possibility of making such a production which would combine footage from military film

Figure 5: Sergeant Mike Lewis filming a mass burial. Former guards can be seen unloading and carrying the corpses of the inmates, 24 April 1945. FLM 1232 (© IWM)

units of all the Allied nations. It is likely that those involved in the making of the atrocity film impressed upon the AFPU the importance of securing a comprehensive film record. As early as the 20 April, Sergei Nolbandov, who had been asked to investigate the atrocity documentary, wrote to the War Office ordering copies of the film shot at Celle and Belsen with all the accompanying dope sheets.[47]

Sergeant Lewis explained in his dope sheet of 16 April: 'It is regretted that separate shots could not be mentioned in writing but so much was happening and so quickly that it was decided to dispense with the captioning of separate shots especially as the material is self-explanatory'.[48] In this regard, they were helped by Lieutenant Wilson, who ensured that the different activities in the camp were properly covered and that the cameramen did not get too close to individual inmates or situations that would have been distressing. Mike Lewis was glad that he was busy filming every day and Sergeant Oakes busied himself with the camera equipment as a distraction.[49] The lens both limited the scenes and operated as a protective barrier for the cameramen; Oakes talked of closing one eye from the horror.[50]

This preoccupation with the job in hand led to a hardening in the men's attitudes: Sergeant Leatherbarrow witnessed an incident when Lawrie was filming the bulldozer filling one of the mass graves, and Lawrie shouted out 'Look out Mike here comes a beauty', within earshot of Ellen Wilkinson MP, one of a party of VIPs visiting the camp. But as Lawrie himself astutely observed, '... if you had become too involved, I think you would have gone mad along with the rest of the people'.[51]

By now it should be obvious to the reader that under the extreme conditions at Belsen the idea that any of the scenes could have been faked or restaged for the camera is preposterous. This was not like the picturesque liberation of the concentration camp at Cosenza near Naples, where the inmates had twice re-enacted the moment of their liberation for Sergeant Hopkinson's camera.[52] As Lawrie recalled, 'Some of them were too far gone to move. There was certainly no way we could have asked them to rehearse a piece for us'.[53] Generally, people involuntarily smiled or at least acknowledged the presence of

Figure 6: Prisoners re-enacting the moment of liberation for Sergeant Hopkinson (AFPU) at Cosenza near Naples, 29 September 1943. FLM 3726 (© IWM)

a camera; even in the oppressive ghettos of occupied Europe the inmates smiled at the camera, making many of these photographs and films unusable for the curators of the Imperial War Museum's Holocaust exhibition.[54] Thus it is an indication of the abysmally low physical and psychological state of most of the survivors at Belsen that they were oblivious of the camera, even though the cameramen were often so intrusive when filming.

Directing the inmates for propaganda purposes was further prevented by the language barrier: Lawrie, Lewis and the rest found that their 'Army German and French' was of only limited use when communicating with the Czechs, Poles, Russians, Dutch and many other nationalities populating the camp. Finally, given the enormous task preoccupying the other British army units at Belsen, there were limits to the co-operation the cameramen could expect of their comrades. They could not, for example, as Lawrie pointed out, have directed the bulldozer driver to restage the sequence in which corpses were pushed into a pit.[55] But perhaps more importantly, faking or restaging scenes for the camera was contrary to the ethos of the AFPU, and during their training the cameramen were instructed to note down in their dope sheets if scenes were staged.[56]

Apart from allocating filming jobs and very general directions, Lieutenant Wilson left decisions about framing to the individual cameramen.

In their dope sheets the cameramen frequently commented on the evidential value of the visual record they were compiling: 'It is impossible to put into writing all that was seen but these pictures should give pictorial evidence of the brutality and callousness of the "Master Race"'.[57] Unlike other camps where instruments of torture and gas chambers had been found, at Belsen the evidence of mistreatment was the condition of the camp inmates, which may partly explain why the cameramen repeatedly filmed sequences documenting the human suffering: heaps of bodies on the ground or in pits; inmates sitting listlessly on the ground; studies of survivors their faces drawn and pinched from hunger. As well as panning and shooting in long and mid-shot to give a sense of the great numbers that had suffered, the cameramen filmed many details in forensic close-up: arms tattooed with prison numbers; portraits of dead faces, mouths gaping open.

Concerned that the scenes in the camps were so terrible that they would not be believed by the general public in Britain and America and would be denied by the Germans,[58] the Allied camera teams filmed visits to the camps by well-known military and political figures such as Eisenhower and the enforced inspections of the camps by German civilians.[59] To corroborate the film evidence at Belsen, it was decided to film sound interviews with various witnesses.[60] Statements from the camp's doctor Fritz Klein, SS guards, former prisoners and members of the British contingent now in charge, were duly filmed with the backdrop of a mass grave or other camp scene. A crucial corroboration aimed at German audiences was film of an enforced visit to the camp by the Bürgermeister and civic officials from Celle, during which they, and men and women of the SS camp guard, were made to listen to an address by the British commander and watch the dead buried in a mass grave. This was sound recorded, the *Movietone* cameramen taking the additional precaution of naming all those filmed in the shot sheet.

Figure 7: A 'corroborating' interview with Franz Hosler (33 years old, Munich), 23 April 1945. FLM 3730 (© IWM)

THE FILMING OF THE LIBERATION OF BERGEN-BELSEN 103

Figure 8: A former prisoner watches a mass burial. A composition which demonstrates the ability of the cameramen to identify with the feelings of the survivors, 18 April 1945. Probably Sergeant Lawrie. FLM 3721 (©IWM)

Sidney Bernstein drew up a set of directives to ensure that the images of the camps could be used to prevent any future German attempts to 'minimise the atrocities or to claim that any particular section of the German population was ignorant of them'.[61] However, this was not released until mid-May 1945, by which stage many of Bernstein's shot suggestions (such as filming Germans visiting Dachau signing statements that they had been there) were no longer possible. Later when advising on the making of the joint Allied film on the concentration camps, Alfred Hitchcock suggested certain techniques such as minimal cutting between sequences so that the filmmakers could not be accused of faking.[62] AFPU practice of taking long and wide shots to establish a scene followed by mid-shots and close-ups of the same subject, helped to deflect possible accusations that the scenes filmed at Belsen were faked. But the cameramen also took special precautionary shots, such as panning up from a mid-shot of a dead child to a general view of the camp and views of the camp from the observation towers.

The filming of the burial scenes enabled the cameramen to record the punishment meted out on the guards by the British and on behalf of the inmates, who had before liberation been compelled to carry out this ghastly task. Thus the cameramen constantly cut from scenes of the burials to the faces of the inmates who looked on, watching their former oppressors, their moods switching between angry jubilation and subdued anguish. In a powerful gesture of identity with the inmates' feelings, the cameramen also filmed the burials from the position of the onlookers, framing sequences of the bulldozer pushing corpses, with the shoulders, heads and faces of the traumatised survivors.

In line with the primary function of the AFPU, there is much coverage of the Army's efforts to bring food and succour to the camp's inmates and, of course, lengthy coverage of all aspects of the

Figure 9: A 'cross' in the foreground of a scene filmed by Sergeant Mike Lewis, in which Father Morrison (left) and Father Kadziolka (right) bless a mass grave, 23 April 1945. FLM 3719 (© IWM)

Figure 10: The corpse of an inmate being dragged to a mass grave. Detail of feet filmed by Sergeant Mike Lewis, 24 April 1945. FLM 3720 (©IWM)

Figure 11: 'Romance in a Romantic Setting'. A former prisoner with a British soldier at Belsen, 15/16 May 1945. Filmed by Lt. Wilson or Sgt. Hewitt. FLM 3723 (© IWM)

medical operation. Not surprisingly, the soldiers and AFPU cameramen took a special interest in the young women at the camp, and there are a number of sequences of women chatting with British soldiers, sleeping and washing.

A common framing device was to film the inmates through the lattice of the camp's barbed wire fence. To give an impression of the terrible smell, they filmed the bulldozer driver grimacing and spitting and he and the onlookers holding handkerchiefs to their faces.

The camera is often very close to the faces of the guards - as if we could spit or strike a blow through the lens. The camera looks in incomprehension at the guards' impassive faces, searching for an explanation, and contrasts the arrogant, stout well-fed guards with the hopeless, emaciated prisoners. The contrast between the conditions inside the camp and the bucolic scenes just outside was also recorded, with Sergeant Lewis filming cows in a lush meadow and a German woman sitting with her children on a sunny lawn.[63]

Figure 12: Study of women showering in the Mobile Bath Unit. Filmed by Sergeant William Lawrie, 22 April 1945. FLM 3724 (© IWM)

When asked about shot composition, Harry Oakes talked of selecting angles that would deepen the horror, and Mike Lewis recalled incorporating a spade that looked like a cross near a grave to give the image extra symbolic power.[64] There are also other allegorical references in the framing, notably naked male bodies splayed, martyr-like, on the ground. Oakes has been honest enough to admit that photographing the camp was a great opportunity: 'We felt in many ways it was a hell of a scoop, to be there at the time, when you think of the newsreel value of such a thing'.[65] New methods were tried to impart the horrors of the camp: both Lawrie and Lewis filmed the zig-zag marks in the soil at the side of a pit, made by the feet of the corpses hanging from the shoulders of the SS, a shot chilling in its sensuous power.

Not surprisingly, the cameramen were relieved to get away from the camp and 'go on to softer things'.[66] They were delighted by signs of the return of normal life, captioning scenes in the dope sheets of 'fraternisation', children playing or women picking out new clothes at 'Harrods', with affection and humour:

> Interior of the stable, the blouse and jumper department. Mrs H.Tanner, of Stoke Rectory, Grantham, Lincs, helps an undecided customer to make up her mind over the important problem of whether green is more becoming than speckled brown.[67]

'The degradation of men and women for years and in spite of this, they still have a spark of decency which asserts itself to wash and clean their bodies and clothes' remarked Lewis in a dope sheet on 16 April.[68] To the casual viewer, the many scenes of naked strangers washing (or even worse *being* washed in the hospital barracks) may seem voyeuristic and intrusive. This may be so but the reverently framed scenes and touchingly respectful accompanying comments in the dope sheets suggest that for the cameramen such scenes were in fact a celebration of life and humanity.

The lack of lights meant that the cameramen could not film inside the huts. Later, as conditions in the camp stabilised and medical wards were set up in the military barracks adjacent to the camp, cameramen were frustrated at being unable to properly record the heroic efforts of the medical staff and the heart-warming scenes of

Figure 13: Former prisoners selecting clothes in 'Harrods'. Scene filmed by Sergeant Harris, 15/16 May 1945. FLM 3722 (© IWM)

the restoration of life and human dignity. When Sergeant Parkinson filmed patients being washed and de-loused by German nurses and orderlies in the Cleansing Centre, he warned the technicians at Pinewood: 'I have shot this sequence having waited several days for the right light. If a suitable occasion arises when the sun shines in through the windows, I will shoot again if required. Please advise'.[69] As a consequence, in the dope sheets there are numerous complaints and warnings to the lab technicians back in England to 'boil' the film negative to ensure that some of the crucial interior scenes were developed.[70] But perhaps the biggest problem was that the unit did not routinely carry sound recording equipment and so Colonel Stewart was thwarted in his desire to arrange to film a sound interview with Belsen's former Commandant, Josef Kramer.

Generally, AFPU dope sheets are fairly impersonal accounts detailing the scenes covered on the rolls of films. But occasionally the writing moved beyond the impersonal shot sheet form, into the first person, giving impressions and opinions. The dope sheets accompanying the rolls shot at Belsen are an especially powerful and rare example of this diary form, the cameramen perhaps seeing their observations on the immoral camp system as a witness statement to stand alongside the film.[71]

In response to those who have criticised the 'liberation films' for ignoring or overlooking the high proportion of Jews in the camp, the dope sheets also reveal that the cameramen were quick to realise that Jews were in the majority at Belsen. Nor did they attempt to conceal this fact. Lawrie noted on his first day's filming:

> The inmates who were called by the Germans, political prisoners, were of all religions and countries, mostly Jews whose only crime lay in the fact that they were Jews.[72]

The cameramen recognised that there was much that could not be conveyed on film. Lawrie apologetically remarked, 'The atmosphere about the whole camp makes the job extremely difficult – it is hoped that some of this atmosphere has got into the pictures'.[73] The dope sheets were where the cameramen supplemented the images on the films with descriptions of the heat, the deathly silence and, most terrible of all, the smell: 'Photographing was not easy as the day became very hot and the hundreds of dead smelt to "high heaven"'.[74]

The Impact of the Belsen Footage in 1945

The footage from Belsen, along with that of other camps and sites of atrocities discovered by the Americans and British, was edited into newsreels and special longer films for screening to German and Allied audiences. These films were immensely important in proving to a previously sceptical public the existence of the camps and the brutal treatment to which the prisoners had been routinely subjected. As Sidney Bernstein remarked:

> The effect of these films on audiences everywhere has been very powerful and has brought home the horror of these camps much more effectively than was possible with still photographs, news stories or radio broadcasts.[75]

As reactions to British films of the camps reveals, many were ignorant of their existence or suspicious that earlier official reports of Nazi atrocities had been exaggerated or were as fallacious as the atrocity propaganda circulated by the British about the Germans during the First World War.[76] Visual evidence from American and British sources was also important in convincing even those in official circles that Soviet reports of the discovery of the extermination facilities at Majdanek and Auschwitz had in fact been genuine. The majority of British people approved of the screening of the Belsen footage and felt that adults should make it their duty to see them.[77]

Not everyone believed the film was genuine.[78] As Leslie Mitchell, the voice of *Movietone News*, recalled when he attended a screening of the newsreels of the liberation of Belsen and Buchenwald:

> Yet when we showed the much-edited pictures in London, there was a crowd of people outside the Empire Cinema with banners proclaiming 'Don't be misled! These films are propaganda. They are fakes!'[79]

AFPU cameramen Charles Hutchinson recalled that after the war he was often asked:

> 'All those pictures about Belsen, they were all faked weren't they?'and they were begging for confirmation of this fact. Now this means that those pictures, although they didn't want to believe them had had such an impact on them that they felt the need to unburden themselves as to whether or not they themselves in their lives had made a real mistake.[80]

Film of the discovery of the camps was a powerful propaganda weapon for the Allies and used as a moral justification for the war. In the issue of the *Gaumont British News* released in April 1945, the commentator reminded the viewers that not only were the scenes in the camp proof of the brutal and evil nature of the Nazi regime, and thus justification enough for the war, but a warning of the fate that was likely to have befallen the British if the war had been lost: 'Never forget, but for the Battle of Britain this might have been you'.[81] Similar sentiments were repeated in the joint Allied documentary account of the campaign from D-Day, *The True Glory* (1945), although in this context, footage of the atrocities discovered in the camps was valuable propaganda coming after a

THE FILMING OF THE LIBERATION OF BERGEN-BELSEN 111

long and hard-fought campaign on continental Europe that had cost thousands of lives.[82]

In these contexts it is interesting to note that the Belsen footage was actually used very sparingly, and that the most offensive footage of the burials in mass graves and the bulldozer scenes, were not released to the public until after the war.[83] In fact the only scenes of the condition of the prisoners used in the first batch of newsreels reporting the discovery of the camps, were from the 600ft of cinefilm shot by Sergeant Haywood on 16 April; all that was included of Lewis and Lawrie's coverage were the close-ups of Josef Kramer and the SS guards being paraded out of the barracks.[84] When the newsreels returned to the Belsen story at the end of May and June to cover the ceremonial burning of the camp huts, scenes of mass burials were included, but these were quite ordered and dignified, with an Army chaplain shown officiating over the burial and the corpses carefully lined up in mass graves and shrouded.[85]

The British intended that general audiences in liberated and neutral countries, as well as Britain and the US, would have the opportunity to see the full extent of the atrocities discovered in Belsen and the other camps in a special documentary (retrospectively titled *Memory of the Camps*). However, this was never completed and the project was eventually shelved.[86] Scenes that had not been passed to the newsreels showing SS guards burying naked female corpses and of mid shots of the tangle of corpses in the mass graves did briefly appear in *The True Glory* which was released to the cinemas in August 1945.

The atrocity footage was also used by Allied propagandists as part of a de-Nazification and re-education programme in Germany and Austria. One would have assumed that in films for this purpose, Allied propagandists would not have demurred from using the most graphic and brutal scenes recorded by the AFPU. However, in the special newsreel screened to German audiences, the editors mainly used the footage shot by Sergeant Haywood. None of the bulldozer sequences were included and the only extra footage consisted of long and mid shots of naked corpses (not that the rest of the material shot by other Allied camera teams was not distressing).[87] *Die Todesmühlen* (Death Mills, 1945) the longer American documentary about the camps, also avoided use of the most extreme views. However, comprehensive coverage of Belsen, including all of the most graphic and damning scenes, did appear in a special mute and untitled compilation of the AFPU footage put together for screening during the Nuremberg Trials.[88]

The Impact of the Belsen Footage since the War and Some Conclusions

Since the early 1950s the footage from Bergen-Belsen has had another 'life' – as an archival record of an historic event, catalogued and conserved in the Film Archive of the Imperial War Museum. Successive uses of the film in numerous secondary productions have kept it as important and influential as it was at the end of the war. Moreover, because this footage was no longer subject to censorship, and access has, in general, been unrestricted, its potential impact on the viewer's sensibilities has been even greater than it was in 1945.

As an archival resource it has been valuable to historians, curators, educators, film and television producers and even survivors. When included in films and television programmes such as *Remember: Richard Dimbleby at Belsen* (1995), *A Passover Remembrance* (1995) or *News 45* (1995) that have related the story of Bergen-Belsen, or prisoners of that camp, the footage has served to inform later generations about the camp, even to ensure that Belsen and the concentration camps became fixed in the collective conscience as a common historical reference point.[89]

A number of survivors have come to the Museum to view the Belsen footage when researching their own life stories, the film helping them come to terms with their traumatic past.[90] Such visits have enabled the Museum's curators to update the catalogue by identifying previously anonymous survivors in the rolls of film.

A Generic Resource for Tales of the Holocaust

Being widely recognised as the 'worst' of all the liberation footage readily available to filmmakers in the west, the Belsen film has proved useful to those who want to represent or illustrate accounts of life in the concentration and death camps under German command – scenes that were never recorded on film. Undoubtedly, by using the archive footage in this manner, a powerful vision of the existence of the prisoners has been evoked, and one that has served to keep fresh the memory of the camps, confounding the intentions of the Nazis that their crimes would never be uncovered.

Although the misuse of film is generally to be regretted, the Belsen footage does provide a first-hand record of the outcome of the Nazis' active neglect of the Belsen inmates, symptomatic of a mindset that saw the prisoners as vermin, to be exterminated, in one way or another.

One must also acknowledge that 'misuse' of the Belsen footage to evoke scenes inside the camps before liberation, has its value to the survivors of the camps. Its exposure in documentaries such as *Night and Fog* has helped to articulate some of the horrors of the camps, sparing the survivors the agony of trying to describe their experiences. It was often only with exposure to images from Belsen that the children of survivors began to know something of the experiences of their parents.[91]

While acknowledging the benefits that this unhistorical use of the archive film may bring, its misappropriation has created a great deal of confusion about the history of the camps and the Holocaust; confusion which could be avoided by the simple practice of sub-titling the footage with the words 'Liberation footage shot by British cameramen at Belsen' (as was done with the Red Army footage shot at Auschwitz in the excellent documentary *Auschwitz: The Blueprints of Genocide*, 1994).[92] There is not space here to explore the ethical aspects of this further but one should be clear that it is not the AFPU cameramen who are to blame for these abuses of the potent visual record that they so earnestly created at Belsen. With great prescience, they grasped that the humanity and individuality of the people they were filming could not be expressed to the viewer, and as a result frequently wrote down accounts of conversations they had with the inmates and named their subjects whenever possible. Although they abandoned the usual guidelines for the portrayal of the dead and indeed the human body, this was not out of callousness towards the camp inmates, but in order to convey the brutality of the camp system and so as to compile a complete and lasting dossier of evidence to indict a regime that they despised.

APPENDIX
BIOGRAPHIES OF THE CAMERAMEN WHO FILMED AT BELSEN

Lieutenant Colonel Hugh Stewart MBE was born in England in 1910 and read English Literature at Cambridge University. After graduating, he entered the film industry as an apprentice editor at Gaumont British. His first big editing job was with Alfred Hitchcock on *The Man Who Knew too Much* (1934). After this he worked at various studios and under various notable producers including Alexander Korda, Eric Pommer and Irving Asher. When the war started he volunteered to join the Royal Artillery and served on an anti-aircraft battery, before being invited by Michael Powell to be the Second Unit director and editor on *The 49th Parallel* (1941). After the film was made, he re-joined the army, and moved to the Army Film Unit in January 1941, where he worked on the production of four short films on various aspects of army life (*A.T.S., Special Despatch, Troopship* and *Street Fighting*). Then in early 1942 Stewart was given the task of setting up and heading the army film and photographic training school at Pinewood. In November 1942, Stewart was sent to Tunisia to command No. 2 Section of the AFPU covering the invasion of North Africa. He was then put in charge of No. 5 Section, which followed the British Army from the Normandy landings through to the fall of Berlin and the end of the war. After the war, Stewart returned to the film industry, working as a producer at Rank from 1947 to 1967. He then went into teaching, lecturing in English literature at Uxbridge Technical College (well into his eighties) and as a visiting lecturer at the Universities of Sussex and East Anglia.

Sergeant Mike Lewis was a Londoner and the son of Polish Jews who had come to Britain before the First World War. As a boy he had wanted to work in an artistic field but the family's economic circumstances had forced him to drop out of his course at the Hornsey Art School, and he worked in various odd jobs before the war. Although not a member of a political party he did become involved in anti-fascist activity (and experienced some antisemitism). He was

THE FILMING OF THE LIBERATION OF BERGEN-BELSEN   115

called up in 1941 and joined the Royal Fusiliers, but volunteered for the Parachute Regiment to escape the boring routine of infantry. He successfully passed through the tough parachute training course, despite a fear of heights, and saw action in North Africa. He was in some extremely tough engagements against the Afrika Corps and was injured in the arms and legs. After hospitalisation in Tunis, Lewis joined the AFU when he heard they were setting up an Airborne Section. He underwent initial training at Sidi Bou Said with the No.2 Section of the AFU and was then transferred to Pinewood for further training in anticipation of the Second Front.

Sergeant William Lawrie was a Glaswegian. After leaving school he trained as a horticulturist for three years in college before being conscripted into the army in September 1939. Following basic training in Stirling with the Argyll and Sutherland Highlanders, Lawrie was sent to France in February 1940 as part of the BEF. He was then withdrawn through Dunkirk and drafted into the Black Watch and was part of the garrison on Gibraltar for three years. He then returned to the UK and joined the Parachute Regiment. After his training he applied to join the AFPU as he had been a keen amateur photographer before the war. After D-day he was sent to France and was attached to the Guards Armoured Division, covering the unit's activities from the Falaise Gap through to the Liberation of Brussels. He was then sent to cover the 6th Airborne Division at Arnhem.

NOTES

1. The figure of 33 rolls of cine-film just accounts for the 100ft rolls of mute footage shot by the AFPU. There are in addition two reels (2,000ft) of film with a synchronous soundtrack held in the Museum's collection.
2. Acknowledgements as to the iconic status of the Belsen images and the recognition that they have come to stand for much more than the story of this camp, are plentiful, but three important examples (all which refer solely to the photographs), are firstly from the historian, Eberhard Kolb, 'These terrible pictures became immediately known throughout the world, and the name of Bergen-Belsen has since then stood as a symbol for the worst atrocities and the inhuman barbarity of the Nazi system of concentration camps', in E. Kolb, *Bergen-Belsen from From 'Detention Camp' to Concentration Camp, 1943–1945* (Göttingen: Vandenhoeck & Ruprecht, 2002), p.11; then another historian Rainer Schulze, 'Largely as a result of the photographs which British war correspondents took immediately after liberation, the name Bergen-Belsen has become the embodiment of the horrors of the National Socialist concentration

camps', R.Schulze, 'Documentation of the History of Efforts to Save Jewish Prisoners in the Bergen-Belsen Concentration Camp,1943–1945', in (ed.), *Gedenkstätte Bergen-Belsen, Newsletter,* No.2 (2003), p.30. A very similar statement also appears on page 67 of the *Explanatory Notes on the Exhibition – Bergen-Belsen* (ed.) (Niedersächsische Lanedszentrale für Politische Bildung, Hannover: 1995).
3. On 5 August 1992, a British news team led by Penny Marshall of ITN (*News at Ten*), her cameraman Jeremy Irvin and fellow reporters Ian Williams (ITN for Channel 4), and Ed Vulliamy (*Guardian*) visited the camp in the Serb territory of northern Bosnia. On 7 August the *Daily Mirror* front-page headline described the resulting images broadcast on television as 'Belsen 92' – 'THE PROOF – Behind the wire, the brutal truth about the suffering in Bosnia'. Other papers saw these images in similar terms: 'Belsen 92' (*Daily Star*).
4. Ronald Tritton, 'War Diary', 19 April 1945, held in the IWM Docs, p.76. Tritton joined the War Office in January 1940 where he was appointed Head of PR2. He set up the Army Film Unit, later the AFPU, and as Director of Public Relations was responsible for the output of the Unit and for 'placing it' for good army relations.
5. Hugh St Clair Stewart, interview record in December 1979, Sound Archive accession no. 4579/06; William Fairlie Lawrie, interview record in April 1989, Sound Archive accession no. 7481/03; Michael Lewis, interview recorded in March 1981, Sound Archive accession no. 4833/09; Ernest Lauret 'Harry' Oakes, interview recorded in 1979, Sound Archive accession no. 4302/6; Harry Oakes, interview recorded in 1999, Sound Archive accession no. 19582/2; Harry Oakes, interview recorded in 1999, Sound Archive accession no. 19888/4.
6. Many of the photos taken by AFPU cameramen are included in Paul Kemp's collection of eyewitness accounts held in the Museum's collections. But there are no details about who took the photos and only two quotes from a cameraman, in this case Sergeant Midgley. See P. Kemp, *The Relief of Belsen, April 1945: EyeWitness Accounts* (London: Imperial War Museum, 1991), pp.12, 19. Neither of the following accounts of the camp published in Germany give any details about the filming and photography: E. Kolb, *Bergen-Belsen: From 'Detention Camp' to Concentration Camp, 1943–1945* (Göttingen: Vandenhoeck & Ruprecht, 1986); W. Scheel (ed.), *Bergen-Belsen: Explanatory Notes on the Exhibition* (Hannover: Niedersächsische Landeszentrale für Politische Bildung, 2002).
7. J. Reilly, D. Cesarani, T. Kushner and C. Richmond (eds.), *Belsen in History and Memory* (London: Frank Cass, 1997).
8. J. Reilly, *Belsen: The Liberation of a Concentration Camp* (London: Routledge, 1998), pp.29–30. It should also be noted that the quote from William Lawrie used by Joanne Reilly is the same one used by Paul Kemp in the brief reference he made to the British Army's filming at Belsen in 'The British Army and the Liberation of Bergen-Belsen April 1945', in Reilly *et al.*, *Belsen in History and Memory*, p.137.
9. A. Insdorf, *Indelible Shadows: Film and the Holocaust* (Cambridge: Cambridge University Press, 2003), p.200.
10. See A. Penrose, *The Lives of Lee Miller* (London: Thames and Hudson, 1985); L. Miller and A. Penrose, *Lee Miller's War: photographer and correspondent with the Allies in Europe, 1944–45* (London: Condé Nast Books, 1992); J. Livingston, *Lee Miller: Photographer* (London: Thames and Hudson, 1989); Scottish National Gallery of Modern Art, *Roland Penrose, Lee Miller: The Surrealist and the Photographer* (National Galleries of Scotland, 2001); V. Goldberg, *Margaret Bourke-White: A Biography* (London: Heinemann, 1987); G. Rodger, *The Blitz: The Photography of George Rodger* (Harmondsworth: Penguin, 1990); B. Hardy, *Bert Hardy: My Life* (London: Gordon Fraser Gallery, 1985); T. Hopkinson, Arts Council of Great Britain, *Bert Hardy: Photojournalist* (London: Gordon Fraser, 1975).

11. T. Kushner, 'The Memory of Belsen', in Reilly *et al.*, *Belsen in History and Memory*, pp.187-8.
12. Letter from Kevin Brownlow to Toby Haggith, 5 July 2005. I am very grateful to Mr Brownlow for giving his agreement to the publication of this quote.
13. Alain Resnais speaking in 1986 and quoted in C. Delage, *'Nuit et Brouillard*: a turning point in the history and memory of the Holocaust', in T. Haggith and J. Newman (eds.), *Holocaust and the Moving Image: Representations in Film and Television since 1933* (London: Wallflower Press, 2005), pp.129-30.
14. Delage, *'Nuit et Brouillard'*, p.130.
15. J. Hirsch, *After Image: Film Trauma, and the Holocaust* (Philadelphia: Temple University Press, 2004), p.ix.
16. *The Angel of Bergen-Belsen* (1998), written and produced by Rob Harris for Loxley Hall Productions. Another example is *Song of Sorrow* (1994), a Danish video documentary about Auschwitz – the makers inter-cut archive footage of the corpses being buried in a mass grave at Belsen with scenes of Auschwitz today, again giving the viewer the impression that the archive film had been shot when this infamous extermination camp was being run by the Germans: *Song of Sorrow* (1994), by Bent Staalhoj and DOK –Film Documentary Group, in co-operation with the Danish Film Institute Workshop. 22mins.
17. Reilly, *Belsen: The Liberation of a Concentration Camp*, p.77. This observation is also made by Tony Kushner, see *The Holocaust and the Liberal Imagination: A Social and Cultural History* (Oxford: Blackwell, 1994), pp.213, 216.
18. TNA INF 1/636 'F3030 Investigation of War Atrocities. Factual Film Report of German Concentration Camps'. At the end of the war, Americans reported to SHAEF that both Nazi and anti-Nazi POWs were disassociating themselves 'almost unanimously from any responsibility for the atrocities depicted. Furthermore, they say that many of the pictures remind them of photographs of the German victims of Allied air raids, which they have seen constantly in the German press and in the Wochenschau' [*Deutsche Wochenschau*, Third Reich newsreel]; Davidson Taylor, Chief of Film, Theatre and Music Control Section of SHAEF to Sidney Bernstein, 25 May 1945. Although Taylor does not specifically cite the Belsen footage here, images from this camp were included in all the newsreels and propaganda compilations of German atrocities shown to Germans at the end of the war.
19. Reilly *et al.*, *Belsen in History and Memory*, p.15.
20. One indication of this process is that, sadly, a common follow-up request by researchers examining the Belsen footage at the Museum, is for something 'worse'.
21. Reilly *et al.*, *Belsen in History and Memory*, pp.13, 187. Another criticism made by Jo Reilly in an essay in this book entitled 'Cleaner, Carer and Occasional Dance Partner? Writing Women Back into the Liberation of Bergen-Belsen', was that the cameramen failed to record the enormous contribution made by women carers to the medical treatment and rehabilitation of the inmates.
22. For this reason, atrocity images do not appear in any of the classroom resources produced by the Imperial War Museum's Education Department. Paul Salmons, Holocaust Education Co-ordinator at the IWM explains this policy in his essay 'Moral dilemmas: history, teaching and the Holocaust', which can be downloaded from the Museum's website, www.iwm.org.uk. This article also appears in 'Teaching History', *The Historical Association*, Vol.104 (September 2001), pp.34-40.
23. See H. Caven, 'Horror in Our Time: Images of the Concentration Camps in British Media, 1945', *Historical Journal of Film, Radio and Television*, Vol. 21, No. 3 (August 2001), pp.205-53; and T. Haggith, 'Filming the Liberation of Bergen-Belsen', in Haggith and Newman (eds.), *Holocaust and the Moving Image*, pp.33-49.
24. See H. Caven, 'Horror in Our Time', pp.205-53. See also A. Reading, *The Social*

Inheritance of the Holocaust: Gender, Culture and Memory (Basingstoke: Palgrave Macmillan, 2002), pp.85–9.
25. Reading, *The Social Inheritance of the Holocaust*, pp.85–9.
26. Sergeant Harry Oakes, IWM Sound Archive accession no. 19888/4, reel 3.
27. Ibid.4, reel 2.
28. Sergeant William Lawrie, IWM Sound Archive accession no.7481/03, reel 2.
29. Sergeant Lawrie filmed scenes of British Commandos crossing the Elbe on 27 April and Sergeant Lewis caught up with the 15th Scottish Division and filmed British troops crossing the Elbe on 29 April.
30. Other filming at Belsen was conducted by Lieutenant Wilson and Sergeants Haywood, Seaholme, Grant, Leatherbarrow, Hewitt and Parkinson. At the request of SHAEF, 2,000 feet of synchronous sound film was also shot by Paul Wyand and Martin Gray of *Movietone News*.
31. Sergeant Harry Oakes, IWM Sound Archive accession no. 19888/4, reel 2.
32. The Soviet army's discovery of Majdanek in November 1944 and Auschwitz in January 1945 were widely reported in the press and in the case of Majdanek supported by radio-photographs, but there was much doubt about these reports.
33. Letter to Tom Williams, 18 April, read during an interview recorded with Richard 'Dick' Williams, IWM Sound Archive, accession no.15437/5, reel 3.
34. AFPU Sergeant Mike Lewis, recorded interview, IWM Sound Archive accession no. 4833/9, reel 7.
35. For example AFPU film, shot by Sergeant Gordon, of the deserted concentration camp of s'Hertogenbosch in southern Holland shows watchtowers, an electrified perimeter fence, a gallows, a crematorium and a heap of ashes, but there is no human evidence or witnesses to explain what had happened (A70 187/6, 31 October 1944).
36. Sergeant Lewis and Sergeant Lawrie's footage shot at Celle on 12 April 1945, appears on A70 297/3–4.
37. From a recorded interview with Sergeant William Lawrie, AFPU, held in the IWM Sound Archive, accession no. 7481/03, reel 2.
38. Secret Caption Sheet No: A700/303/3, Sergeant Ian Grant, 15 April 1945.
39. 'Notes for Instructors', IWM Department of Documents.
40. Caven, 'Horror in Our Time', p.227.
41. More than 37 Units of the British Army became involved in the work at Belsen. This figure does not include units from voluntary organisations such as the FRS, UNRRA, the Red Cross etc. Units from other Allied armies also contributed to the operation. See Kemp, *The Relief of Belsen*, p.31.
42. One of the earliest examples is found in Kino Khronika No.9 (February 1943, IWM catalogue no. RNC 9), which includes footage of a mass grave and various exhumed corpses of locals killed by the Germans at the village of Vorontsovo-Alexandrovskoe, North Caucasus. Among the bodies identified were those of Matvei Stepanovich Kip, a 'non-party activist of the local collective farm' and communist Tatiana Ivanovna Kornienko. One of the first Soviet-discovered sites of atrocity to appear in British newsreels was the massacre of 600 forced-labourers at the Lublin Castle. This item appeared in a number of newsreels including the War Pictorial News issue released on 25 December 1944 (IWM catalogue no. WPN 190).
43. From page 18 of 'Notes for Instructors' for the seven week course for AFPU trainees at Pinewood. This undated document is held in the IWM Department of Documents.
44. Lieutenant Colonel Hugh Stewart was the officer in command of No. 5 Section of the AFPU, the Unit responsible for covering the British Army's activities in the North-western European theatre, IWM Sound Archive accession no. 4579/06, reel 4.
45. Sergeant William Lawrie, IWM Sound Archive accession no. 7481/03, reel 2.

THE FILMING OF THE LIBERATION OF BERGEN-BELSEN   119

46. Paul Wyand (*British Movietone News* cameraman) in a letter to Frank Chisnell (News Editor at *British Movietone News*), 22 April 1945. IWM Department of Documents.
47. TNA INF 1/636 'F3080 Investigation of War Atrocities. Factual Film Report on German Concentration Camps'. Sergei Nolbandov to Ronald Tritton, PR1 War Office, 20 April 1945.
48. Secret Caption Sheet No: A700 304/1 & 2, sheet 2, Sergeant Mike Lewis, 16 April 1945.
49. Harry Oakes, AFPU, Imperial War Museum Sound Archive Interview accession no. 19888/4, reel 4.
50. Strictly speaking, Oakes may be talking metaphorically here, as the AFPU cameramen were trained to film with both eyes open when filming.
51. Sergeant William Lawrie, AFPU, Imperial War Museum Sound Archive Interview, accession no. 7481/03, reel 2.
52. AFPU Secret Dope Sheet, AYY 556 1/3, Sergeant Hopkinson, 29th September 1943. This footage subsequently appeared in an issue of the *Warwork News* (IWM catalogue no. S15 33).
53. Sergeant William Lawrie, AFPU, Imperial War Museum Sound Archive Interview, accession no. 7481/03, reel 3.
54. An observation made by James Taylor in a conversation with the author. James Taylor is a member of the Imperial War Museum's Department of Research and Information and was one of the team responsible for mounting the Holocaust Exhibition.
55. 'There was no direction. You couldn't direct the fellow driving the bulldozer. He had a job to do and he jolly well got on and did it. You couldn't say "Look go back and do that again" in the circumstances'. From the transcript of the recorded interview with William Lawrie, IWM Sound Archive accession no. 7481/03, reel 3.
56. According to Hutchinson, that 'faking' would have had serious consequences for the cameraman: 'in fact if one had got caught out really badly faking something that never happened, I think you'd have been out on your ear'. Charles Ronald Hutchinson, who was a Sergeant cameraman with the AFPU, from a transcript of a recorded interview held in the Imperial War Museum's Sound Archive, accession no: 4477/07, p.41.
57. Secret Caption Sheet No: A700 304/3, 17 April 1945.
58. To counter these doubts, camera teams filmed visits to the camps by well-known Allied political and military figures and enforced inspection of the camps by German civilians. General Eisenhower was filmed visiting Ohrdruf on 7 April 1945, along with German citizens and a Wehrmacht officer who was forced to inspect the dead. (IWM film catalogue no. A70 514-14). This item later appeared in issue 210 of War Pictorial News (IWM catalogue no. WPN 210). A delegation of British MPs was filmed visiting Buchenwald, see IWM film catalogue no. A70 514-72. This footage was edited into the *Gaumont British News* and *British Movietone News* issues released at the end of April (IWM catalogue nos. RMY 144 & NMV 830A).
59. General Eisenhower was filmed visiting Ohrdruf on 7 April 1945, along with German citizens and a Wehrmacht officer who were forced to inspect the dead (IWM film catalogue no. A70 514-14). A party of British MPs was filmed visiting Buchenwald, (IWM film catalogue no. A70 514-72).
60. As the AFPU did not routinely record sound, *Movietone News*, which had cameramen and the bulky recording equipment in Germany, was asked to go to the camp to film these scenes: PRO INF 1/636. On 22 April Sidney Bernstein (SHAEF) arrived at Bergen-Belsen, writing the same day to Paul Wyand at *Movietone*, 'I would appreciate you taking sound interviews of the British official and German SS men etc. at the Belsen concentration camps'. He also instructed Wyand that 'Shooting you arrange should be co-ordinated with the work done by AFPU'. Wyand and the Sound man Martin Gray filmed 'sound shots' for the 'M.O.I. SPECIAL ON BELSEN' on 23 and 24 April. The two reels of synchronously recorded film runs for 2,000 ft, about 20

minutes in running time. The AFPU cameramen shot additional mute reels of many of the scenes covered by the sound team. These sound reels are held in the IWM Film and Video Archive and numbered A70 514/97 & 98.

61. TNA INF 1/636 'F3080 Investigation of War Atrocities, Factual Film Report on German Concentration Camps': Sidney Bernstein to Dr G. S. Wagner , 12 May 1945.
62. A full account of the efforts to make this film (retrospectively titled *Memory of the Camps*) and the involvement of Alfred Hitchcock has been written by Kay Gladstone, 'Separate Intentions: The Allied Screening of Concentration Camp Documentaries in Defeated Germany in 1945–46: Death Mills and Memory of the Camps' in Haggith and Newman (eds.), *Holocaust and the Moving Image*, pp.50–64.
63. These scenes were used with devastating irony by the editors and scriptwriters of *Memory of the Camps/A Painful Reminder* (IWM catalogue no. MGH 3320A).
64. This sequence appears in reel no. A70 308/3–4. The handle of the spade is in the foreground with Father Morrison and Father Kadziolka in the background standing at the edge of one of the mass graves, presumably blessing the grave.
65. Sergeant Harry Oakes, AFPU photographer, IWM Sound Archive Interview, accession no. 19888/4, reel 3.
66. Ibid.
67. Sergeant Hewitt, Secret Caption Sheet A700 335/4, 15/16 May 1945.
68. Sergeant Mike Lewis, Secret Caption Sheet A700 304/1–2, 16 April 1945.
69. Sergeant Parkinson, Secret Caption Sheet A700 322/1, 1 May 1945.
70. When Lieutenant Wilson filmed some Christening ceremonies for children miraculously born in the camp, he warned the technicians at Pinewood: 'This roll is all interior shots. The light was very poor indeed and it is understood that although it was shot wide open, some, or perhaps all may be underexposed. I suggest that the negative be boiled'. Secret Caption Sheet A700 355/1, 5 June 1945.
71. 'I understand from the women imprisoned in the concentration camp that these SS women committed many cruelties upon them. For instance, the women could only get their very meagre portion of food if they carried away at least one dead body a day'. Sergeant Mike Lewis, Secret Caption Sheet A700 304/1& 2, 16 April 1945.
72. Sergeant Lawrie, Secret Caption Sheet A700/304/3, 17 April 1945.
73. Sergeant Lawrie, Secret Caption Sheet A700 304/4, 18 April 1945.
74. Sergeant Lawrie, Secret Caption Sheet A700 304/1+2, 16 April 1945.
75. TNA INF 1/636 [F3080] Sidney Bernstein, Chief of Film Section, SHAEF, London, to Brigadier A.G.Neville, MC, HQ 21 Army Group of the British Liberation Army, 2 May 1945. The special power of cine-film was also remarked on in *The Times*, 'These films should be shown throughout the world and nowhere more than in Germany. The printed word can glance off an inattentive mind, but the moving picture bites deep into the imagination', 1 May 1945, p.8. This quote appears on p.250 of Hannah Caven's article, 'Horror in Our Time'.
76. Caven, 'Horror in Our Time', p.229.
77. Ibid., p.248.
78. According to a Mass Observation Survey, an average of 3 per cent of those consulted after visiting an exhibition of photographs from Belsen (organised by the *Daily Express*), thought the atrocity stories were false. See Caven, 'Horror in Our Time', p.244.
79. L. Mitchell, *Leslie Mitchell Reporting: An Autobiography* (London: Hutchinson, 1981), p.145.
80. From a recorded interview with Charles Ronald Hutchinson, held in the Imperial War Museum's Sound Archive accession no. 8254/2, reel 07. Hutchinson was a cameraman with the AFPU and served in the UK, Sicily and Italy between 1941 and 1945.

THE FILMING OF THE LIBERATION OF BERGEN-BELSEN   121

81. The *Gaumont British News* issue 'Horror in our time', is catalogued as RMY 144. The *Movietone News* treated the Belsen footage in a similar manner, the commentary pointing, 'If the Hun had invaded Britain this [close up of Josef Kramer] might have had the power to torture and to starve any one of us. Yes such atrocities might have been inflicted on the people of these islands. They were inflicted on the people of Belsen... Can anyone any longer doubt the truth of German atrocities – yet shall we remember these things in ten, fifteen, twenty years time?' *Movietone News* Issue no. (IWM catalogue no. NMV 830A).

82. An American voice accompanying footage of camps liberated by the US forces, explained: 'The government sent a few of us Congressmen over to see those camps and if there's anybody left who wonders if this war was worth fighting – well I wish they could have been along – there it was right in front of us fascism and what it's bound to lead to wherever it crops up...'. From the soundtrack of *The True Glory* (8/1945), production sponsors Ministry of Information and Office of War Information; co-directed by Garson Kanin and Carol Reed; script Irwin Shaw; music composer William Alwyn. run time: 84mins. This film is accessioned in the IWM collection as CVN 319.

83. The photographs were also censored, with the most upsetting withheld from publication or only shown in special public exhibitions to which children were not admitted.

84. After shooting this reel Sergeant Haywood moved on, and by 18 April was covering scenes of the British Army around Uelzen. Haywood's reel is catalogued as A700 302/1.

85. See *War Pictorial News*, 18 June 1945, (IWM catalogue no. WPN 215); see also *Movietone News*, 31 May 1945, (IWM catalogue no. NMV 834A).

86. In 1985 the draft commentary was read by the actor Trevor Howard for a television broadcast in the USA of the rough cut which is held in the Imperial War Museum's archive.

87. *Welt im Film* No. 5 (15 June 1945), 19mins. IWM accession no: WIF 5.

88. The title allocated for this film by IWM curators is: Composite Material of Belsen Atrocities (1945), 2 reels, accession no. MGH 114.

89. *Remember: Richard Dimbleby at Belsen* (9 January 1995), BBC2; p.c. Panorama; producer: Carol Sennett; run time: 15mins. *A Passover Remembrance* (13 April 1995), BBC1, producer: Valetta Stallabras; run time: 15mins; *News 45* (2 May 1995), BBC1, presented by Sue Lawley, run time: 15mins.

90. Two recent examples are Dita Kraus and Gaston de Wit. Dita Kraus (née Polachova) was born in Prague and interned in Terezin's ghetto, Auschwitz and a labour camp near Hamburg, before ending up in Bergen-Belsen. After a period as an interpreter she fell ill with typhoid. She can be identified as the woman with the polka-dot scarf in the following reels held in the IWM archive: A70 307/40 and A70 308/03. A recorded interview with Dita Kraus is held in the Museum's Sound Archive, accession no. 23090. During the war, Gaston de Wit was a courier for the Belgian resistance, helping British pilots whose planes had been shot down to get back to Britain. In March 1944 he and his father (also in the Resistance) were arrested by the Gestapo and sent to Dora via Buchenwald. He eventually ended up in the military barracks at Bergen-Belsen. Although Gaston de Wit remembered that the group of prisoners from Belgium and Luxembourg were filmed by the British Army when they went home, we could not find this sequence. However, the opportunity to view a related scene at this time was none the less a very valuable experience for Mr De Wit.

91. Susan Sontag famously came across photographs from Belsen and Dachau in a bookshop in Santa Monica in July 1945. This was so traumatic for the 12-year-old that she divided her life into before and after viewing these images. See S. Sontag, *On*

Photography (New York: Anchor, 1990), p.20. Annette Insdorf in the Preface of her book *Indelible Shadows*, recalled how seeing the film *Night and Fog*, had given her 'an inkling' of what her parents had endured (see p.xiii). For Joshua Hirsch whose father was a survivor of Auschwitz, viewing the bulldozer sequences at Belsen in *Night and Fog* as a child was a way of identifying with his family members who had perished in the camps. In fact the Belsen images substituted the non-existent images of his grandparents who had perished, giving him a strong sense of identity with the emaciated corpses. See J. Hirsch, *After Image*, p.ix.

92. *Auschwitz: The Blueprints of Genocide*, produced by Horizon and broadcast on BBC2 on 9 March 1994, produced by Isabelle Roslin and directed by Mike Rossiter, 50mins.

What Wireless Listeners Learned: Some Lesser-Known BBC Broadcasts about Belsen

SUZANNE BARDGETT

Richard Dimbleby's account of the scenes he witnessed at Bergen-Belsen in April 1945 – recorded on what the famous broadcaster called 'the most horrible day of my life' – has acquired an iconic status in British popular memory. Less well known is the work of two other experienced BBC programme-makers who compiled accounts for radio of Belsen in the weeks and months after the camp's liberation.[1] This essay looks at their efforts to bring to British audiences a deeper understanding of what Belsen signified and of the suffering of those imprisoned there.

Patrick Gordon Walker's 'sections of the jigsaw'

As the Allies advanced across the Low Countries in 1944, experts in psychological warfare moved in their wake, bringing the propaganda effort which had been waged from mainland Britain right up to Germany's borders. Patrick Gordon Walker – an Oxford don before the war, fluent in German – was part of this campaign.[2] As the BBC's German Service's Workers Programmes specialist, he had since 1941 been at the heart of the section of the European Service based in Bush House which provided a formidable daily output of news and features to Germany.[3]

In late 1944 a number of the German Service personnel found themselves in demand by the newly formed Psychological Warfare Department under the joint Anglo-American-Canadian command of SHAEF (Supreme Headquarters Allied Expeditionary Force). Their brief was to use Radio Luxembourg, the newly captured second most powerful radio station on the continent, to broadcast to the twelve

Figure 14: Patrick Gordon Walker. (© Robin Gordon Walker)

and a half million foreign workers estimated to be living and working inside Germany.[4]

Gordon Walker arrived in Luxembourg via Paris on 21 October 1944, enjoying a rapturous welcome from Luxembourgers who had regularly tuned into his programmes.[5] With the battlefront initially just ten miles away, and events moving fast, he spent the next six months using liaison officers, translators and interpreters to provide news commentaries and classical and light entertainment from dawn till one in the morning.

On 17 April he and his American driver, Sergeant Princie, left Luxembourg in a recording van for a 'dash into Germany' to make recordings. It ended up being a 1,250 mile trip. They headed first for Brunswick where the newly captured main prison at Wolfenbüttel was now under the charge of a British captain. He showed them the terrifying detritus of the prison's wartime history – torture instruments, and a guillotine. A rough memorial had been put up to the 550 prisoners who had been executed at the prison. They were shown a Czech and a Polish prisoner – in an appalling state of malnutrition.[6]

The next day they tried to reach a camp they had heard about at Salzwedel, but were turned back, and instead recorded the stories of some of the people of Brunswick: a lawyer who had defended political prisoners; and the Bürgermeister, whose interview was 'long, nervously delivered, unclear and self-justificatory. I did not form a good impression of the man'.[7]

On Friday 20 April they arrived at Celle, 30 kilometres from Belsen and the following day drove to the camp.

After four intensive years at Bush House, Gordon Walker was probably the most expert in German affairs of the Allied commentators who visited the camp, and his deep curiosity can well be imagined.

What levels of knowledge would he have encountered among the British soldiers who guided him when he arrived there? It has been said that British press reports of Belsen in 1945 failed to give a full account of what the camp signified, and in particular did not acknowledge the high proportion of Jewish inmates in the camp. Certainly newspaper accounts were limited by the fact that most journalists visited for one day only – and, with the fast pace of events in the closing weeks of the war, had little time for in-depth interviews and analysis. But in the camp itself, soldiers and relief workers – who had been specially reinforced by Jewish personnel – had started to grasp the essentials of what had happened to thousands of the inmates. As one Jewish relief worker commented: 'the camp which is spoken of most frequently... and with the most dread, is Auschwitz, and it was here that many of the internees were branded with their numbers'.[8] Nor were the liberators naive about the fact that 'official agendas' would very likely ensure that certain facts were censored. A captain in REME (Royal Electrical and Mechanical Engineers) reported:

> I've been talking today to our officer who has been organising the water supply to a concentration camp. Here are some details that were not given in the account on the wireless tonight. 40 per cent were Jews. The bulk of the inmates were Germans but most nationalities including British and American were represented. There were no lavatory arrangements whatever in the camp and most of the inmates had dysentery.[9]

One of the Intelligence Corps officers who was Jewish, Arnold Horwell, was even allowed to give special briefings to press and others arriving at the camp – a clear recognition, it would seem, that the specifics of the Jewish survivors' situation needed to be made clear.[10]

Gordon Walker set to work and in just two days got a good deal of very usable material. He called several soldiers of the Oxfordshire Yeomanry together in a tent and interviewed them as a group – perhaps to obtain more relaxed responses.[11]

In his fluent German he interviewed Anita Lasker and her sister Renate, and several others, including Hetty Werkendamm, a Dutch girl whose parents had been in a work camp. Her father had been half strangled by the SS and made to shovel human excreta in 'the shit pit': 'the little girl's stories went on endlessly', he wrote in his diary.[12]

His tape recordings of these conversations have survived although sometimes with little documentation. One captures the moment when a survivor was reunited with his wife – the man sobbing terribly. The wife is not heard – her appearance may be guessed at.[13]

Two survivors were recorded in English – Gitta Cartagena and Helen Kulker, both originally from Czechoslovakia, and both saved from the gas chambers at Auschwitz by being sent to join labour detachments in Hamburg. Kulker described how the gas 'camera' had dominated Auschwitz, and how the chimneys could be seen smoking all day. Gordon Walker asked her to explain for the benefit of listeners the term 'camera' – 'it's an odd word in English'.

As Gordon Walker made his way around the camp a pattern emerged:

> Over and over again I was told the same story – of the parades at which people stood naked for hours and were picked out arbitrarily (allegedly incapable of work) for the gas chamber and crematoriums, where many were burnt alive. Only a person in perfect health survived. Life and death was a question of pure chance.[14]

Word got around that Gordon Walker would record messages to relatives which would then be broadcast on the BBC. (Messages to relatives of German prisoners of war had been an important feature of the German Service's output, so Gordon Walker would have been familiar with the drill for this.) Anita Lasker later recalled that it was no easy task to be confronted by a microphone, but with repeated transmissions the message that she and Renate were alive in Belsen camp eventually reached their third sister, Marianne, in Britain.[15]

That evening Gordon Walker recorded the first eve of Sabbath service held in the camp:

> A group of a hundred or so in the open air, amid the corpses. Two or three women sang duets and solos. The padre read the service in English and Hebrew. No eye was dry. Certainly not mine. Most of the celebrants were in unconcealed floods of tears.[16]

The following Saturday morning, he recorded another Jewish service where 'all around women and men burst into tears and cried openly':

> Then we collected the orchestra together. They had got their instruments from the old camp band. Some of them played very well. They loved old jazz and played such tunes as 'I can't give you anything but love'.[17]

The mood to play was infectious – the atmosphere in the camp must have been quite extraordinary at this point – and Gordon Walker collected together some Russian girls and Dutch boys to sing. The Russians sang partisan songs, and the Dutch what appears to have been a specially composed short song 'the English: long may they live in glory'.

On the last evening Gordon Walker was given access to some of the Nazi guards who were being held in custody. With a borrowed pistol for protection, and back-up from the British military, he tried to find an SS member ready to describe what had gone on in the camps. A medical doctor who had been at Auschwitz tried to claim that he had only tended the sick, but another – a Romanian – agreed to talk. A woman prisoner, Elizabeth Volkenrath – who had overseen the women's camp at Auschwitz-Birkenau and subsequently held a similar post in Belsen – was also with considerable difficulty persuaded to speak on tape.[18]

During his time at the camp Gordon Walker realised that the rescue efforts of the British medical personnel were not progressing as fast as they should.

The concluding passages of the typescript of his diary are prefaced with the words 'FROM HERE ON NOT FOR PUBLICATION' and document the 'serious shortcomings' which delayed decisions so that the evacuation of the military training school happened more than a week later than it might have. 'The main cause was that there was no person *in the camp* who was of high enough authority to take decisions and to put in his requests to the proper authorities'. He emphasises in a later paragraph that 'it's a question of decision and authority'.[19]

What had happened? A report in 224 Military Government Detachment's war diary shows that there had indeed been 'frequent changes of command' and that this lack of authority had meant that fewer lives had been saved than might have been. It is clear that it was those in overall authority rather than the medical personnel on the ground who bore responsibility for the slowness of response.[20]

Gordon Walker left Belsen on the Sunday morning and he and Princie drove to the virtually flattened town of Hamm, where eight out of ten of the population were living in cellars. In the days that followed, Gordon Walker wrote up his visit to Germany as a slim book, *The Lid Lifts,* for the publisher Victor Gollancz, finishing the first draft just as news came of Germany's unconditional surrender.

The radio programme for which he had made the recordings was assembled and broadcast in the evening of Sunday 27 May as 'Belsen Concentration Camp: Facts and Thoughts'.[21]

Although the organisational failings of the rescuers had obviously perplexed Gordon Walker, it would have been unthinkable to mention any such shortcomings on air, and its overall thrust was to highlight the British Army's role in saving lives and the gratitude felt by the camp's inmates. The programme opened with 'God Save the King' – played on a very out-of-tune canteen piano by Fania Fenelon (one of the 'musicians of Auschwitz' who would later write a book about that camp's orchestra) – and closed with the children's songs and three 'hip-hip-hoorahs' for the British.

Two witness statements feature. Driver Mechanic Payne of the Oxfordshire Yeomanry describes seeing a woman who had completely lost her mind and who insisted on feeding milk to her long dead baby. Gitta Cartagena tells of her certainty in Auschwitz that she would be gassed and how she kept a record with notches on her bunk post of the days she had left to live.

SOME LESSER-KNOWN BBC BROADCASTS ABOUT BELSEN 129

Elizabeth Volkenrath's testimony was not used – perhaps because it was in German. The fact that she was in custody and awaiting trial would in any case have prohibited it.

The Jewish Sabbath open-air service conducted by Leslie Hardman is given several minutes. A moving observation by Gordon Walker – that everyone was in tears but struggled on to show the outside world that they were still alive – was omitted from the final recording, presumably simply to shorten an overlong script.

A lengthy central section is taken up with Gordon Walker's own thoughts on the German camps and what they meant: 'whoever of us has shut his ears to these things, or flinched from whatever effort was necessary to put an end to them – now carries part of the responsibility for these things'.

Knowing the extent of material which Gordon Walker uncovered, one looks – with the benefit of hindsight, of course – for more signs of understanding of the Jewish tragedy. On his last night in the camp he had spoken privately with Leslie Hardman, who 'broke down and sobbed out loud' – a heart-rending scene which made it into *The Lid Lifts*, but not the BBC programme. He knew that many of the prisoners were there because they had been marched there, but did not attempt to build up a picture of this forced migration of prisoners from Auschwitz and other camps in the east to the western part of Germany. He perhaps felt that the recordings were so unusual as to require no further embellishment or conjecture, and was acutely conscious that it was simply too early to provide a full perspective:

> In my diary I have set down things as I observed them as honestly as I could… For this is, I think, the best service you can give to a democracy at the moment on the German problem. To give the facts as accurately as possible and to let each draw his conclusions. But the diary method produces a jigsaw that is still in its box. The representative observer has one further task – to fit together some corner and sections of the jigsaw that belong together. This is still in the realm of fact reporting.[22]

The programme got a favourable reaction, according to the BBC Listeners' Report, with three out of four of the 9 o'clock News audience listening to it. 'Its APPRECIATION INDEX was 83 … the recordings of the British Soldier's evidence, the singing of the children, the Jewish service, and the Czech girls' story were all singled out for praise, as was Patrick Gordon Walker's narration'.[23]

Realising that the children's songs offered a child's perspective on freedom from Nazi tyranny, Gordon Walker wrote a further talk based solely on these, and suggested it to the BBC programmers for Children's Hour. It was broadcast on 14 June 1945, giving younger Home Service listeners their own version of the horrific news story which had so perplexed their parents in previous weeks.[24]

'That was the message in song', Gordon Walker closed the programme, 'of these children from this terrible concentration camp to the children in Britain. I suppose they are the saddest songs you will ever hear. All these Russian and Dutch children had lost their fathers and mothers, murdered by the Nazis'.[25]

Figure 15: Patrick Gordon Walker (lying on the floor) with fellow BBC colleagues, the new voices of Radio Luxembourg, now a 'vital weapon in the Allied radio war against the Nazis'. (© Robin Gordon Walker)

Leonard Cottrell's 'The Man from Belsen'

In April 1946 BBC listeners heard the first full-length drama documentary account of daily life in the Nazi camps as experienced by prisoners, when the Home Service broadcast a dramatised feature about the experiences of a British survivor of Belsen, Harold Le Druillenec. It was written and produced by Leonard Cottrell – writer of a number of talks, plays and adaptations for the BBC who in later decades would find fame as the author of several popular histories of the ancient world, among them *The Bull of Minos* and *The Lost Pharoahs*.

Le Druillenec was a schoolmaster in Jersey, and during the Channel Islands' occupation had been arrested, together with his sister, Louisa Gould, for helping to shelter an escaped Russian prisoner of war. His trial took place just two weeks after the Normandy landings – the sounds of the fighting on the nearby French coast could actually be heard in the St Helier courtroom – but the Nazi administration were still sending convicted Channel Islanders to the French mainland, and Le Druillenec was taken off the island to begin his five-month sentence in a prison near Rheims. From there he was sent to Neuengamme, on the outskirts of Hamburg, where he was selected to join a slave labour detachment in the naval port of Wilhelmshaven. As the Allies approached, he was transported to Belsen, arriving there on 5 April 1945.[26]

After the liberation Le Druillenec had been nursed back to health in a hospital at Epsom, Surrey. He was briefly heard on the Home Service when the Belsen Trial – at which he was a witness – was reported from Lüneberg. Then on Christmas Day 1945 he was heard by millions of wireless listeners in Britain and abroad when he broadcast live from Castle Cornet in Guernsey on 'Wherever you may be' – an hour-long sharing of greetings from different locations which directly preceded King George VI's Christmas message.[27]

Cottrell presumably interviewed his subject at length and drew out from these conversations a narrative and a cast of characters. The 'little band of friends' Le Druillenec had made during his captivity helped shape the piece: Colonel Reynaud, a First World War veteran and 'very much the old type of cavalry officer'; the bluff, sturdy American, Lloyd Gybels, who advised newly arrived inmates 'don't judge things by the standards of ordinary life'; the pale aristocrat Jean de Frotté whose privileged background made him least adaptable to the privations of camp life; and 'little Baudu', a tough Breton cattle-breeder whose humanity and resourcefulness kept the others going.

The BBC must have been impressed by the script for they gave it a strong cast of actors including Valentine Dyall (familiar to Home Service listeners as 'The Man in Black' in the popular thriller series *Appointment with Fear*, then five years into what would be a 12-year run). Le Druillenec himself was persuaded to participate as narrator. A musical accompaniment was commissioned from the distinguished composer William Alwyn, and Eugene Pini, the well-known violinist, engaged to play it. Sound Effects were briefed to produce a hissing steam train, marching feet, the hum of planes and the distant thud of bombs.

And so it would have been quite a large group of actors, technicians and musicians who gathered together with Cottrell and Le Druillenec in Studio 8 at Bush House on 11 April 1946 for two full days' rehearsals, culminating in the live broadcast on the evening of Friday 12th – just three days before the first anniversary of Belsen's liberation.[28]

To listen to the feature today is to experience a highly accomplished piece of radio – slightly old-fashioned in style, perhaps, but its spare construction and fluid dialogue make for a timeless and moving piece.

Listeners hear the angry surprise of the prisoners as the train on which Le Druillenec and his friends are being transported slows down and they realise that they are being taken to a concentration camp, not a Stalag. In measured tones Le Druillenec recalls how concentration camps were well organised and run with efficiency; how their inmates had their belongings confiscated and were made to lose their identity: 'I want you to imagine the scene: Naked men – all nationalities moving forward in a crocodile. Trousers, tunic, shirt, clogs. Trousers, tunic, shirt, clogs. Trousers, tunic, shirt, clogs. All with the characteristic stripes'. The *Blockälteste* barks at them 'like a vicious public school headmaster': 'From now on you have to be concerned with furthering the interests of the Third Reich'.

The American character, Lloyd Gybels, has been in Neuengamme for some while, and from him the new arrivals learn the rules of camp life: 'you'll see things going on here that'll drive you nuts if you try to figure them out – guys beaten to death for stealing a swede; guys tortured for weeks and then killed because the Camp Chief didn't like their faces'. The past history of the group's *Blockälteste*, Omar, once a radical journalist, is used to illustrate how the concentration camp system could take away the values of a civilised man and make him into a monster.

In the feature's second half, Le Druillenec is transported in a cattle wagon to Lüneberg where the train is bombed by American planes, and the inmates of an adjoining wagon killed. The following day Colonel Reynaud, Baudu and Le Druillenec are packed into a truck and driven to another camp – Belsen.

They realise that buildings adjoining their hut are crammed with dead bodies. The overcrowding is serious, yet more convoys arrive each day.

Le Druillenec narrates the painful progress of the ten days: on the second night the huts are too crowded for them to lie down and they have to sit 'with legs apart, the next man between your knees'; on the sixth day the SS order them to start dragging the bodies to pits for burial; on the eighth Colonel Reynaud dies; on the ninth Le Druillenec says 'I am finished'.

But on the tenth day distant rifle shots are heard, and Baudu shakes his friend and tells him that the British are coming. At the end of the programme Le Druillenec manages to get the attention of Derrick Sington, the officer in charge of the Loudspeaker Unit which announced that the camp had been liberated. He tells Sington that he is British and is driven away on the bonnet of the loudspeaker van, Baudu shouting out to him: 'Goodbye Harold, you'll write to me won't you'.

The recording of this last section of the programme must have been extraordinary to witness – with Harold Le Druillenec describing his ordeal of just a year past, the passing of each day marked by the soaring notes of Eugene Pini's violin.

The programme did not portray the years of imprisonment and degradation in Auschwitz that had been the experience of many of Belsen's inmates, or make clear the fact that so many of the prisoners had been Jewish. Being delivered in rather clipped, 'public school' English, moveover, Le Druillenec's narration sounds strange when compared to the testimonies given in later years by 'continental Britons'. But as an attempt to explore the concentration camp experience it was a thoughtful and highly professional piece.

So what do these two programmes tell us about the BBC and its approach to the revelations made at Belsen in 1945? There is no doubt that the terrible facts were seen, certainly by the European Service, first and foremost as a story to be brandished at the defeated Germans:

> The European Service must give the fullest possible attention today to the concentration camps. Bullock will write a special report which should be run at some length. Establish the war guilt. This was the system which the quislings supported and was the basis of the Nazi regime. Show that this was the justification for the war.[29]

But the news controllers acknowledged that the wider story was not a straightforward one:

> In fact the guilt spreads over us all. Even Britain, who declared war on this evil before she was herself directly attacked and who did so much to secure the victory should not forget that she herself negotiated with Adolf Hitler in 1938, turning a blind eye to Buchenwald and Dachau and the Jewish pogroms, and that a British trade delegation was visiting Germany when the Nazi pestilence was taken into Czechoslovakia. This is not to induce an exaggerated feeling of self-reproach but only to show that the essential evil is Nazism and that it is not only the German people who need to walk through these prison camps.[30]

And they knew that a large part of it had yet to be told:

> While we are giving the details as we learn them about the concentration camps in Germany, it should not be forgotten that the extermination camps in Poland were even more frightful and that there millions of people were slaughtered.[31]

Gordon Walker's 'Facts and Thoughts' shows that – within the limitations of a very short programme and to a degree constrained by the mood of triumph in spring 1945 – a serious effort was made to move beyond the horrific images of the first reports, and to explore the identity and experiences of Belsen's inmates. The phenomenon of 'the concentration camp' was a new, dark arrival in Europe's history, and – as the elaborate production 'The Man from Belsen' shows – the best brains and talents were put to help public understanding of it.

NOTES

1. Recordings were also made at Belsen by Wynford Vaughan Thomas on 28 April, covering the visit to the camp of the nearby town of Soltau.
2. *Patrick Gordon Walker: Political Diaries 1932–1971* (hereafter *Diaries*), edited with an introduction by Robert Pearce (London: The Historians' Press, 1991).
3. Gerard Mansell, *Let Truth Be Told: 50 Years of BBC External Broadcasting* (London: Weidenfeld and Nicolson, 1982), pp.147–64.
4. TNA, FO 898/404. Summary by Peter Ritchie Calder, 10 March 1945.
5. 'They all know my name. It's often quite touching. When I told the porter of the hotel I was here, he became very excited and sought out some woman in the office, crying out "come quickly, Gordon Walker is here."' PGW to Audrey Gordon Walker, 21 October 1944, in the Papers of Baron Gordon Walker, GBR/ 0014/ GNWR, Churchill Archives Centre.
6. *Diaries*, p. 140.
7. Ibid., p 142.
8. IWM Department of Documents, 91/21/1, papers of Dr A. R. Horwell, Report by Jane Leverson to Joint Committee for Relief Abroad, 6 May 1945.
9. IWM Department of Documents, 91/21/1, Captain M F Jupp, HQ REME, 6th Airborne Division, 19 April 1945
10. IWM Department of Documents, 91/21/1, papers of Dr A. R. Horwell, to his wife, 16 May 1945. 'Bird has assured me that I shall have them for a few hours to "drill" them on my pet subjects – Jewish problems, DP problems, moral aspects of ex-concentration camp inmates etc. It will be another unique chance to drive certain points home, of which press and public are not aware yet'.
11. British Library Sound Archive, BBC 8684.
12. *Diaries*, p.149. See also Hetty Verolme, *The Children's House at Belsen* (London: Methuen, 2005).
13. British Library Sound Archive, BBC 8683.
14. *Diaries*, p.147.
15. Anita Lasker-Wallfisch, *Inherit the Truth* (London: Giles de la Mare, 1996), p.99.
16. Patrick Gordon Walker, *The Lid Lifts* (London: Gollancz, 1945), p.46.
17. Ibid., p.47.
18. National Sound Archive, T 8691. See also *Diaries*, pp.150–2. For more on Elizabeth Volkenrath, see Raymond Phillips (ed.), *The Belsen Trial* (Edinburgh: William Hodge, 1949), pp.213–22.
19. Papers of Baron Gordon Walker, Churchill Archives Centre. Gordon Walker omitted this critical section from the copy of his diary which he lodged with the BBC.
20. See Joanne Reilly, *Belsen: The Liberation of a Concentration Camp* (London: Routledge, 1998), pp.34–6; and 'Frustrations, 18–23 April 1945', Ch.5 in Ben Shephard, *After Daybreak: The Liberation of Belsen, 1945* (London: Cape, 2005). Captain Gluck's Progress Report of 29 April – two weeks after the camp was discovered (WO 219/3944) stated: 'feeding and fair distribution of food still a problem'.
21. 'Belsen Concentration Camp: Facts and Thoughts', Sunday 27 May 1945, BBC Written Archives Centre, Caversham.

22. Gordon Walker, *The Lid Lifts*, p 73.
23. BBC Written Archives Centre, Listener Research Report, Belsen: Facts and Thoughts, 14 June 1945 (based on 274 questionnaires returned by the Talks and Discussions Panel).
24. BBC Written Archives Centre, 'Children's Belsen' by Patrick Gordon Walker, 2 May 1945.
25. Gordon Walker – who had been much involved in Labour politics in Oxford in the 1930s – won the seat for Smethwick in the 1945 General Election, and began a third career in politics. It would span nearly three decades, and make him an expert in Commonwealth affairs, and briefly – in 1964 – Foreign Secretary.
26. Paul Sanders, *The Ultimate Sacrifice* (Jersey: Jersey Museums Service, 1998), Ch.5, 'Compassion with a Capital C: Louise Gould's "Family Affair"'.
27. *BBC Yearbook*, 1946.
28. Script: 'The Man from Belsen', 12 April 1946, BBC Written Archives Centre, Caversham.
29. BBC Written Archives Centre, E2/131/22, Assistant Director, European News Directorate, 19 April 1945. 'Bullock' is Alan Bullock, later to become one of Britain's leading historians.
30. E2/131/22 Foreign General Directives, European News Directives, File XXII, March – August 1945, Memo from Director of European News Department.
31. General Directive in same file, 26 April 1945.

Lesser-Known BBC Broadcasts: The Scripts

The Script of 'Belsen Concentration Camp: Facts and Thoughts' by Patrick Gordon Walker

Sunday, 27th May, 1945: 9.15-9.30 p.m. Home Service: London.

>   DISC: DBU 63285 .. disc 1 .. band [1]
>
>   ('God Save the King' – played on a rather tuneless piano in the SS canteen at Belsen)
>   Fade........

Have you recognised that? It's God Save the King as it was played in honour of the British liberators at Belsen Camp on April 15. I reached the camp on the fifth day, and made a number of recordings there.

>   DISC: (ditto)   Up........
>
>   Fade........

So that is God Save the King as it was played on the fifth day of liberation at Belsen, by Fania Perla, a Frenchwoman whose mother was English – on the piano – rather a tuneless one, I'm afraid – in the SS canteen, which had been taken over by the prisoners.

Already in five days many of the prisoners had made a remarkable recovery. They were determined to use again to the full the lives that the British Second Army had returned to them. It's quite certain, I think, that if we had not come when we did – very few of the 30,000 survivors we found there would have left the camp alive. When our spearhead entered the camp there were actually more dead than living. We found the bodies of 35,000 dead lying about the camp, and among them 30,000 living, just living.

What I saw there myself will always haunt me. Living people too weak to move the dead off them. Living people lying on the dead as pillows. Heaps of raw mangold wurzels among the dead – the only food the prisoners had had for days before our arrival. Human beings had fought each other for half a raw mangold wurzel. There had been cannibalism in the camp. Typhus everywhere. Fifteen hundred young children.

I would like you to hear the evidence of a British soldier, a gunner in the Oxfordshire Yeomanry. What he describes happened on the first day of liberation.

DISC: DBU 63284 .. disc 1 .. band 2

I'm Driver Mechanic Payne, of the Oxfordshire Yeomanry. I live at Mansley Woodhouse. I want to tell you a tale – just one tale – out of many hundred of horrible sights and atrocities I saw. I myself was driving a milk stall, and round this milk stall was a screaming crowd of women with babies. I kept picking a few babies out and feeding them. One woman who was – I think she was mad – kept kissing my feet, hands and clothing. So I took the baby from her, and when I looked at the baby its face was black – it's been dead for a few days. I couldn't convince her it was dead – so I pressed the lips open and poured the milk down its dead throat. The woman crooned, gibbered with delight. I gave her the baby back and she staggered off, and lay in the sun. And when I next looked she was dead with the baby in her arms, and so I put her with a stack of other dead bodies – two or three hundred, and I turned away. That's all I have to say, but I'm a British soldier, and it's not propaganda, it's the truth.

Our men got fresh water all over the camp in a day – hoses, water-tanks, water-carts. They brought in food. They gave up fifty-thousand of their blankets. They gave up their Naafi rations of cigarettes and sweets.

All the British soldiers I talked to said the same thing to me: will the people at home believe these things?

I think most people in this country do believe these things – now. But belief is not enough. We have next to ask questions.

What is the meaning of these camps?

All countries have known occasional descents into cruelty. In Belsen and Buchenwald and the other camps, it seems to me that men undertook perfectly deliberately and with cold calculation to assault the foundation of Western civilisation – which is respect for the individual life – which distinguishes us from the animals.

In these camps the SS knew what they were doing. Deliberately to treat human beings like animals was part of their attempt to destroy Europe. At Belsen I spoke with an SS doctor who had at Auschwitz performed experiments on women, twins and deformed people – as if those people had been guinea-pigs.

These things have happened in the midst of Europe. It seems to me that whoever of us has ever shut his ears to these things, or flinched from whatever effort was necessary to put an end to them – now carries part of the responsibility for these things.

The world can and must, in a tremendous act of justice, stamp out this horror, and punish the guilty. But may I add this? I have seen these things myself and perhaps because I have I am convinced that vengeance must not be indiscriminate. We must not punish innocent and guilty alike. There were Germans in these camps. At Belsen I met German victims – not Jews but political prisoners. But I do not only mean that. I mean that if we do not discriminate in our vengeance we shall be doing what the SS would have wanted us to do, namely, as they did, to destroy the respect for human life.

What I saw in Belsen – and not only there – has convinced me absolutely, as if it were one of the stones civilisation itself rests on, that there must always be – not unnecessary delay, but order, formality and proven guilt before any human life is taken away.

And now may I come back to what I recorded. This is an interview with a Czech girl as we stood among the corpses and the filth. Her name is Gitta Cartegena. Gitta had spent three years in seven different concentration camps, including Auschwitz – worst of them all, she said:

DISC: DHU 63284 .. disc 1 .. band 3 .. & disc 2 (whole)

How long were you at Auschwitz?

I was there exactly 6 months. From the day these 4,000 people left, we knew the date of our death. We knew we had to live 3 months more. I myself was making marks on my bedstead, how many days I had still left to live, and every night I went to sleep I undercut one mark, that was one day gone and one day less to live.

How many days were there left when you left Auschwitz?

The first month we hoped – excuse me for speaking so... the first month I hoped there would be a miracle. The second month we thought, why all the people before us went to gas, why not we – our fate, you can't change anything from that; and then when you are young – I am 21 – you want so terribly to live and you never know what value life has got, then when you know that you'll lose it to the exact date; so if they told me I was to get my hair cut as they did in many cases, or they would do me something terrible, I would say yes, just so they would let me live, and all the young people like me. In two days before we had to go to the gas there was – there came a law that young people from Auschwitz went to work in Germany to clean Hamburg and these towns that are so terribly bombed by your soldiers, these months, from after the bombardment. So the miracle came that we had waited for.

And now one of the most moving sights I have ever seen – the first Jewish Sabbath Service in Belsen. Something less than half the prisoners in Belsen were Jews. The Jewish chaplain to the British Second Army:

> DISC: DBU 63284/A 3 & 4
>
> We are assembled together in this now liberated concentration camp where so many thousands of our brothers and sisters have been incarcerated, to hold the first Saturday or Shabath morning service... We will now sing... Grant peace, welfare, blessing unto us and unto all Israel thy people. <u>Singing</u> ...

One of the most horrible things about these camps were the orchestras maintained by the SS, made up of the prisoners. Terrible things happened to music. The parade where the women had to stand naked in the open for hours, while some were arbitrarily picked out to be gassed or burned alive – this parade happened to music.

But now in Belsen the musicians were free. The little orchestra was eager to play for me. It wanted to play the old English dance tunes it remembered from before the captivity.

DISC: DBU 63284 .. disc 6 .. band 2 (20 seconds)

('<u>I can't give you anything but love</u>')
<u>Fade</u> ....

Seven countries were represented in the orchestra. There were French, Dutch, Hungarian and German women, with Czech and Polish men.

And here is a last scene from this place of horror, which has now been burned and blotted from the earth.

There was a children's block – where orphaned children (that is, children whose parents had been gassed and burned) were looked after by self-appointed foster mothers – looked after with unbelievable tenderness against starvation.

The children said they would like to sing. I took them as far away from the corpses as I could – fifty yards, perhaps – and there, near the barbed wire fence amidst pines and young birch trees, they sang for me and for the world outside.

Here are a dozen Russian children – from nine to fourteen – singing a Partisan song that they remembered from before their captivity.

DISC: DBU 63284 .. disc 8 .. band 1 (28 seconds)

And here are some Dutch boys and girls of about the same age. They were Jews looked after by a Russian woman. They are singing a song in honour of the British liberators, who had given these little children a chance to live out their full lives: 'The English – long may they live in glory!'

DISC: DBU 63284 .. disc 8 .. band 2 (25 seconds)

ACKNOWLEDGEMENT

Reproduced by kind permission of the BBC Written Archives Centre, Caversham, and Robin Gordon Walker.

The Man from Belsen, **the BBC's First Anniversary Feature, Broadcast 15 April 1946**

The concluding quarter of this hour-long feature is reproduced here.

<u>TRAIN WHISTLE. DISTANT SHOUTING. FADE.</u>

10. LE DRUILLENEC: That was the last time I saw my friend, de Frotté. Next morning we were divided into two parties. Of the 450 prisoners who had set out from Wilhelmshaven, about 200 died on the journey, or were killed in the raid. Of the survivors, 150 were left behind on the field at Luneberg, among them was my friend, Jean de Frotté. I will tell you later what happened to those who remained behind. I was in the other party, together with Colonel Reynaud and Baudu. We were packed into a truck and a lorry and driven away. We thought we were going back to the Neuen Gamme, but when the truck stopped...

<u>LORRY SLOWS DOWN.</u>

3. REYNAUD: Thank God! Thank God! They're slowing down. Where are we? This isn't Neuen Gamme.

<u>LORRY STOPS. ENGINES STILL RUNNING. FADE UP SHUFFLING TRAMP OF FEET. KEEP BEHIND:</u>

4. LE DRUILLENEC: It was not Neuen Gamme. It was Belsen.

BRING UP TRAMP OF FEET.

5. GERMAN VOICE: Vom Lastwagen Herunter! Schnell! Zu fuenft den anderen Gefangenen!

MURMUR AND SHUFFLING OF MEN. FADE, WITH TRAMP OF FEET.

6. LE DRUILLENEC: You have heard so many general descriptions of Belsen that I will not bore you by repeating them. You know about the decay, the filth, the stench from the unburied dead, although you cannot imagine these things. All I will tell you now, very briefly, is what happened to my companions and myself during those last terrible days.

MUSIC BEGINS, VERY QUIETLY, NOT HORRIFIC: A MONOTONOUS, SLOW LINKING THEME WITH A SUGGESTION OF COLD IN IT, AND A STEADY, WELL-ACCENTUATED RHYTHM. FADE BEHIND:

First night. Crowded into a dark hut, filled with bunks. Colonel Reynaud and I find one empty bunk.

7. REYNAUD: As we've only one blanket between us, Le Druillenec, I suggest we share it.

8. LE DRUILLENEC: We got into bed. Then ...

DOOR IS FLUNG OPEN. ANGRY SHOUTS AND MURMURS.

1. GERMAN VOICE:	Heraus aus den Betten! Aufstehen! Die sind nicht fuer Euch! Sie gehoeren den Chefs! Ihr gehoert auf den Boden! Heraus! **GOES OFF MIKE AS HE SPEAKS.**
2. REYNAUD:	These beds are for the Camp Chiefs, Le Druillenec. We must get out.
3. GERMAN VOICE:	Heraus! Ruehrt Euch!
4. REYNAUD:	(<u>angrily, to Guard</u>) So gehoert es, ihr unzivilisierten – **BLOW AND GROAN.** Le Druillenec, let's find the other French prisoners. There must be more. (<u>raises voice</u>) Y a-t'il des prisonniers français ici? Y a-t'il des prisonniers français? Nous sommes français.
5. FRENCH VOICE:	Oui, ici dans ce coin – par ici! **FADE MURMURING AND SCUFFLING. MUSIC. REPEAT THEME. KEEP BEHIND:**
6. LE DRUILLENEC:	Second morning. Driven out with blows at 3.30 a.m. Standing in the cold and driving rain for hours, waiting for food, nothing but a few scraps since leaving Wilhelmshaven. Colonel Reynaud very weak. **MUSIC INTO MURMUR OF WAITING CROWD. FADE.**
7. REYNAUD:	At least they might give us some coffee – at least that.

BBC BROADCASTS: THE SCRIPTS

8. BAUDU: (approaching) Harold, have you seen that hut over there – the brick one? Have you, Colonel?

9. REYNAUD: No.

10. BAUDU: Come over with me. I'll show you.

UP CROWD NOISE, THEN DOWN.

11. LE DRUILLENEC: Fifteen long low rooms, each filled with dead. Stacked in neat, systematic rows, the crown of each head touching the chin of the next. Maybe 700 corpses per room. Fifteen rooms.

CROWD NOISE, INTO BRIEF MUSIC, THEN BACK INTO CROWD AGAIN. FADE CROWD NOISE INTO MUSIC.

5. LE DRUILLENEC: Second night. More convoys arrive, filling the already overcrowded hut. Cannot lie down. Have to sit with legs apart, the next man between your knees. Daren't try to rise or your space will be filled, the congestion is so great. Overhead, lying on planks, the sick and dying, most of them with dysentery. No escape. Locked in every night. Colonel getting weaker. Boudu still keeps his strength and spirits.

MUSIC UP, THEN FADE.

2. LE DRUILLENEC: Fifth night. Still more men crammed into Hut 13. Every morning more men are too weak to crawl out. Even if they are still alive, they are officially dead and are carried to the mortuary. Colonel too weak to move. Baudu and I carry him out. They must not take Colonel Reynaud.

	MUSIC UP AND OUT BEHIND:
3. LE DRUILLENEC:	Sixth day.
	FADE UP LARGE CROWD NOISE
4. GERMAN GUARD:	Zu fuenfen antreten! Schnell, schnell!
	MURMURING AND SHUFFLING OF MEN. C/F TO SHUFFLING MARCH. FADE IN CROWD NOISE AGAIN BEHIND:
5. GERMAN GUARD:	Tragt die Toten zu den Leichengraeben. Reisst diese Decken in Streifen, bindet die Streifen um die Knoecheln und schleppt die Leichen durch die Lagerstrasse! Schnell!
6. LE DRUILLENEC:	The crematorium had stopped working. The corpses are to be buried in great pits at the far end of the camp. We are ordered to drag the dead from the mortuary to the pits, tying strips of blanket around their ankles.
7. GERMAN GUARD:	Keine Zeit verschwenden! Zupacken! Tragt sie in die Grübon!
	FADE MURMUR INTO MUSIC, WHICH FADES BEHIND:
8. LE DRUILLENEC:	Seventh day. They're filling the fourth pit. The number of bodies seems endless. Ten thousand men are at this task all day, yet there seems no end to it. Getting very weak. So is Baudu. We left Colonel Reynaud outside our hut this morning. Then, as we're passing through the mortuary yard...
1. BAUDU:	Harold! Look! It's Colonel Reynaud!

BBC BROADCASTS: THE SCRIPTS

2. LE DRUILLENEC:	Colonel Reynaud, lying in a stream of filth, among the dead.
3. REYNAUD:	(<u>weakly</u>) I've been here all night. Can you get me some water?
4. BAUDU:	We're going to get you out, first.
5. REYNAUD:	No use – you'll have to go against the traffic – the guard will stop you.
6. BAUDU:	Will they? We'll see. Take his shoulders, Harold.
7. REYNAUD:	It's no use, my friends. I'm finished anyway.
8. LE DRUILLENEC:	Both of us are so weak that we can hardly lift the Colonel, thin as he is. By luck we get past the guard in a blanket and take him back to the hut. He is in great pain. Baudu has one cigarette. He tries to barter it for one litre of soup for Reynaud. He fails. Then the guards come with sticks and drive us back to the mortuary. When we get back that night, we find that our friend has been taken back. He lies there all night and dies at mid-day on the following day.
	<u>MUSIC UP AND DOWN</u>
9. LE DRUILLENEC:	Ninth day. I am finished. I have not eaten for five days, nor had a drink for six days. The work of filling the pits go on, but we dodge it. Ostrich-like, we hide our heads under a blanket, perfectly convinced that even though the rest of our bodies are visible, the guards will not see us. They beat us and drive us out again. We pretend to go. Then when

they've gone we go back to our blankets.

MUSIC UP AND DOWN

1. LE DRUILLENEC: Tenth day.

FADE UP MURMUR AND DISTANT RIFLE SHOTS.

2. BAUDU: Harold, the S.S. have gone. Have you seen the new guards? They're Hungarian. They're worse. They're shooting at the prisoners. But if the S.S. have gone, maybe that means the British are coming. Harold! (trying to make him understand) I say the British may be coming!

MUSIC UP AND DOWN

3. LE DRUILLENEC: (to himself, dully) What if the British are coming? They'll be too late. We shall die before they arrive, or be shot. The Hungarian guards are now killing whole batches of prisoners. They call them out and shoot them. As they go forward, knowing it will be to their death, they rub their hands together. If I'm called, I will not rub my hands together ...

MUSIC UP AND DOWN
HEAVY EXPLOSIONS DISTANT, THEN NEARER.

4. BAUDU: Harold, it's true! The British must be very near! Those are their guns! They must be all around the camp. (pause) There's some fresh grass outside Block 26. I've eaten some. It's good. Try it. It'll do you good.

BBC BROADCASTS: THE SCRIPTS

<u>MUSIC, MORE EXCITED, EXPECTANT, C/F TO GUNFIRE. LOUDER.</u>

5. BAUDU: There are tanks on the Coller-Vinsen road. Harold – I said tanks! British or American tanks, with a white star on them! Harold, wake up and listen! The guards have gone! People are looting the kitchens! Come with me – quickly! The gates are open! …

<u>FADE.
BRING UP EXCITED MURMUR, MIXED WITH DISTANT CHEERING.</u>

1. LE DRUILLENEC: With little Baudu by my side, I staggered to the compound gateway. It was open. Prisoners were pouring on to the central road of the camp. I saw, drawn up by the roadside, a British radio truck, with the officer sitting in it. I <u>thought</u> I rushed up to them, but they told me afterwards that I crawled there on all fours. The car was just going to move.

<u>BRING UP EXCITED BABBLE OF CROWD.</u>

2. LE DRUILLENEC: Wait! …. Wait, please! I am a British subject!

3. CAPT. SINGTON: What's your name?

4. LE DRUILLENEC: Harold Le Druillenec. I'm from the Channel Islands.

5. CAPT. SINGTON: Harold Le Druillenec? Well, I'm not making a practice of this, but you'd better come with us. No, I think you'd better sit on the bonnet.

	That's better! No, I'm sorry I can't take your friend. He'll be seen to very soon. Drive on, Briggs!
6. BAUDU:	Good bye Harold. You'll write to me, won't you?
	FADE CAR AND CHEERING CROWD.
7. LE DRUILLENEC:	So, on April 16th, I left Belsen, sitting on the bonnet of a British radio truck because I was too lousy and dirty to be allowed inside. I weighed ninety pounds, and when I saw myself in the mirror for the first time, I looked behind me to see who was there. The army treated me with infinite kindness and in a few days I was in a hospital in England. Some months later, when I returned to give evidence at the Belsen trial, I went to Luneberg to discover what had happened to my 150 comrades who had been left behind, only to find their graves. We learned from a signalman whose box overlooked the field that after a fortnight the S.S. guards lined up the prisoners, then shot them in batches. Among these who perished was my dear friend, Jean de Frotté, who had endured and suffered so much. Of the 450 men who left Wilhelmshaven, about twenty-five survived. Of the 12,000 Frenchmen who entered Neuen Gamme only 600 returned to France. Such is my story.
	Now, my experience, terrible as it was, was no worse than that of millions of other concentration camp prisoners. Why, you may ask, should we wish to recall these horrors? Why not forget? I can sympathise with such a viewpoint. I, too, often wish I could forget. And yet, at other times, I think that such

stories should be remembered. There is a danger that these camps may come to be regarded as part of a fantastic nightmare from which mankind has awakened. This, I believe, is an over-optimistic view.

Though the Germans perfected the Concentration Camp, it was not a German invention, and I saw men of other nationalities employed in the camps, behave as brutally as the Germans.

No, the Concentration Camp is a new weapon, as new as gunpowder was in the fifteenth century. It is a scientific instrument of domination by which a Totalitarian state can control millions through fear: not fear of death, but of a living death. I believe that wherever a State achieves total power, wherever free speech and criticism are denied, and power is not subject to democratic control, unscrupulous men will be tempted to use this weapon again. Surely, if civilisation is to survive, we must preserve at all costs a humane and liberal way of life.

Finally, may I ask you to regard this programme, not as a record of one man's personal sufferings, but as a memorial to all the millions who perished in that twentieth-century hell of man's creating, the Konzentrationslager.

1. ANNOUNCER: That was "The Man From Belsen", a Feature programme, based on the experiences of Mr. Harold Le Druillenec, the only British survivor from the Belsen Concentration camp.

Mr. Le Druillenec himself was the narrator. The programme was written by Leonard Cottrell.

There is an alteration to the cast as

published in the "RADIO TIMES" – Colonel Reynaud was played by Leslie Porrins. The rest of the cast was as follows:

Bernard Dupuys	Bernard Robel
Jean de Frotté	Valentine Dyall
Doctor Moreau	Lewis Stringer
Lloyd Gybels	Tommy Duggan
Omar, the Block Chief	Esmé Peroy
Jean Baudu	Philip Wade
Taprell	David Ward
French Professor	Carleton Hobbs

The musical effects were arranged by William Alwyn, and played by James Blados and Harry Taylor.
The violinist was Eugene Pini.
"The Man From Belsen" was produced by Leonard Cottrell.

ACKNOWLEDGEMENT

Reproduced by kind permission of the BBC Written Archives Centre, Caversham.

'And I was only a child': Children's Testimonies, Bergen-Belsen 1945

BOAZ COHEN

My sweet parents, Dad, Mum and a sister died in the destruction of the Krakow ghetto. In all these camps I worked very hard, went without clothes and was beaten up severely, I was also ill with many ailments, *and all this when I was only a child.*[1]

Most of the personal recollections of the liberation of Bergen- Belsen were put down or recorded several decades after the end of the Second World War. They are thus affected both by distance from the event itself and the 'processing' of many years' thought and retelling. The lack of earlier testimonies can be easily explained: survivors were trying to recover from their ordeals, to find a country that would take them in, and eventually to build new lives, families and careers. The liberators – soldiers, relief workers and medical students – were likewise busy forging their lives after the war. It took many years of digestion, and coming of age for the memories of Bergen-Belsen to be told to the world.

It appears though, that a set of survivor testimonies collected just after the camp's liberation lay dormant in the archives for many years. These are the testimonies of children and teenagers, taken in the camp, in 1945 and 1946 set down on paper at the instigation of Helena Wrobel (later Wrobel-Kagan) in a high school she set up for young survivors in Belsen. The testimonies, titled 'My Way from Home to Bergen-Belsen', are unique therefore in their closeness to the events described.[2]

Bergen-Belsen Child Survivors

Who were the children and teenagers in Bergen-Belsen? Where did they come from, and how did they survive? The bitter truth is that there was little chance of survival for Jewish children in Nazi-occupied Europe. This explains why there were so few children at the concentration camps at the time of liberation. In December 1945 there were only 1,800 children in the DP camps of the American zone. It is difficult to come up with exact numbers for Bergen-Belsen. Since early 1945, the camp, used for neutrals and other 'exchange Jews' did have a *Kinderbaracke* with 52 Dutch children of Jewish families from the diamond trade and some 30 children from Poland and Slovakia. Upon liberation, the Dutch children were repatriated and not many others remained. The nursery and primary school that was up and running in May 1945 initially had only 30 children. Most of the children and young people at the camp at the time of liberation, however, had arrived there with the massive influx of survivors of other camps in the last months of the war. They had experienced the Nazi hell as children in ghettos and in camps. Many had matured early and had seen much, and their testimonies enable us to see these experiences through children's eyes. They also demonstrate the unique and intense nature of the few weeks spent in Bergen-Belsen during those last weeks of the war. Although many of the children were veterans of Auschwitz and of the death marches, their encounter with Bergen-Belsen was highly traumatic and figures prominently in their testimonies:

'Only here we felt that five years of war were "nothing" compared with four weeks in Bergen Belsen', recounted Regina G. (46) in her testimony.[3] 'There was hunger, filth. Typhoid was rampant in the camp and "devoured" people who no longer wanted to live'.

Lea H. (35), 13 years old at the time of liberation, wrote: 'We slept on bare, wet and dirty floors fainting with hunger, and the lice were eating us. A horrible epidemic of typhus was taking its toll like a burning fire. I never believed I would survive this Gehenum [hell]'.

Edyta R. (11), 15 years old, arrived at Bergen-Belsen from Groß-Rosen:

> This was the worst camp I was in during the war. There was terrible hunger and people died in droves ... all night you could hear people dying ... during work we were set upon by dogs

and were tortured cruelly – people were half dead. In the morning 10% of us were dead. Everyone wanted to die, no one believed it would ever end.

In contrast with the harrowing descriptions of the camp's horrors, the day when liberation finally came is hardly mentioned in the testimonies. Only 14 of the 46 testimonies discuss it. Some were ecstatic. 'There were no limits to our happiness' wrote Lea H. (35). 'We were running around the whole lager like madmen'. Others could only describe their pitiful condition: 'I was so ill I wasn't able to see', wrote 13-year old Gutka F. (17). Most children were too ill and numb to remember anything about the day.

Liberation brought a massive effort at rehabilitation. Doctors and medical students were brought into the camp. Their devoted work came too late for thousands, but many were nursed back to health. But what were the young survivors to do once their weight had returned to normal and they were free of lice and typhoid? How could they be prepared to rebuild their lives? The question bothered many of the survivor leaders in the camp and their response was to set up a nursery and primary school, both of which were in place by May 1945.[4] In July when the first soldiers of the Jewish Brigade arrived at the camp they were astounded to hear from one of the houses, 'a Hebrew song, the children are welcoming us with Hebrew singing ... who created this wonder?'[5]

Environment for Testimony: The Hebrew Gymnasium

But what was to be done with the older children and the teenagers who 'continued to roam around with their pots to the communal kitchen to receive their bread and soup, from there to the clothing warehouse. And so day after day aimlessly and purposelessly'.[6]

Dr Helena Wrobel had taught geography at the Gymnasium in Tarnow, Poland, before the war. She hid in the woods with the partisans and was later incarcerated in several work camps. She was liberated at Bergen-Belsen and became one of the teachers in the primary school. Seeing the plight of the teenagers she decided to open a high school.

She put up notices all over the camp: 'In a short time a

Gymnasium will be established in the camp. Interested pupils should contact Helena Wrobel'.[7] Her friends laughed at her, but in the morning there were 31 teenagers outside, 30 girls and one boy. She asked the camp's Jewish administration to send a Jewish Brigade soldier to help her. By that time a number of soldiers from the Brigade were in the camp helping with education and community work. She was joined by David Littman of the 606th Field Artillery Regiment. Littman had grown up in Poland but had emigrated to Palestine with his family in 1934. By the time he joined the Jewish Brigade he was two years into his studies at the Hebrew University in Jerusalem.

Running a school in a DP camp was no mean task. There were no books, paper or pencils and Wrobel and Littman used their cigarette rations to fund the school activities. Teachers had to teach 'from their heads' – with all the difficulties this involved. The testimonies themselves testify to the scarcity of paper. They are written on all sorts of stationery – often on pages torn from the former Camp administration's accounting books.[8] Books were scrounged in every possible way: Littman's letters home to his family in Tel Aviv abound with requests for books.[9] Books were also bought from German teachers in the locality and bookshops using cigarettes and food parcels allocated by the camp's committee.

The school was named the Hebrew Gymnasium 'The Jewish Brigade Bergen-Belsen' and grew rapidly.[10] In February 1946 there were 104 students in the Gymnasium, and 19 teachers. By the end of 1946 the total number of pupils in the camp's educational system had grown to 880 – largely due to the arrival in the camp of Jewish refugees from the Soviet Zone. The teaching at the school had strong ideological underpinnings that are echoed in the testimonies. Bergen-Belsen DPs, led by Josef Rosensaft, were combative and vocal on Zionist issues, especially on policy decisions concerning children, and the school was, in the eyes of its teachers, 'the hotbed for the nurturing of a national Jewish spirit'.[11] The school was named after the Jewish Brigade, thus positioning the young, brave, Zionist soldiers as the children's role models. Ideological factors were at play in the choice of Yiddish (and later Hebrew) as the teaching language for the school. The first students spoke mainly Polish as did the teachers who had also taught in this language before the war. Still, it was decided that teaching would be carried out in Jewish languages. This was deemed more appropriate for the school's educational message of Jewish nationalism and Zionism. The decision had its practical benefits as well - especially when more and more children from Hungary and Romania joined the school. One of the testimonies shows the students' identification with the school's language policy:

> Unlike the need we had for using Hungarian and Polish, we can now speak in Yiddish or Hebrew. It's much nicer to hear Yiddish. We have nothing to thank the Poles and Hungarians for. They are the diligent disciples of Hitler's annihilation ideology. It's wrong and unneeded to use these languages, especially after the pogroms there.[12]

Zionist ideology was even more apparent in the school's curriculum and educational values. While there was much general education with classes in physics, maths, archaology and botany, particular emphasis was placed on Hebrew, Jewish History and Palestinian geography, and the like. Special school gatherings centred on the land of Israel, Eretz Israel, and the Jewish return there. One such event ended with the words: 'The whole land is our home. She is waiting for us, she needs sons to build her, sons to defend her. May we soon reach the day when we will all work together in building our homeland and defending it'.[13]

But how did the children respond to such education? Did they identify with its underlying values? From the testimonies it seems that they did. In the 'My Way from Home to Bergen Belsen' testimonies, some of the students ended their essays with the hope to go to Eretz Israel. 'Now my aim is Eretz Israel', wrote 13-year-old Pola Z. (15) after recounting the loss of her family. 'Just like we waited for liberation from the Germans', wrote Lea H. (35) 'we're waiting 100 times over for the day when we will come to our beautiful and faraway homeland'. These aspirations were not just the product of successful brainwashing by their teachers. The students' wartime experience brought them to these conclusions themselves. A student who returned to her hometown only to find that no one from her family had survived, wrote: 'I decided to go to Palestine because we had too many casualties in the Galus (exile). I want to live with my brothers on my land and to build my life' (56).[14] 'I know that there I'll be treated as a human being', wrote 15-year-old Syma G. (27), reflecting on her experience in Europe.

The Testimonies

In the first days of the school's existence Helena Wrobel made the students write essays titled: 'My Way from Home to Bergen Belsen'. Forty-six such testimonies were taken between December 1945 and February 1946 and many more were taken later. While most students wrote essays, some were asked to fill in personal questionnaires.[15] The later testimonies and questionnaires include comments and criticisms on the current situation of the children and on the school solicited by Wrobel-Kagan and her staff. Many of the testimonies give the children's age. Most had been born somewhere between 1928 and 1933, were children during the Second World War and at the time of writing were teenagers aged 13–18. They entered the adult world at an early age.

The majority of the first testimonies are in Polish – the language most children still felt most comfortable with, but some are in Yiddish. They are handwritten and on a variety of types of paper – many on pages torn out of German accounting books.

They are short, ranging from half a page to three pages, and usually the style is laconic - even dismissive: 'Everybody knows how life in the ghetto was - there was a terrible famine and hundreds of people died', wrote Syma G. (27). In a similar vein Edzia J. (41) wrote, 'What life was like and how everybody worked is known to everyone'. It is as if the students were 'skimming' over what they saw as the mundane in order to get to the harrowing stories of the war's final days of which they write extensively.

Many things were left unsaid – they were just too painful to remember and were left out in a process of self-censorship. A 13-year-old girl (9) recounted her arrival with her family at Auschwitz: 'When I stood in the *Apell* I was shaking from the cold. When I looked up I saw smoke-filled skies. With this I'm finishing the account of my life during the war'.[16] The clipped style stemmed, it seems, from the writer's awareness of the magnitude of their experience – it just couldn't be wholly told. 'I have kept what happened to me short', concluded Estera (Edzia) Z. (8), 'because otherwise I would have to write without end'. Occasionally there are attempts to describe emotions: Edyta R. (11) recalled that she was 'lonely and lived in fear of death by gas and of the crematorium'. Students related to feelings of degradation: 'this was the end of our self-respect, our feminine identity', wrote another (50) of her treatment in Auschwitz, 'we were not humans anymore'. 'What we felt in the camp was depression and degradation', wrote one of the other girls (55). Another recalled the moment her brother was taken to his death. 'From that moment', she wrote, 'I was finished'.[17]

Much has been written in the last years on the construction of survivor testimonies and life stories.[18] It is commonplace to see them as attempts at a coherent exposition of one's life: constructed narratives with background and conclusions. The Bergen-Belsen testimonies are different – the students say almost nothing about their pre-war lives. Sometimes they provide basic information about family members, pre-war addresses, etc., but no more. Most start their narrative from the moment their community fell under Nazi control: 'On the 18th of February there was a general resettlement of Jews from our town Chrzanow', 15-year-old Taube W. (37) opened her essay, 'Our family fell apart'. It may be claimed that, obviously, when the students were asked to write about 'the way from home to Bergen Belsen' they concentrated on the 'way' and not on the 'home'. Still, there was their pre-war life, the home they came from, whose invisibility in the testimonies cannot be discounted. Likewise, liberation and its aftermath hardly appeared in the testimonies. These focus primarily on the wartime experience and on specific episodes at that. The last days of the war figure prominently. Evidently, the death marches and the last weeks in Bergen-Belsen eclipsed much of what happened before that.

We have to bear in mind that we do not know how these testimonies were taken and what instructions were given to the students. Were they receiving help from their teachers in constructing and writing the testimonies and if they did, were they asking for it or was it offered to them? Did they compare notes and stories with their schoolmates or with family members who survived? These questions have to be borne in mind when reading and analysing the testimonies.

The testimonies offer a wealth of information on childhood experiences of occupation and persecution. They relate to many aspects of the children's lives and the horrors they saw around them. In the following pages three major issues prominent in the testimonies will be described: the death marches, family and loss, and moral and immoral behaviour.

The Death Marches

The descriptions of the death marches, given as they were, only a few months after the events, provide a clear and poignant view of the last months of the war as witnessed by the children.

'On the 3rd of February 1945, when the guns of the approaching Russian army could be heard very clearly, we left the lager setting off for a terrible journey', wrote Taube W. (37). It was to be a six week march from Neusalz to Flossenberg from where she and those of her friends who survived the journey would be taken by train to Bergen-Belsen. Conditions were harsh:

> 900 girls were divided into three transports and were sent off for a long journey with one loaf of bread and wearing makeshift shoes. We were walking fast, rushed by the SS-women, who didn't care about food for us, only to make us walk as many kilometres as possible in one day.

Similarly, Pnina J. (39) set off from the camp in Peterswaldau (a part of the Groß-Rosen complex) on 21 January 1945. 'We were given bread for two days and started marching', she wrote. 'The cold was terrible and after two days there was nothing to eat. Death and fear were in our eyes. We had to do 30 km. a day. Many girls dropped down of hunger and exhaustion. After a week I could walk no more'. Other students also mentioned the intense cold and lack of clothing and shoes. 16-year-old Miriam B. (14), was on the death march from Neusalz to Bergen-Belsen: 'We started off in January, it was terribly cold. The girls had no clogs, we walked barefoot'. It was not hunger but thirst that was the most painful to bear. More than one student wrote of eating snow. 'Snow was like drink for us, because we were suffering from thirst', wrote Lea H. (35).

The last leg of the journey to Bergen-Belsen had been by train, and was remembered as even worse than the foot march. Miriam B. (14) remembered:

Walked so for 10 days and then reached the train cars, it was there that the nightmare began – an endless journey. The cars were open, we sat glued to one another. Our backs and bones broke. We were suffocating.

16-year-old Sara G. (44) similarly described her train transport from Auschwitz to Bergen-Belsen:

We were driven into cattle cars. They didn't count, just pushed in as many as possible. We stood for three days and three nights. Some were on their knees. Sitting was out of the question. On the way scores of bodies were hurled out. There was a terrible smell in the cars, filth. Some were crying, asking for some breathing space. Many jumped to their deaths because they couldn't breathe inside for lack of air.

As well as underscoring Nazi inhumanity, the testimonies record the general chaos and breakdown of the camp system in the last months of the war. 'We were walked towards the little town of Goben, where the K. D. was situated', wrote Taube W. (37), 'but the Russian army conquered this lager from a different direction and we had to go back'. Then, 'a real miracle happened: the SS-women were commanded to leave us immediately. We remained alone, 200 girls under the supervision of 2 men'. The guards allowed the girls to forage for food but then continued the march. They had nowhere to flee to.

Family and Loss

For the children caught up in the horrors of this period, the family was the one single factor enabling a sense of security in insecure times. Students wrote extensively about their fathers, mothers and siblings. Even in cases where the family had eventually perished, students recalled how, in times of deep uncertainty, the fact that the family had been together had empowered them and enabled them to face the threatening future. 'In spite of everything I feel relief because I'm with all my family', wrote Jona B. (36) of her feeling when her family and herself were transferred from the ghetto to the camp (probably from Lodz to Birkenau). 'Come what may but we are together. We survived the ghetto and will survive this'. Similarly, 19-

year-old Fira P. (5) who went through several work camps in Estonia with her family wrote of their importance for her: 'Fate was kind to us. We passed all the selections and I stayed with my parents. These were terrible times indeed. Hunger and hard work sucked up all our spirit. But I was with my family all the time and therefore very happy'.[19] These lines were written after the students had lost their families or most of them, and show just how meaningful this issue was for them.

Most painful to describe was the last sight of their families. Stela L. (42) wrote of her separation from her father and brothers on the platform in Auschwitz:

> I didn't have enough time to kiss Daddy, he quickly disappeared... I didn't see where the brothers went and didn't realise that I remained alone with Mummy.... In my ears I could still hear my brothers' words: 'Our dearest Mummy, come with us'. And in my eyes I can still see my Daddy's sad eyes.

Jona B. (36) also wrote of her family's arrival at Auschwitz: 'The first blow: we are separated from our father and brother. But it doesn't end here. Selection, I'm separated from my Mummy. In one minute they took all I had'.

The loss of family was remembered by the students as a distinct breaking point. 15-year-old Estera (Edzia) Z. (8) had been incarcerated with her family in the Lodz Ghetto. In July 1944, while searching for bread for her family, she was rounded up and deported to Auschwitz. 'The journey was horrible for me', she wrote, 'I cried all day and night with no break, because I knew that I would not see my parents and my brothers again'. The realisation that now they were alone was excruciating: 'I was so shocked I didn't know what was happening to me', wrote 15-year-old Syma G. (27) about her mother's death in the camp: 'Later I felt lonesome and miserable for remaining alone in the world'. Upset at the prospect of having to cope alone was even stronger after liberation. 'It's so tragic to be left alone, without parents', wrote one of the students (19), 'and to lose all the family in such a terrible way'.[20] Another girl (50) wrote in retrospect: 'On September 1942 I was taken to the camp. I was there alone for three years. I lived in terrible conditions. I was in seven camps. I've been through a lot. The hardest part was being alone, so young and without parents'.[21]

Many youngsters assumed the role of parent to younger family members: 'In our first year in the ghetto I lost my parents', wrote one of the girls (55). 'As an 11-year-old orphan I had to be a mother to my 6-year-old brother. We were separated in Auschwitz in 1944. From that moment I was finished'.[22]

The sense of being alone in the world was accentuated after liberation, as students realised that they had to build their lives anew without a family to support them emotionally and materially. 'It's so tragic to be left alone, without parents and to lose all the family in such a terrible way' (19).[23]

Moral Evaluation: Good and Evil

In the introduction to a book on children's testimonies published in Poland in 1947, Maria Hochberg-Marianska attempted to characterise their moral approach:

> Every time a child came across noble people, where it found help and heart, it expresses its gratitude with the words filled with best feelings. Every gesture, giving a piece of bread, a word of sincere compassion – these responses of the heart in the awful days of destruction – did not disappear from the memory of the children... Children speak about the bad deeds and the awful people with the same honesty and directness.[24]

Many of the testimonies describe cruel or selfish behaviour among prisoners – sometimes involving discrimination against particular groups. 'The Gypsy women are distributing the food' wrote Jona B. (36) of her experience in Birkenau, 'and because they "like to eat" we get less than half of the food we deserve'. Pola Z. (15) recounted her arrival in Bergen-Belsen: 'We were attacked by Russian women who took all we had left, it was very hard'.[25] This was not an isolated encounter. Another of the girls (2) told of continuous strife: 'We had to fight for our lives and for food', she wrote. 'To be five Jewish girls among many wild Russians was no great pleasure. They took the water we got with such great pains'.[26] Problems were first and foremost caused not by national rivalries but by the impossible conditions. Miriam B. (14), whose account of the death march from Neusalz to Bergen-Belsen was mentioned above, wrote of the conditions in the train cars taking her and her friends on the last leg of the journey: 'Strong and weak began to battle for space. We were no longer humans but animals. Each one of us fought for some air to breathe and for space. We were woken many times at night by our thirst and started fighting for the snow that fell upon us'.

But the testimonies are also replete with description of humane behaviour and of prisoner solidarity. Many of the students – especially the younger ones – owe their lives to aid given to them by adults. 15-year-old Edyta R. (11) and her aunt were the only survivors of their families. In September 1943 they were sent to Plaszow. Edyta, 12 years old at the time, was to be sent to death, but she wrote, 'My loving aunt saved me [from selection], at a very great risk for her'. Similarly, 15-year-old Syma G. (27) was watched over in the camp by a cousin: '[she] watched over and took care of me in the camp, only because of her I'm still alive'. 16-year-old Sala R. (12), survived the last weeks in Bergen-Belsen through a chance meeting with 'a friend of my mother, she gave me some bread and promised to help'.

From the pages of the testimonies come some extraordinary acts of kindness. In one selection at Auschwitz, wrote Ruita S. (1): 'I was to go to death and my mother to the transport. The *blukova* [woman in charge of the block] moved me from oven to oven (it was very dangerous). When she gave me a sign I ran to my mother'. She was 12 years old at the time. Stela L. (42) was also 12 years old and in Birkenau when her mother was taken from her. In her testimony she recounts that 'I wanted to throw myself on the barbed-wire, other women held me back with difficulty, comforting me by saying that I would see my Mummy in a few days' – surprisingly she did.

Sara G.'s (44) description of the harrowing conditions in the train cars to Bergen-Belsen was mentioned above. Yet, she does not fail to recount that, in spite of the unbearable thirst, 'a bucket of water was brought to the wagon but no one dared drink because we saved it for the people who fainted'. 16-year-old Bronka S. (45) remembered the *Judenaltëste* (senior Jewish inmate) in the Neusalz forced labour camp. 'She was always on our side. She was a 22-year-old girl to whom we owe our lives'.[27]

Why Children's Testimonies?

The children's testimonies of Bergen-Belsen are a unique cultural and historical document. It still has to be asked why were they taken at all? What were Wrobel's aims in collecting the testimonies? Why did she make students, all trying to open a new page in life, open their wounds and recount their horrendous experiences?

We have nothing from Wrobel or her co-workers on this subject. In the 1950s she had the testimonies typed up with a view to publication but nothing came out of it. Neither Yad Vashem nor a mysterious British professor who allegedly offered to work on them were interested enough in publishing them.[28]

Wrobel's initiative was in fact another manifestation of a more general phenomenon: the collection of children's testimonies in the Jewish post-war world.[29] This work was done mainly by the Historical Commissions established by Jewish survivor historians and memory activists.[30] The leading commissions, those in Poland and in Munich (working in the American zone) targeted children, developed research methodologies, and published children's testimonies.

How much was Wrobel informed about this work? It's hard to know. Bergen-Belsen's DP community was isolated from the majority of Jewish DPs concentrated in the American zone and from its cultural and historical centres. This was due to British policy, which would not accept Jewish self-determination and therefore worked to isolate 'its' Jewish DPs from the huge and thriving Jewish DP population in the American Zone, and to Bergen-Belsen's camp leadership which, because of this British policy, developed independently from Jewish leadership in the American Zone. It seems that while Wrobel's work developed in isolation, it nonetheless reflected the general mode of thinking at the time.

The issue of surviving children held a special place in survivor culture. The suffering of children epitomised the enormity of German evil. The innocence of the children targeted by the Nazis, and the horrible fate they suffered during the war were the culmination of the Jewish tragedy. Their plight had political implications as well, and the testimonies could be used in the ongoing political struggle. A paper on the collection of children's testimonies was published by the Polish Central Historical Commission in 1945. In typical communist rhetoric the first goal of such testimonies was the anti-fascist struggle:

1. To give – as much as possible – a rounded picture of the criminal Nazi activity, whose purpose was to first morally corrupt and physically exterminate the young Jewish generation.
2. The ultimate tasks of the research are to provide material for an accusation against fascism and to convince the world that it must mercilessly and finally eliminate every trace of fascism.[31]

And there were also issues of Jewish rebuilding to consider. Adults were awed by the children and their stories. The children and their survival played a major role in fulfilling the need for Jewish heroism in the Holocaust. Jewish children survivors were also the nation's hope for the future. Their tragic life during the Holocaust was the backdrop for the building of their new lives. Historically, the aim was to integrate the children's stories into the Jewish narrative of the Holocaust.

But Wrobel and her fellow teachers were not historians and did not see themselves as the chroniclers of the Holocaust. Neither were they political leaders needing the testimonies in order to underline the plight of the Jewish people. They were teachers, interested first and foremost in giving their pupils some sense of normality, and a basis on which to build their future. They had to understand what went on in the not-so-distant past. Without such understanding the students could not be helped, for how can you help a student if you do not know the emotional baggage he is carrying? An acknowledgement that the testimonies were a crucial tool in understanding the students appears also in the Polish Central Historical Commission's paper on children's testimonies. There it was claimed that the testimonies were needed in order:

3. To establish the psychological and physical state of the Jewish youth after living for a period of several years under the conditions of the Nazi regime (ghetto, bunker, 'Aryan side', camp, forest, partisans, etc.).
4. To gather together information about the plans and aspirations of the Jewish youth, investigate their political convictions, their attitude towards other nations, etc., in order to obtain informative material for the direction of our further educational work.[32]

CHILDREN'S TESTIMONIES 167

But there were other important reasons for getting students to write their testimonies. Israel Kaplan of the Central Historical Commission in Munich claimed that the Holocaust was an important and far-reaching chapter in the life of the children and that they should not be made to forget it. As grown-ups, he continued, 'the children will probably thank their teachers for these memoirs'. He also suggested something that Wrobel did intuitively: establishing a school archive containing all the students' testimonies. As a teacher, Wrobel must have been no less interested in having the students 'work out' their experiences. Survivors collecting testimonies, such as Rachel Auerbach in Poland and later in Israel, spoke of the act of testifying as an essential catharsis on the way to building a new life.

In conclusion, it can be said that the collection of testimonies from children survivors of Bergen-Belsen by the adult survivors is a fascinating historical and cultural phenomenon. The testimonies themselves enable us to see the camp and the last months of the war through the eyes of a distinct group of victims. Even more so, they offer an insight to the unique Holocaust experience of children and young people, and enable us to integrate their story into the historical narrative of the Holocaust and of Bergen-Belsen camp.

NOTES

Support for the research and writing of this essay came from the 'Documentation and Education: Children's Holocaust Testimony Project' of Bar-Ilan University, which was supported by a grant from the Rabbi Israel Miller Fund for Shoah Research, Documentation and Education of the Conference on Jewish Material Claims Against Germany. I would like to thank professors Joel Walters, Hagit Lavsky and Dov Levin for their comments on this essay.

1. Testimony no. 70, name unknown to us, see note 3. Emphasis added.
2. I was introduced to these testimonies by Mr Yosi Shavit, the director of the Ghetto Fighter's House archives where the testimonies are deposited. His co-operation has been vital for the success of this project. I'm indebted to the work of Ms Edna Elazari in her MA thesis: 'The Hebrew Gymnasium "The Jewish Brigade" in Bergen-Belsen, December 1945–March 1947' (Hebrew), Hebrew University of Jerusalem, 1988. Elazari had access to personal papers of the Gymnasium staff and her work is invaluable. She is also the last researcher to see the whole set of testimonies in the Yad Vashem branch in Givatayim. The file has since disappeared and only an incomplete copy exists in the Ghetto Fighters House archive. Elazari's own collection of material on the Gymnasium was destroyed in a flooding of her basement. I have therefore used excerpts of sources and testimonies from Elazari's work in places where the original is unavailable.

3. Testimonies were numbered and named by Wrobel-Kagan. Where possible the number and name of witnesses are given. For testimonies not available in the archives today, only numbers are given as in Elazari's work. Much thought had been given in the preparation of this project to the question of unveiling the full names of witnesses. On one hand these testimonies are accessible to the public in the archives and (partially) on the net. Sixty years had passed since they were taken and they are now in the public domain. Publishing the names would have made the paper much more humane as befits its subject matter. It would also be a great help to historians to have the full name of witnesses. On the other hand the testimonies were taken when the witnesses were young, some were even minors. They were taken at a time of great emotional upheaval and at a very sheltered setting. At the time, the issue of publication was not on the children's minds. It has therefore been decided to use first names and initials of the surname. The full names of the witnesses are available for further research.
4. Elazari, 'The Hebrew Gymnasium', p.53.
5. Yehudah Tubin, Elazari, 'The Hebrew Gymnasium', p.51.
6. Wrobel-Kagan, Elazari, 'The Hebrew Gymnasium', p.83.
7. Littman's letter to his family, 28 November 1945, Elazari, 'The Hebrew Gymnasium', p.87.
8. Elazari, 'The Hebrew Gymnasium', pp.83–6.
9. Littman's letter to his family, 28 November 1945, Elazari, 'The Hebrew Gymnasium', p.87.
10. Other educational institutions opened in the camp: the 'She'eris Israel' yeshiva opened in November 1945, the ORT vocational school in June 1946 and later a 'Beis Yaacov' girls' school and seminary.
11. Elazari, 'The Hebrew Gymnasium', p.89. See also Hagit Lavsky, *New Beginnings: Holocaust Survivors in Bergen-Belsen and the British Zone in Germany 1945–1950* (Detroit: Wayne University Press, 2002), esp. chs.8-11.
12. Testimony no.60, Elazari, 'The Hebrew Gymnasium', p.89.
13. Private papers of David Littman, Elazari, 'The Hebrew Gymnasium', p.96.
14. Elazari, 'The Hebrew Gymnasium', p.98.
15. One such questionnaire exists in the Ghetto Fighters House archive, file no.5592.
16. Elazari, 'The Hebrew Gymnasium', p.70
17. Ibid., p.78.
18. See Gabriele Rosenthal, 'Reconstruction of Life Stories: Principles of Selection in Generating Stories for Narrative Biographical Interviews', in Amia Lieblich and Ruthellen Josselson (eds.), *The Narrative Study of Lives* (Thousand Oaks, CA: Sage, 1997), pp.59-91; Charlotte Linde, *Life Stories: The Creation of Coherence* (Oxford: Oxford University Press, 1993).
19. Jona B. 'lost everything – dad, mom and brothers and sisters' in Auschwitz. Fira P.'s father was murdered in Stutthof.
20. Elazari, 'The Hebrew Gymnasium', p.80.
21. Ibid., p.79.
22. Ibid., p.78.
23. Ibid., p.80.
24. Maria Hochberg-Marianska and Noe Greuss (eds.), *The Children Accuse* (Polish edn., Warsaw, 1947; English edn., trans. Bill Johnston, London: Vallentine Mitchell, 1996, 2005).
25. Interestingly, she uses a Polish-Catholic expression 'The cross was horrible', meaning hard work.
26. Elazari, 'The Hebrew Gymnasium', pp.64, 70.
27. Ibid., p.66.
28. In years of extensive work in Yad Vashem's archive I did not find any mention of this

matter. The 1950s were years of internal and public conflict concerning the institution's goals and it had a very poor publication record. Elazari recalls that Wrobel mentioned she had an interested British professor but refused to divulge his name.
29. For an extensive coverage of this issue, see Boaz Cohen, 'The Children's Voice: Post-War Collection of Testimonies from Child Survivors of the Holocaust', *Holocaust and Genocide Studies* (forthcoming, 2007).
30. In the early post-war years Jewish survivors all over Europe organised historical commissions aimed at documenting the Jewish tragedy. These commissions collected thousands of survivor testimonies, unearthed documentary evidence built up by Jews during the Holocaust, and collected German documents. For more information on the commissions see Boaz Cohen, 'Holocaust Survivors and the Genesis of Holocaust Research', in Johannes-Dieter Steinert and Inge Weber-Newth (eds.), *Beyond Camps and Forced Labour: Current International Research on Survivors of Nazi Persecution* (Osnabrück: Secolo Verlag, 2005); Shmuel Krakowski, 'Memorial Projects and Memorial Institutions Initiated by She'erit Hapletah', in Yisrael Gutman and Avital Saf (eds.), *She'erit Hapletah, 1944–1948: Rehabilitation and Political Struggle* (Jerusalem: Yad Vashem, 1990), pp.388-98.
31. Gita Selkes, 'General introduction to the Questionnaire for Children', Central Jewish historical commission, Warsaw 1945.
32. Ibid.

The Liberation of the Bergen-Belsen Camp as seen by Some British Official War Artists in 1945

ANTOINE CAPET

It seems that the extensive discussion now taking place on the impact of the images of Belsen, then and now, tends to neglect the drawings and paintings made by the Official War Artists, most of which are now in the collections of the Imperial War Museum.[1] It is not clear why these other visual testimonies are left aside while a lot of attention is – justifiably – devoted to photographs and films.[2]

An examination of this question takes us into the realm of 'representation', where a fundamental question may be asked on the function of art: should it present a ready-to-digest representation of reality? Many great film directors of the past were reluctant to adopt Technicolor – and some today continue to refuse the 'colourising' made possible by modern technology even though they know that this will preclude broadcasting their works on popular television networks. It seems that they want to emphasise that their 'art' does not consist in depicting reality as closely as possible – suggestion rather than demonstration seeming to be their common motto. But for a subject as serious as Belsen, is it possible – is it desirable – to leave anything to suggestion? The fact that historians know that photographs and films are also 'artificial' in the real sense of the word, that is to say man-made rather than from the natural world – and therefore submitted to distortions of reality – is of no importance here: the 'general public' is convinced that 'seeing is believing'[3] and that 'the camera does not lie'. Thus the creator's awareness of the limits of his/her art – whatever his medium – is in conflict with the average viewer's firm belief that the cinema conveys reality more

THE LIBERATION AS SEEN BY BRITISH WAR ARTISTS 171

accurately than the theatre, or that a photograph will always be a more reliable source of information than a drawing or painting.[4]

This difficulty over the function of art as a faithful representation of reality is compounded by the widespread perception of 'art' as a superficial – or at least non-essential – pursuit, which belongs to a realm which has nothing to do with everyday life and nothing to tell 'ordinary people', what we could call the 'not-for-people-like-us' syndrome. One can therefore understand the reservations of those engaged in 'Holocaust education'. In their public lectures and publications, they have to face the indifference, or even scepticism, of generations which have other preoccupations. If they show slides or include illustrations, their choice will be 'indisputable historical documents' like photographs. In other words, first things first: Holocaust Education cannot be transformed into courses in Art Appreciation to fill the void left by the public educational system. For all these reasons, one can suppose that only a limited number of people are in fact familiar with the works of art left by the Official War Artists in connection with the liberation of Belsen, as opposed to the many for whom 'Belsen' primarily calls to mind what has unfortunately become 'the iconic

Figure 16: 'A British Army Bulldozer pushes Bodies into a Mass Grave at Belsen'. BU 4058 (© IWM)

bulldozer scene',[5] a phrase which, alas, undoubtedly represents the reality of the perception of the camp by the general public – and the photograph does not seem to be disappearing from recent publications.[6]

This raises all sorts of questions. The paintings might present a vivid depiction but do they not also run the risk of seeming disrespectful to the thousands of dead? Even though the official caption of the photograph, 'A British Army Bulldozer pushes Bodies into a Mass Grave at Belsen' (Figure 16), does not describe the scene in human terms, there is no mention of the driver, as if the bulldozer ran automatically, and the victims have only become dehumanised 'bodies'. The kerchief worn by the soldier to protect his health, erecting a literal and metaphorical barrier between their two worlds, further distances him from his fellow-creatures. As all modern authors on Belsen and/or the Holocaust indicate, the Jewishness of the majority of these victims was not perceived, or at least not publicised. Today, everyone knows that the corpses being callously bulldozed are in fact in the main the bodies of Jews. Hence the danger that the scene could now be misinterpreted as showing contempt for Jewish people. Moreover, even if one does not always subscribe to the psychological theories of modern semiologists on the role of the subconscious in the perception of images, there is no denying that the British soldier on his bulldozer suggests macho brute force.[7] The psychological transgression of the age-old taboo – respect for the dead – becomes a physical act of aggression. Whether one likes it or not, up on his bulldozer, the driver visually represents the 'Upper Race', while the bodies on the ground represent the 'Lower Race' – and therefore the Nazi relationship between the 'Master Race' and the 'Slave Race' can most unfortunately, at a subconscious level, be replicated in this scene. Understandably, then, Tony Kushner speaks of the 'lack of sensitivity in the use of such images',[8] while Jo Reilly describes the scene as 'that of a British soldier bulldozing bodies unceremoniously into a mass grave'.[9] But once again, the danger comes from the excusable unpreparedness of the public and the banality of the captions or comments offered ('A British Army Bulldozer pushes Bodies into a Mass Grave at Belsen' or such like are obviously cruelly inadequate). In fact, as Jo Reilly explains, the scene was not a routine one, but only took place on two occasions, and she gives the reasons for resorting to such extreme measures:

THE LIBERATION AS SEEN BY BRITISH WAR ARTISTS 173

> Two of the huge piles of bodies to be buried had become very decomposed. Blankets could not be spared and without blankets the bodies could not be handled. As the only solution, pits were dug alongside the bodies and they were then pushed in by the bulldozer.[10]

Pursuing the thread of semiology as an interpretive tool, one sees the difficulty of using images like 'A British Army Bulldozer pushes Bodies into a Mass Grave at Belsen' out of context – or rather in the context of inadequate media. Marshall McLuhan's otherwise controversial theories on individual participation in mass communication here prove of some help if we follow his well-known reasoning on the effort required by, say, the viewer of a photograph:

> There is a basic principle that distinguishes a hot medium like radio from a cool one like the telephone, or a hot medium like the movie from a cool one like TV. A hot medium is one that extends one single sense in 'high definition.' High definition is the state of being well filled with data. A photograph is, visually, 'high definition.' A cartoon is 'low definition,' simply because very little visual information is provided. ... And speech is a cool medium of low definition, because so little is given and so much has to be filled in by the listener. On the other hand, hot media do not leave so much to be filled in or completed by the audience. Hot media are, therefore, low in participation, and cool media are high in participation or completion by the audience.[11]

Thus a photograph, as a 'hot' medium which does not leave much 'to be filled in or completed', induces low participation in the viewer. This, of course, does not mean that a photograph is such a perfect reflection of reality that the viewer requires no effort in reconstructing that reality – it simply means that the viewer feels satisfied with what he sees and does not need further contextualisation (historicisation) to understand the message. The average consumer will therefore, rest content with what he 'sees' on 'A British Army Bulldozer pushes Bodies into a Mass Grave at Belsen'. It would obviously be insensitive to offer it 'in the raw', outside a carefully-written publication – for instance as a brief 'illustration' in a television programme. 'The medium is the message', so 'A British Army Bulldozer pushes Bodies into a Mass Grave at Belsen' will have a different impact depending on the medium in which it is reproduced.

Narrowing the problem strictly to that of 'A British Army Bulldozer pushes Bodies into a Mass Grave at Belsen' and how it would/could be received today, we can transpose the issue raised by Jo Reilly:

> In the spring of 1945 the British press was awash with images of the concentration camps. There can be no doubt they made a great psychological impact on almost everyone who saw them. The question, however, of whether these images brought the British people any nearer to an understanding of the Holocaust, in a way that the newspaper reports of the massacres had not, is debatable ...[12]

The answer given by some authors and editors of books on Belsen published recently is that they feel that the publication of such photographs risks undermining their objectives of educating people about the Holocaust. But this does not explain why the war artists' record has been ignored, because the same criteria of immediacy in the perception do not, of course, apply to them – in McLuhan's vocabulary, they are 'cool' media.

One can perhaps try to discuss this by comparing and contrasting photographs and paintings which have exactly the same theme, starting with *One of the Death Pits, Belsen: SS Guards collecting Bodies* by Leslie Cole (Plate 10) and *The Liberation of Bergen-Belsen Concentration Camp, 1945: One of the Mass Graves partially filled with Corpses* by Sergeant Morris (Figure 17).

Leslie Cole (1910–1977) had a background in the decorative arts, as a mural decorator and fabric painter. From 1941, he worked for the War Artists Advisory Committee, receiving an honorary commission as a captain in the Royal Marines. After a long period in Malta, he went to record the scenes found during the liberation of Belsen, before going on to Japanese prisoner-of-war camps in Singapore. Until he reached Belsen, Cole had only painted what we could call 'classic' scenes of war activity, like the unloading of ships under enemy attack (*Malta: No Time to lose – Soldier Dockers unloading a Convoy during a Raid*[13]), but now he was confronted with the atrocities of war, and gave posterity two of the most powerful testimonies given by artists (the other one being *Belsen Camp: The Compound for Women* (Plate 9), which will be discussed later in this article).

What makes *One of the Death Pits, Belsen: SS Guards collecting Bodies* so powerful? Probably the gripping visual reconstruction, not of reality – as we have argued, this is impossible – but of the accounts of the burials given by witnesses and by photographers like Sergeant Morris. Readers of the grim statements given by liberators and survivors during the Lüneburg trials may well remember the deposition given by Harold O. Le Druillenec, a late British deportee from Jersey, who had been made to drag dozens of corpses to the pits for burial.[14] Now it was the former SS guards who had to drag the corpses – this is clearly visible on the picture, like the British soldiers with guns who watch them.

Figure 17: 'The Liberation of Bergen-Belsen Concentration Camp, 1945: One of the Mass Graves partially filled with Corpses'. BU 3778 (© IWM)

This irony is totally absent from Sergeant Morris's photograph for the simple reason that he chose to take his picture at a time when that gruelling activity was suspended. And imagining this reinforces the cruelty of it all: how could the SS troopers – human beings whatever their crimes[15] – eat their midday lunch? How could the soldiers? The absence of all living presence sets our minds thinking, trying to fill the gaps with what we know from other sources. Since the framing of the image leaves out everything not connected with Morris's immediate theme, the death pit, it leaves out the context: the viewer concentrates on the result, not on the process which led to it. The only allusion to that process is in the caption, with the all-important word 'partially': we know that Morris concentrated on this corner because the others were empty, waiting to be filled with more of these horribly distorted shapes which used to be living human beings. The modern commentator is painfully reminded of that very common phrase in today's vocabulary, 'work in progress' – and yet this is what Morris actually shows us, a 'snapshot' both in the literal and figurative meaning.

Historians familiar with the work of official artists will be reminded of a type of genre scene which we could call 'the beehive': a large narrative composition of group activity, each individual busy with a separate task. The archetype is possibly Barnett Freedman's *The Landing in Normandy: Arromanches, D-Day plus 20, 26th June 1944*.[16] In his Belsen painting Cole has adopted this classic composition, with the centre and foreground describing exactly what his title suggests, while the upper part constitutes the literal, physical background. But this physical background also provides context. One can clearly see the rows of barracks – typical of any POW or concentration camp (contextual information in the usual sense) – but then in the upper middle of the composition, he gives a detail which forcefully reminds the viewer that this is no ordinary POW or concentration camp: a barely identifiable conglomeration of human shapes in what looks like a dustbin. Their identification is left to the viewer: they are bodies waiting to be thrown into the pit, like those in the foreground. The lorry in the upper middle right hints at how the process is ordered: the bodies come from the barracks – they are carried by lorry near the mass grave, temporarily piled up in the container, then dragged along before being thrown into it on the

THE LIBERATION AS SEEN BY BRITISH WAR ARTISTS 177

right, the captive ex-guards returning to the precinct on the left, to go and fetch new bodies. One of the SS troopers (identifiable by his jackboots) is in the pit, carrying one of the thrown bodies to fill the centre.

In this complex narrative composition Cole has tried to encompass all the facets of the mass burials at Belsen. The smoke in the background, probably coming from the huts burning after being emptied of their dead occupants, cannot fail to suggest the crematorium of the camp when it was still in Nazi hands, and beyond that the mass combustion of gassed corpses in Auschwitz. Without going as far as Picasso in 'Guernica', the artist has chosen a colour scheme based on only two series of gloomy hues outside white (infrequent), grey and black: light brown-medium, brown-dark brown and several shades of blue and green. The skies, which constitute only a small area of the composition, are extremely menacing, and the fumes merge into the clouds, especially on the left. The landscape is bare of grass, bare of trees – except for the vaguely threatening dark masses at the back and the gaunt trunks and rickety branches of the three birches on the edge of the pit, whose barren forms replicate those of the human beings in the pit. The landscape is de-natured in the etymological sense. Among other inter-textual references in literature and the arts, people familiar with the Authorised Version of the Bible will be reminded of the Valley of the Shadow of Death – not the version of hope in the Psalms[17] taken up in Bunyan's *The Pilgrim's Progress* – but the grim description in Jeremiah 2–6:

> either said they, Where is the LORD that brought us up out of the land of Egypt, that led us through the wilderness, through a land of deserts and of pits, through a land of drought, and of the shadow of death, through a land that no man passed through, and where no man dwelt?[18]

The most horrid 'detail' is of course the actual throwing of a female body into the grave by a former SS guard. To make things even more horrible, Cole has chosen to draw her in a position which suggests somebody diving into a swimming-pool. But of course the swimmer is dead and the reception material will not be water but a sea of corpses. The bizarreness of the scene can introduce in the viewer a sense of guilt, and more than that – as underlined by Tony Kushner in the very first sentence of *Belsen in History and Memory* – the feeling of voyeurism.[19] Now, if initially the word 'voyeur' only had sexual connotations, as indicated in the *Oxford English Dictionary*, which assimilates it to 'peeping Tom',[20] its meaning has now been extended to include interest in morbid scenes[21] – a curious reverse process since the voyeur of today can satisfy his lust by watching other people both having pleasure and suffering pain. Of course the sane viewer of Cole's painting does not derive pleasure from what he sees, but there is no denying that the picture arouses an unhealthy curiosity in him. How was the 'diving' woman seized by rigor mortis in that position? And the most prominent body in the pit, the erect torso and head on the bottom left-hand corner, which almost seems alive? These questions refer us back to the descriptions which we have read relating to what the liberators discovered in the barracks of Camp 1,[22] and one finds oneself trying to reconstruct the circumstances of their death – which immediately provokes a sense of guilt. Faced with a picture like *One of the Death Pits, Belsen: SS Guards collecting Bodies* or a photograph like 'The Liberation of Bergen-Belsen Concentration Camp, 1945: One of the Mass Graves partially filled with Corpses', the viewer seems to be in a no-win situation: either he only considers the global scene, laying himself open to the accusation of callousness or he starts to consider the individual bodies, trying to imagine their life stories – including, of course, the circumstances of their death – and may feel that he is intruding into their privacy. Such pictures are obscene in the first English meaning of the word: 'offensive to the senses' before they are obscene in the second, current meaning of 'offensive to modesty'.[23]

The same feeling of unbearable unease comes from looking at Cole's other painting, *Belsen Camp: The Compound for Women*. This time it is not so much the entanglement of corpses in the foreground on the right that creates this malaise as the appearance of the survivor who occupies the centre of the composition. Her emaciated face and sallow complexion are cruelly banal in the context: what immediately strikes the viewer, however, is her gait, her bent knees suggesting leg muscles too weak to support even her meagre weight,[24] the fleshless wrists and fingers protruding from the sleeves of her camp uniform. Contrary to most other women shown on the picture, she wears

9 'Belsen Camp: The Compound for Women'. Leslie Cole, oil on canvas, 660 x 901mm © IWM ART LD 5104

10 'One of the Death Pits, Belsen: SS Guards collecting Bodies'. Leslie Cole, oil on canvas, 622 x 901mm
© IWM ART LD 5105

11 'Belsen: April 1945'. Doris Clare Zinkeisen, oil on canvas, 622 x 698mm © IWM ART LD 5467

12 'Human Laundry, Belsen: April 1945'. Doris Clare Zinkeisen, oil on canvas, 804 x 1000mm © IWM ART LD 5468

13 Aerial view of Bergen-Belsen: the concentration camp is set into the wider area showing the German *Wehrmacht* barracks (where the DP Camp was set up), the village of Belsen, the railway ramp (where prisoners arrived) and the southern part of the town of Bergen.
© for the historic photographs (RAF flights of 13 and 17 September 1944): The Aerial Reconnaissance Archives, Keele; for the aerial photographs of the wider area (digital orthophotos DOP of May 2001 and September 2004): Landesvermessung und Geobasisinformation Niedersachsen, Hanover, Germany; for geodesy: HafenCity Universität Hamburg, Fachbereich Geomatik; for the photomontage: Juliane Hummel, Stiftung niedersächsische Gedenkstätten – Gedenkstätte Bergen-Belsen

14 The ceremonial burning down of the last hut at Belsen. Photograph taken by Sergeant Bert Hardy of No. 5 Army Film and Photographic Unit, 21 May 1945. BU 6674 © Imperial War Museum

15 The extension of the new Documentation and Information Centre (artist's impression, wide view)
© KSP Engel und Zimmermann Architekten, Brunswick, German

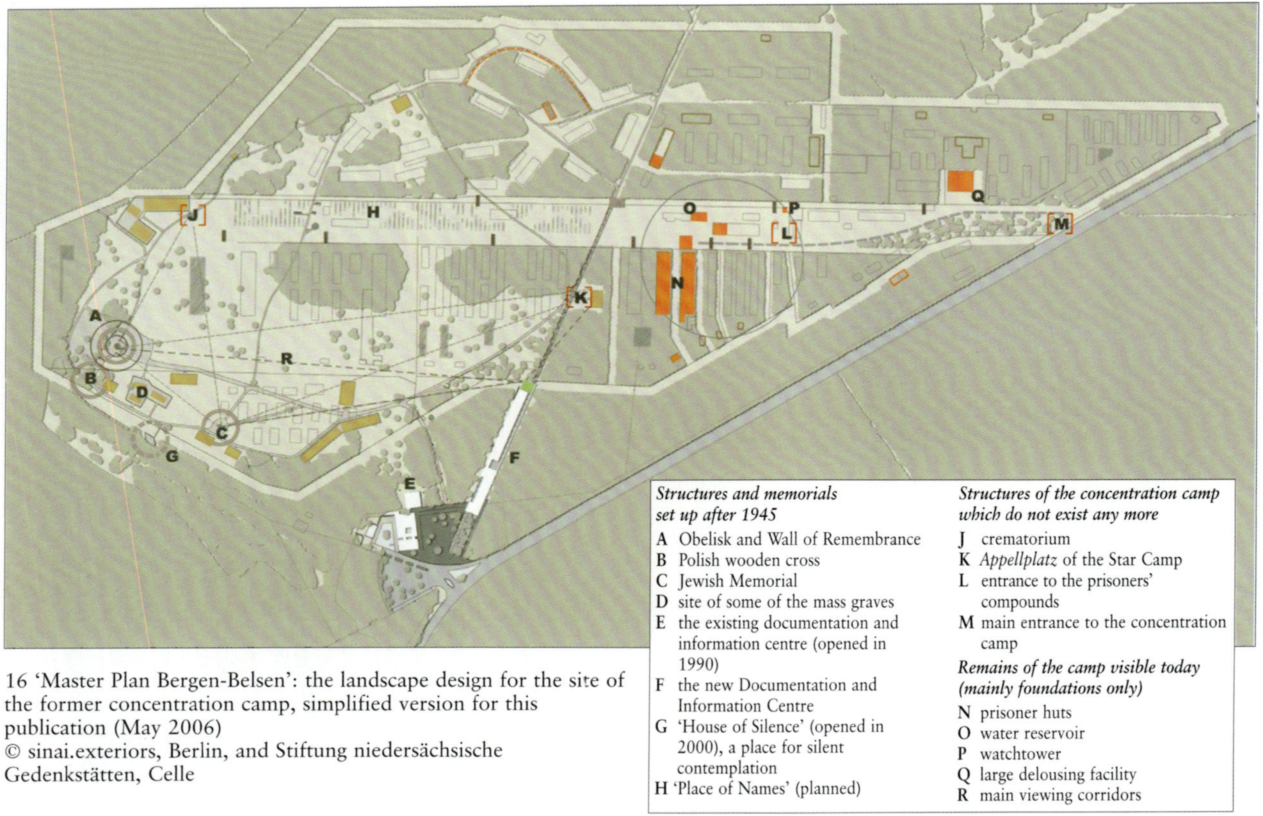

16 'Master Plan Bergen-Belsen': the landscape design for the site of the former concentration camp, simplified version for this publication (May 2006)
© sinai.exteriors, Berlin, and Stiftung niedersächsische Gedenkstätten, Celle

Structures and memorials set up after 1945
A Obelisk and Wall of Remembrance
B Polish wooden cross
C Jewish Memorial
D site of some of the mass graves
E the existing documentation and information centre (opened in 1990)
F the new Documentation and Information Centre
G 'House of Silence' (opened in 2000), a place for silent contemplation
H 'Place of Names' (planned)

Structures of the concentration camp which do not exist any more
J crematorium
K *Appellplatz* of the Star Camp
L entrance to the prisoners' compounds
M main entrance to the concentration camp

Remains of the camp visible today (mainly foundations only)
N prisoner huts
O water reservoir
P watchtower
Q large delousing facility
R main viewing corridors

trousers, and the only sign of femininity left in her is her long hair. The three women who follow her seem to have less difficulty walking, and the two women talking near the hut's door on the left almost seem 'normal'. By a deliberately gruesome contrast in the composition, however, the artist shows in the foreground the horribly distorted body of what we may imagine was once a beautiful middle-aged woman, judging from her fine black hair and quietly resting face, which contrast with her skinny arm raised as if calling for help. What distress is expressed by this raised arm? What kind of prolonged starvation can have reduced her poor thighs to such unimaginable thinness? What story is told by rigor mortis intervening in such an 'unnatural' position? These are questions which the woman sitting on the ground behind her may or may not be asking herself. The expression on her face is such that it is impossible to tell whether she is looking at her or staring at the ground, lost in thoughts which we shudder to imagine. The triangular composition of the foreground therefore encompasses a variety of the human cases found outside the huts on 15 April and the following days and described by liberators and survivors: individual dead women, bodies in piles, 'apathetic' survivors, recent internees in reasonable health, able to have normal social relations like talking to others.

The atmosphere of despair is reinforced by the uniform tonality, with the same choice of colours as in *One of the Death Pits, Belsen: SS Guards collecting Bodies* – only there is even less light, and no white at all. The leaden skies, the fumes emanating from the compound, the dark shapes in the tents, the indistinct details in the background – except for the watchtowers which remind us that this was a concentration camp – create an effect of 'Night and Fog' which forcefully reminds the viewer that the scene is the result of Nazi barbarity, which had still ruled supreme in the camp only a few days before.

What is not shown are the scenes in the huts where conditions, as we know from contemporary accounts, were very much worse. It was left to Doris Zinkeisen, another official war artist, to provide a pictorial record of the scenes found there with *Belsen: April 1945* (Plate 11).

Doris Zinkeisen (1898–1991) came from a well-to-do family in Scotland, went to art school and studied at the Royal Academy. She was the costume designer for the 1936 musical 'Show Boat' and also decorated the luxurious Verandah Grill on the *Queen Mary*. In 1938 she published *Designing for the Stage*. During the war, she became a nurse for the Red Cross and an Official War Artist, which explains her presence in Belsen shortly after its liberation. We know from information given by her son to the Imperial War Museum that, psychologically, she never recovered from the shock. 'They are truly heartrending', he says of the letters she wrote to her husband while she was at Belsen, 'and reflect the agony she endured while doing her work as a war artist. She always told us that the sight was awful, but the smell she could never forget. She had nightmares for the rest of her life until she died'.

It must be emphasised that *Belsen: April 1945* both reflects this shock in her and produces an effect of shock on the viewer who sees it for the first time. The picture is not on permanent display[25] at the Museum – its last appearance was during the 'Women and War'

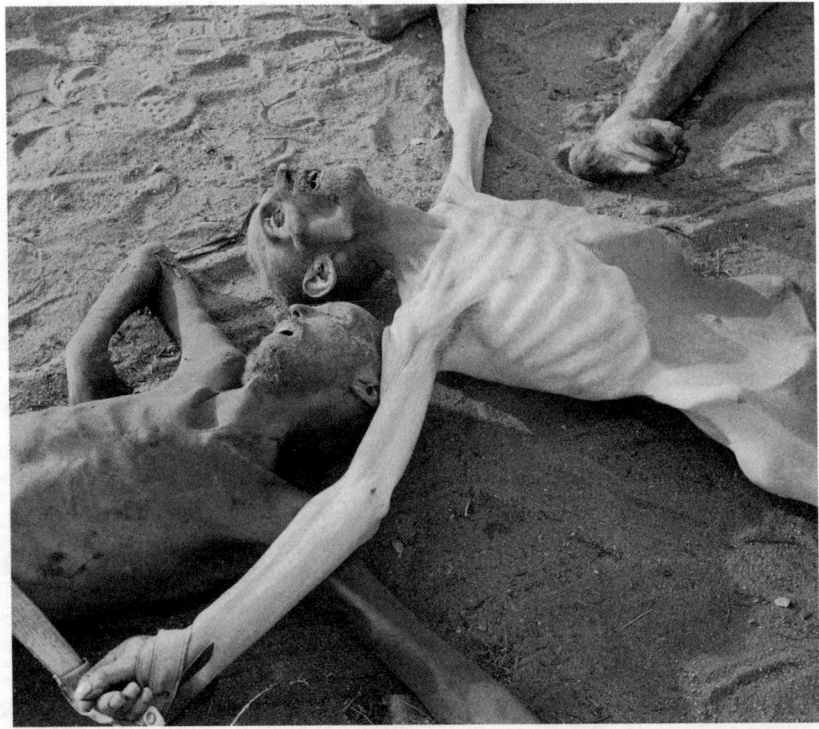

Figure 18: 'The Bodies of Victims in Bergen-Belsen Concentration Camp'. BU 3760 (© IWM)

exhibition of 2004, on a small wall of its own, in a deliberately dark corner, which enhanced the chiaroscuro nature of the painting. Here again we have a triangular or diagonal composition, with the relatively well-lit area – the area with the bodies, the main subject – in the right hand bottom triangle, the remaining surface showing an undetermined background of undetermined colour. All we can say is that the colour is dark, with very small relieving touches of light grey, once more suggesting smoke.

The viewer who has never seen close-up photographs of actual Belsen corpses, as for instance 'The Bodies of Victims in Bergen-Belsen Concentration Camp' by Lieutenant Wilson (Figure 18), cannot make sense of Doris Zinkeisen's rendering of the two human bodies on the right – the first reaction is to believe that she has not studied anatomy properly. The reason is that the eye expects a protruding or at least a flat stomach between the thorax and the hip bones. Instead, in the Belsen victims, the abdomen is in fact a huge hollow – it is as if the man in Lieutenant Wilson's photograph had been disembowelled live by some diabolical vacuum process.

One, therefore, has to surmount one's instinctive incredulity, and the eye has to forget the acquired memory which it has of the familiar shape of the human body, before it becomes possible to comprehend Doris Zinkeisen's composition in all its horror: these are not shapes distorted for some noble artistic purpose as in, say, Francis Bacon's paintings. No, though these distortions are also artificial, they are the result of deliberate starvation by the Nazis. Anybody at all familiar with the abstract art of the twentieth-century is thus forced to reconsider his artistic values by this uneasy coexistence between the now usual abstract artist's licence and the ghastly reality of the camp as shown on *Belsen: April 1945*. Moreover, as if to make the interpretation even more complex, Doris Zinkeisen has chosen a deliberate mixture between 'realism' for the men and 'abstraction' for the backdrop: the scene could take place anywhere, and contrary to Cole's pictures, there are absolutely no 'clues' on the canvas indicating that we are in Belsen – we have to take her word for it when she says so in the title. This makes it both 'universal' – a general testimony on the Holocaust – and less effective as a 'document' on Belsen proper. Could that be the reason why it is so little known in spite of its extraordinarily powerful nature? If we bear in mind that, contrary to this, Cole provides his background with the most 'figurative' details imaginable, one sees the difficulty for the commentator who tries to show the fundamental unity of purpose, if not of effect, of painters like Leslie Cole and Doris Zinkeisen.

If we now go back to our initial discussion, it seems remarkable that visual testimonies of such importance should continue to be neglected as aids in Holocaust education. Looking back in 1997 on events since 1945, Tony Kushner wrote: 'The newspaper reporters, broadcasters, photographers and camera-crews, as well as the various individuals involved in liberation, would shape the memory of the Nazi concentration camps for generations to come',[26] thus rightly implying that the Official War Artists had been absent from this process. It is obvious that the three paintings examined here are too shocking and graphic to be casually included in school textbooks. But they seem to suffer from a form of de facto ostracism whose roots are not easy to determine. The accusation of callous disrespect for the Jewish victims is not really convincing as an explanation because it could equally be levelled at 'A British Army Bulldozer pushes Bodies into a Mass Grave at Belsen', which has had an enormous diffusion.

A few hypotheses have already been formulated above, and in the final analysis it seems that these works of art are deemed to be too demanding for general educational use. Of course, one has to be at least reasonably conversant with the facts of Belsen in 1945 to approach them, but this holds good in all other forms of document analysis. One thing is sure: in spite of McLuhan's correct judgement that in 'a cool medium of low definition' like a piece of graphic art, 'so little is given and so much has to be filled in' by the viewer, it cannot be said that paintings *intimidate* writers and publishers of twentieth-century history books. One only has to see how often *Ruby Loftus screwing a Breech-Ring*[27] is used to illustrate 'women at war', by people who are obviously not all specialists of the semiology of the image. But then, the work is a reassuring one, on a consensual subject. The paintings of Leslie Cole and Doris Zinkeisen on the other hand are on possibly the most 'disturbing' subject of twentieth-century history, and cannot leave even the dispassionate historian emotionally unaffected. The impact they have had on the few privileged people who have seen them paradoxically prevents them from having a wider impact among the general public.

It is to be hoped that this fragmentary and incomplete attempt to draw attention to the undeserved oblivion into which they have largely been relegated will contribute to renewed interest in and analysis of their multifaceted significance by more competent commentators, in spite of all the difficulties.[28]

NOTES

1. This contribution could not have been written without the unstinting technical assistance of the Imperial War Museum, notably in its Photograph Archive and Department of Art. I would also like to gratefully acknowledge the invaluable support provided by Suzanne Bardgett and her Personal Assistants, Naomi Blum and Luke Sunderland.
2. For film, see Toby Haggith's contribution in the present volume. For a wider discussion, see Hannah Caven, 'Horror in our Time: Images of the Concentration Camp in the British Media, 1945', *Historical Journal of Film, Radio and Television*, Vol.21, No.3 (2001), pp.205–53. We could add contemporary cartoons, notably those of Carl Giles in the *Daily Express*, 1944–45. See Peter Tory, *Giles at War* (London: Headline, 1994), which has many reproductions.
3. This was, in fact, the name of a contemporary exhibition of photographs organised by the *Daily Express*. See Caven, 'Horror in our Time', p.246.
4. Curiously, the cartoonist Giles seemed to subscribe to this belief, according to his biographer Peter Tory: '"What could I have drawn," he asks, "that would have told anything more vivid than the dreadful photographs which continue to haunt us?"' (*Giles at War*, p.150). Still, his cartoon of Kramer as a family man (see note 16) possesses levels of meanings impossible to find in a photograph.
5. Tony Kushner speaks of 'the Belsen bulldozer-pit imagery', in Jo Reilly *et al.* (eds.) *Belsen in History and Memory*, (London: Frank Cass, 1997), p.187.
6. It is not used in *Belsen in History and Memory*, even though, as already indicated, Tony Kushner refers to it in the text. Likewise, although Eberhard Kolb reproduced three extremely gruesome photographs in the fifth enlarged edition of his *Bergen-Belsen: Vom 'Aufenthaltslager' zum Konzentrationslager, 1943–1945* (Göttingen: Vandenhoeck & Ruprecht, 1996), pp.140–1, he chose not to include *A British Army Bulldozer pushes Bodies into a Mass Grave at Belsen*. The photograph, however, is reproduced in Ben Shephard, *After Daybreak: The Liberation of Belsen, 1945* (London: Jonathan Cape, 2005), with a slightly different caption: 'The clear-up begins. A bulldozer pushes bodies into a mass grave, 19 April 1945'. In 1991, the photograph occupied a full page of Paul Kemp's *The Relief of Belsen, April 1945: Eyewitness Accounts* (London: Imperial War Museum, 1991), p.21. This gave it special prominence, as only one other photograph was given full-page treatment.
7. See Paul Kemp's caption in *The Relief of Belsen*, p.21: 'Burial of the dead using a bulldozer. This brutal method was used when it became clear that there were too many bodies to be individually collected'.
8. Kushner, *Belsen in History and Memory*, p.4.
9. Joanne Reilly, *Belsen: The Liberation of a Concentration Camp* (London: Routledge, 1998), p.28.
10. Ibid.
11. Marshall McLuhan, *Understanding Media: The Extensions of Man* (New York: McGraw-Hill, 1964), pp.22–3.

12. Reilly, *Belsen: The Liberation of a Concentration Camp*, p.55.
13. Oil on canvas, 1943 (IWM ART LD 3257 – visible on the Imperial War Museum website, www.iwm.org.uk).
14. Raymond Phillips (ed.), *Trial of Josef Kramer and Forty-Four Others: The Belsen Trial* (Edinburgh: William Hodge, 1949). Trial held 17 Sept.–17 Nov. 1945 at Lüneburg before a British military court for the trial of war criminals for atrocities committed against Allied nationals in the concentration camps at Belsen and Auschwitz; also R. Phillips, *War Crimes Trials*, Vol.2. (Edinburgh: William Hodge, 1949). Another transcript is now available in digitised form on the University of the West of England site: *United Nations War Crimes Commission. Law-Reports of Trials of War Criminals. Volume II: The Belsen Trial of Joseph Kramer and 44 Others*, edited by George Brand, foreword by Lord Wright of Durley (London: HMSO for the United Nations War Crimes Commission, 1947; reprint New York: H. Fertig, 1983). http://www.ess.uwe.ac.uk/WCC/belsen1.htm (August 2005).
15. Kolb reminds us that in his undated report written shortly after 15 April, Lieutenant-Colonel Taylor mentions that one of these SS troopers committed suicide and two others attempted it (*Bergen-Belsen : Vom 'Aufenthaltslager' zum Konzentrationslager*, p.157, note 14). This is confirmed by Chief Nurse Doherty, who writes in a letter dated 16 July 1945: 'One SS man hanged himself and several others committed suicide by trying to escape. Those who attempted to escape were shot by our men, as they knew they would be, but evidently preferred this to burying the dead, which was the task allotted to them by the British'. Muriel Knox Doherty, *Letters from Belsen 1945: An Australian Nurse's Experiences with the Survivors of War*, ed. Judith Cornell and R. Lynette Russell (St Leonards, NSW: Allen & Unwin, 2000), p.36. In *The Strange Case of Dr Jekyll and Mr Hyde* (London: Longmans, Green, 1886), R.L. Stevenson (1850–94) adumbrated the modern psychoanalytical theories on the duality of man. In this context the cartoonist Giles remarkably described Josef Kramer, whom he met when the camp was liberated, in terms of this good/evil polarity (*Giles at War*), pp.150–2. And his horribly effective cartoon of Joseph Kramer for the *Sunday Express* (30 September 1945), 'He was always so kind to me and the three children' (*Kramer's wife*) powerfully encapsulates the disquieting/fascinating dual persona which he seems to have perceived in him (cartoon reproduced in *Giles at War*, p.145). I am indebted to Hannah Caven for drawing my attention to Giles's treatment of Kramer.
16. Oil on canvas, 1944 (IWM ART LD 5816 – visible on the Imperial War Museum website).
17. 'Yea, though I walk through the valley of the shadow of death, I will fear no evil; for thou art with me; Thy rod and thy staff, they comfort me'. *Psalms*, 23–4.
18. Modern Biblical scholarship has led to a critique of the translation, arguing that the original word *tsalmavet* should be pronounced *tsalmut*, meaning *darkness*, not *death*. Thus it would be the Valley of the Shadow of Darkness. But this does not affect the analogy between the Biblical passage and Cole's composition.
19. 'In a century that has witnessed ever-increasing opportunities for voyeurism, the liberation of Bergen-Belsen concentration camp by British forces in April 1945 has special significance'. Kushner, *Belsen in History and Memory*, p.3.
20. 'A person whose sexual desires or sexual activities are stimulated or satisfied by covert observation of the sex organs or sexual activities of others. Cf. 'peeping Tom'. *Oxford English Dictionary, Compact Edition*, 1991.
21. Tony Kushner seems to consider only the former aspect. When he writes 'The pictures of naked women particularly were prone to exploitation as pornography, starting a trend of the female victim as a titillating sexual plaything of the Nazis which is still alive in cultural representations of the Holocaust today', Kushner, *Belsen in History and Memory*, p.192, this does not in any way apply to the dead bodies of *One of the*

Death Pits, Belsen: SS Guards collecting Bodies – where we have only a purely morbid version of voyeurism. But this does not invalidate his general point on voyeurism.
22. See, for instance, the deposition of the senior medical officer, General H.L. Glyn Hughes, during the Lüneburg Trial: 'The conditions in the camp were really indescribable; no description nor photograph could really bring home the horrors that were there outside the huts, and the frightful scenes inside were much worse. There were various sizes of piles of corpses lying all over the camp, some in between the huts. The compounds themselves had bodies lying about in them. The gutters were full and within the huts there were uncountable numbers of bodies, some even in the same bunks as the living'. *Trial of Josef Kramer and Forty-Four Others*, pp.31–2; *United Nations War Crimes Commission Report*, p.9.
23. 'Obscene' entry, *Oxford English Dictionary, Compact Edition*, 1991.
24. In Leslie Cole's correspondence on his work now at the Imperial War Museum, he, indeed, writes: 'the woman in the centre of the picture actually collapsed while I was drawing'. See Cole's full comment in Caven, 'Horror in our Time', p.216.
25. The Belsen paintings by Cole and Zinkeisen were frequently displayed in the Imperial War Museum in the 1980s, and indeed almost formed the only reference to the Holocaust in the Museum in those years. For a wider discussion of the past policy of the Museum, see Suzanne Bardgett, 'The Depiction of the Holocaust at the Imperial War Museum since 1961', *Journal of Israeli History*, Vol.23, No.1 (2004), pp.146–56.
26. Kushner, *Belsen in History and Memory*, p.184.
27. Oil on canvas, 1943 (IWM ART LD 2850 – visible on the Imperial War Museum website).
28. The Imperial War Museum also has the following drawings and paintings on Belsen: Edgar Ainsworth, *Belsen 1945* [drawing, IWM ART 16555]; Mary Kessell: *Notes from Belsen Camp, 1945* [seven drawings, IWM ART LD 5747 a–g; visible on the website]; Eric Taylor: *Dying from Starvation and Torture at Belsen Concentration Camp* [drawing, IWM ART LD 5584]; *A young Boy from Belsen Concentration Camp* [drawing, IWM ART LD 5585]; *Liberated from Belsen Concentration Camp, 1945* [drawing, IWM ART LD 5586; visible on the website]; *A living Skeleton at Belsen Concentration Camp* [drawing, IWM ART LD 5587]; *Human Wreckage at Belsen Concentration Camp* [drawing, IWM ART LD 5588]; Doris Zinkeisen: *Human Laundry, Belsen: April 1945* [painting, IWM ART LD 5468; visible on the website]. The British Red Cross Museum and Archives (44 Moorfields, London EC2Y 9AL) have another painting on Belsen by her, *The Burning of Belsen Camp (Huts in Camp 1)* [Ref. LDBRC 0012/4; visible on http://www.redcross.org.uk/standard.asp?id =51854].

PART III
PRESERVING THE MEMORY

From 'This Belsen Business' to 'Shoah Business': History, Memory and Heritage, 1945–2005

TONY KUSHNER

Introduction

> Seeing films one also saw – always saw the newsreels, though only one remains in my memory. It would have been sometime in 1945 and it was at the Playhouse, a cinema down Guildford High Street. Before the newsreel began there was an announcement that scenes in it were unsuitable for children and that they should be taken out. None were; having already waited long enough in the queue nobody was prepared to give up their hard-won seat. It was, of course, the discovery of Belsen with the living corpses, the mass graves and the line-up of sullen guards. There were cries of horror in the cinema, though my recollection is that Mam and Dad were much more upset than my brother and me. Still, Belsen was not a name one ever forgot and became a place of horror long before Auschwitz.[1]

Alan Bennett was ten or 11 years old, his brother three years older, when they saw this Belsen newsreel. Colin Richmond, later a history postgraduate with Bennett, was similarly 'one of the many', who remembers exactly where he was when the footage was shown. Aged eight, 'I sat in about the tenth row (in an aisle seat on the left-hand side) of the circle, the Regal Cinema, High Street, Sidcup, Kent'.[2] The impact of the camp disclosures in 1945, both immediate and long term, is undeniable. The meanings attached to such imagery, however, have been complex and fluid. The purpose of this article is to unravel the many strands that have been incorporated into the memory of Belsen. It focuses especially on the years between 1995 and 2005, analysing what impact more reflexive approaches to

Holocaust remembrance have had on a popular level. The interplay of heritage and history, as manifested in a variety of cultural forms, is explored, revisiting the question of the appropriate manner and mode to represent the Holocaust. Finally, a close reading of texts drawn from literature, film and television, will enable a comparison of the memory work from 'then' – 1945 and the immediate post-war period – and now – the postmodern-influenced era.

In 1945, Belsen, whether described or portrayed in newspaper articles, photographs and newsreels, was understood through the prism of atrocity. As John Horne and Alan Kramer have highlighted in their work on the First World War, 'Atrocities are a culturally constructed and historically determined category'.[3] In Britain, stories first about atrocities committed against Belgians by German soldiers, and then the mass murder of Armenians in the Turkish Empire made a huge contemporary impact.[4] After the war, the Belgian atrocity stories were largely (and to an extent, wrongly) discredited and the fate of the Armenians increasingly subject to amnesia. In Britain, lack of faith in government propaganda (especially in the light of the enormous losses on the western front that had devastated so many families) led, after 1918, to suspicion about any official or media reports about 'atrocities'. Aware of this incredulity, the British government during the Second World War decided to be sparing in its use of atrocity propaganda, in spite of the opportunities provided for this by the brutality of the Nazi regime. If atrocity propaganda was to be used, then it had to be selective and frugal. 'Horror stuff', according to a now infamous Ministry of Information memorandum in July 1941, was to be used 'sparingly and must deal with undisputably innocent people. Not with violent political opponents [ie socialists and communists]. And not with Jews'.[5]

The stark discrimination outlined in this memorandum is at total variance with later constructions of the British war effort in which the saving of the Jews has become a symbol of the country's moral righteousness in a world otherwise gone mad or bad. It does not follow, however, as some polemicists have suggested, that because Britain was not fighting *for* the Jews it must have been fighting *against* them. Nevertheless, why Jews, now accepted as *the* major victims of the Nazis, were not regarded as 'undisputably innocent victims' by British officials (ironically at the very point when mass murder was beginning on the Eastern Front) requires some explanation. In so doing, the combination of a range of factors, reflecting both long-term tendencies and more immediate concerns relating to the war, have to be taken into consideration.

First, Jews, especially foreign Jews, were not trusted or regarded as trustworthy. Many senior government officials believed that Jews tended, through their perceived 'oriental' characteristics, to 'exaggerate' their suffering. Past stereotypes of Jews as financially dubious, disloyal and subversive undermined unconditional acceptance of their victim status.

Second, it was deemed inappropriate, within the dominant liberal ideology in Britain, to separate out Jews from the countries in which they lived – even if only to highlight their suffering under the Nazis and their collaborators. Jews, according to the standard British governmental line, 'must be treated as nationals of existing states and are not to be regarded as having a distinct Jewish nationality'. To treat them otherwise would 'perpetuate the very Nazi doctrine which we are determined to stamp out'.[6]

Third, and more pragmatically coming out of the second point, was a desire to avoid anything that might provide intellectual or emotional ammunition for those supporting the Zionist cause – a factor of increasing importance as British–Jewish clashes over Palestine intensified towards the end of the conflict and immediately afterwards.

Fourth, during the war itself, the government wanted to avoid any impression that it was fighting a war on behalf of the Jews – it feared that the Nazis would exploit such a linkage within their own propaganda, stimulate British antisemitism and thereby help to undermine morale on the 'home front'. Whilst, for reasons of external pressure ultimately out of its control, government attention *was* publicly directed, at the end of 1942, towards the plight of European Jewry, this particularistic focus was treated as an unfortunate and counter-productive development which was not to be repeated. In particular, the Allied Declaration on behalf of European Jewry, announced in the House of Commons on 17 December 1942 by Foreign Secretary, Anthony Eden, and outlining the mass murder that had already taken place, was regarded in Whitehall circles as having created unwanted headaches at a crucial point in the course of the war. The Declaration led to demands for action to save the Jews which were regarded by the British government and its state apparatus as both impossible and/or dangerous.[7] Never again during the conflict were Jewish sufferings the focus of official British discourse aimed at a domestic audience. In April 1945, however, the British government faced a dilemma – its policy of not mentioning Jews as singular victims of the Nazis was challenged by the horrifying reality of the liberated concentration camps.

Belsen was the only major Nazi concentration camp liberated by the British army. Uniquely, amongst the western camps, it had evolved so that by early 1945 the large majority of its inmates were Jewish. These Jews were either those who had survived there with 'privileged' status from 1943 onwards, or the more recent arrivals, those from the death camps, especially Auschwitz, who came to Belsen through the death marches in the winter of 1944/45. In contrast to the inmate make-up in 1945 of other notorious western camps such as Buchenwald and Dachau which were liberated by the Americans, roughly two thirds of the 60,000 found alive in Belsen by British soldiers at the time of liberation were Jewish.[8]

Through the determination of those surviving to explain who they were and where they had come from, and the efforts (in spite of language and experiential differences), of those who came to report from Belsen, the Jewishness of its victims was communicated within the confines of the liberated camp. That this ethno-religious particularity was not largely passed on to a British audience at home was due to informal censorship and self-censorship. For example, dope sheets from the British cameramen who provided the material for the newsreels made explicit references to Jews. Hannah Caven, in her archaeological re-construction of this raw data, provides many such examples, including that written by Sergeant Oakes of the British Army Film and Photographic Unit (AFPU) on 24 April 1945: 'An inmate tells the world. Helen Goldstein, a Pole – Her crime: being born from Jewish extraction. Four years in concentration camps, but was only here two weeks before the British arrived'.[9] Such labelling was, however, removed and the newsreels as shown in Britain were essentially de-racinated.

This process of universalisation was also at work in the most famous, indeed iconic piece of journalism emerging from Belsen – Richard Dimbleby's remarkable radio broadcast from the camp. It is well known that initially the BBC refused to use Dimbleby's script and that only a truncated version was actually used, broadcast on 19 April 1945.[10] What has remained hidden, until disclosed by the forensically precise research of Judith Petersen, is that Dimbleby made *two* recordings at Belsen. One of these referred explicitly to the Jewishness of the victims but that part of his description of the camp was not used at the time or for many years after.[11] The possibilities that these alternative Dimbleby recordings have enabled in subsequent Belsen-related memory work will be explored later in this article.

The key factor in representations of Belsen in 1945 was that they were framed as atrocities, but atrocities that had to be accepted as genuine: 'seeing is believing', as one exhibition was labelled, or 'Proof positive', to quote the title of Paramount's newsreel.[12] Indeed, the power of Belsen imagery as 'proof positive' extended into the courtroom – a compilation of liberation footage, entitled *Nazi Concentration Camps*, was used as illustrative evidence at both the Nuremberg and Eichmann Trials.[13] The purpose of the newsreels and other representations of Belsen was to show the nature of the Nazi regime and/or the German people, although the logic of the Cold War ensured that the former, rather than the latter would soon officially (though not popularly) be blamed for such cruelties and suffering. There was no interest in the victims as such, other than to illustrate the bestiality of the perpetrators.

Moreover, the Jewishness of the victims was, as throughout the war, potentially problematic. The narrative presented had to be straightforward – an evil enemy, a humane, liberating force of British soldiers and victims who, whilst lacking any individuality, were undeniably victims. And on a crude level, the aims of those representing Belsen to the British public – atrocities that *had* happened – were met: just three per cent of a sample interviewed by the social anthropological organisation, Mass-Observation, at the end of April 1945, believed that the stories were false.[14] The very fact, however, that such surveys, in Britain and America, were regularly carried out in the last six months of the war shows the concern on both sides of the Atlantic that the reality of atrocities should be accepted.[15] Yet the images portrayed and described were so powerful that Belsen, as Bennett insists, 'was not a name one ever forgot'. Indeed, the impact was such that in the immediate post-war years and beyond, the word 'Belsen' had a life of its own.

Case Studies from 1945 and the Post-war Era

The ease with which 'Belsen' could be disconnected not just from the fate of the Jews, but from Nazi atrocities more generally, is neatly illustrated through the writings of James Lees-Milne. During the Second World War, Lees-Milne was a major figure within the National Trust. Travelling the country, his job was to find a tenable future for stately homes suffering from decay and at risk of abandonment. A self-conscious snob and a reactionary, Lees-Milne's mission, in the words of David Cannadine, was 'to preserve these "secular shrines" from twentieth-century barbarism. As he candidly admitted, his priorities were the country houses, their traditional owners, and then the National Trust – in that order of importance'.[16]

Aside from his work with the National Trust, Lees-Milne is also remembered now as one of the major diarists of twentieth-century Britain, publishing volumes from the Second World War onwards. Lees-Milne was, to an extent, self-reflexive in his diary writing, aware of the different dynamics of the genre in contrast to other forms of autobiographical discourse. He had intended finishing his diary writing at the end of the Second World War but three months later returned to it commenting 'There is no explanation. I merely missed it like an old friend'.[17] The longevity of this mode of literacy practice confirms Lees-Milne's rationale although it must be suggested that other factors were at work. Lees-Milne was socially well-connected and he must have been aware of the future publishing potential of his diaries – their narrative coherence and constant engagement with the rich and famous points in that direction. Indeed, the theatre critic, James Agate, who matched the buildings' conservationist for his waspish pen, had effectively made a living from publishing his diaries. Agate's diaries appeared from the mid-1930s, with little chronological delay, in a series suitably entitled *Ego*.[18] The strong possibility that Lees-Milne was writing with an eye on a future audience for his diaries – or at least was self-important enough to want them read in some form in posterity – inevitably made an impact on what was included in them and how they would be constructed. Lees-Milne's inclusion of a diary entry from 22 May 1945 relating to Belsen has to be seen partially in this light – its infamy was something that *should* be commented on at this point in time by any serious social commentator. His diary provides a classic example of the framing of the camp purely as horror, with no empathy revealed whatsoever for its victims.

The context for the entry was a meeting with fellow conservationist, John Wilton, who had recently returned from Belsen. Lees-Milne's normal chatty, gossipy style is replaced by stark reportage of Wilton's account of the camp that in many ways replicated the unemotional, factual and mechanistic approach of the newsreels:

> The stench was so overpowering that he and others were physically sick. Then they became accustomed to it. The atrocities committed there were worse than the press disclosed. He saw several corpses with deep cuts across the small of the back. Starving fellow-prisoners had done this in the attempt to extract human liver and kidney to assuage their hunger. Other corpses had their private parts torn off. He himself saw a wooden shield, the sort on which we mount a fox' mask, with a man's chest impaled upon it, the nipples and hair intact. He saw a torture chamber with stone bench, troughs and channels for the blood to run into.[19]

Two years later, in the heart of the misery of austerity-driven Britain, Lees-Milne returned, within his writings, to the notorious concentration camp, but now the reference point was no longer the impact of its commandant, the 'Beast of Belsen', or for that matter, 1945. Instead it was the neglect of what Lees-Milne treasured most, the stately home, and the heritage abuse of the inter-war years.[20] In an architectural study of eighteenth-century Britain, *The Age of Adam* (1947), Lees-Milne examined the fate of Landsdowne House in London, begun by Robert Adam in 1762 and completed six years later. Lees-Milne could not contain his anger at the twentieth-century treatment 'of this excellent building'. In the late 1920s 'by some extraordinary process of the commercial conscience', most of the original building was demolished: 'the facade of Portland stone was taken down, the foundations pushed back several feet, and the front partially re-erected, only in another composition, to adorn an amorphous mess of glazed brick, steel, and concrete that dares to parade the title of a luxury club'. His final analysis shows the potential of atrocity discourse, when alienated from the victim (as exemplified by Lees-Milne's diary entry), to lose focus of time and place, let alone moral authority:

> No more Belsen-like treatment of a work of art by speculative Philistines was ever tolerated in the decadent inter-war period by a smug and cynical public. Notwithstanding this nation's indifference to the fate of Landsdowne House, the Americans were allowed, at no little expense to themselves, to salvage a few pickings out of the holocaust.[21]

This was not an isolated example of 'Belsen' simply becoming a word used to describe *anything* in an abused state. Indeed, Lees-Milne was not alone in exploiting the concentration camp imagery to make a point about the decline of the built English heritage. In a diary entry written ten days before that of Lees-Milne in May 1945, James Agate reported a journalist's description of Eaton Square in Belgravia, London: 'In 1939 those houses were alive. They had personality and spirit as well as nurseries and kitchens. Now they have been occupied by the Army. They are almost as horrible to look at as the corpses at Belsen or Buchenwald'.[22]

At this point it is worth returning again to Alan Bennett's comment that Belsen 'became a place of horror long before Auschwitz'. Belsen from 1945 onwards had a particular resonance and centrality in the British imagination. It took many years before Auschwitz would become a metonym either for the crimes of the Nazi regime or more generally as a symbol of mankind's capacity to commit evil deeds (or, as we have seen in the everyday use of 'Belsen', simply architectural vandalism).

The Meanings of Auschwitz

Auschwitz did not, as Martin Gilbert rather overstates, keep its existence secret throughout 1942 and 1943 in the west.[23] For those communicating Nazi horrors to the outside world, and the campaigners receiving such information, it, or its original Polish name, Oswiecim, had become familiar.[24] Nevertheless, it was not, in Britain, at least until the postwar trials, a household name. In the Houses of Parliament in 1945 it was referred to briefly only twice, and then erroneously as 'Aeuschwitz' and 'Aeschwald'. At this point there was little understanding in Britain that the western concentration camps such as Buchenwald, Dachau and Belsen were not the major sites of Nazi mass murder or that the extermination programme had taken place largely in the east. 'Aeschwald' was thus largely an amalgam of Buchenwald and Dachau and thereby presumably sited within Germany itself – as was 'Aeschwitz Camp in Germany'.[25] Such geographical and conceptual confusion in 1945 can be easily understood given the chronological proximity to the events and the enormity and complexity of what had taken place.

There were some like the British activists Victor Gollancz, Eleanor Rathbone and James Parkes who could quickly piece together the confusing elements into a coherent narrative and recognise the full impact of Nazi policies on European Jewry. Such individuals, however, were exceptional.[26] It is not clear, however, how much difference several decades (from the late twentieth to the early twenty-first-centuries) of increasingly intensive educational and cultural attention to the Holocaust has made to this state of immediate post-war ignorance. Is there now widespread understanding of the key role Auschwitz was to play in the 'Final Solution' of the Jewish question and the differing, if linked, history and function of Belsen?

Laurence Rees, Creative Director of History Programmes for the BBC, writes in the book version of his critically acclaimed television series *Auschwitz: The Nazis and the 'Final Solution'* that the appalling film images from Belsen 'of emaciated bodies and walking skeletons rightly shocked the world when they were shown'. He adds that they also created an image of Belsen 'that does not reflect the reality of its original conception, and in the process the film adds to the confusion that exists in many people's minds over the difference between a concentration camp and a dedicated death camp'. Rees traces the 'inception' of Belsen to 1943 when it was intended to act as an exchange camp for 'privileged Jews'.[27] In fact its origins can be taken back a further two years when it was used for Soviet prisoners of war – thousands died there of starvation and disease. It is a neglected aspect of Belsen's historiography and memorialisation. Like Auschwitz, Belsen had a complex and multi-layered history even within the few years of the war. What Rees attempts and succeeds in doing within his six part BBC 2 programme is to show the evolution of Auschwitz from a camp for Polish prisoners in 1940 through to its increasingly important role, during the second half of the war, in the extermination of the Jews.

In December 2004 the BBC released details of an opinion poll that revealed that 45 per cent of 4,000 adults in Britain surveyed had not heard of Auschwitz. For those under 35, the figure rose to 60 per cent. This was in advance of Rees' documentary series which was broadcast in January and February 2005, part of the commemorations to mark the sixtieth anniversary of the camp's liberation. After Holocaust Memorial Day on 27 January 2005 the BBC carried out a follow-up poll which found that 94 per cent of the 4,000 questioned had heard of the death camp, with half believing that they were well-informed about it. Karen Pollock of the Holocaust Education Trust told the *Jewish Chronicle* that this was 'an astonishing change in statistics and very encouraging ... It is our challenge and responsibility to build on this success.'[28]

Some 27 years earlier, before Holocaust education had been developed in Britain, the perverse and disturbing alter egos of Peter Cook and Dudley Moore, 'Derek and Clive', pondered 'how much television affects people ... they watch television and they get very influenced by it'. As an example, Cook referred to the Hollywood mini-series, *Holocaust*, starring Meryl Streep, and how by episode three he had 'got on a number 18 [bus]... to Golders Green ... and I must have slaughtered about eighteen thousand before I realised ... what I was doing ... [and] I thought the fucking television has driven me to this'.[29]

However obscene and inappropriate, Peter Cook had a point. Children did not, as a result of watching the television programme, *Andy Pandy*, 'jump in a glove and rush down the road'.[30] Nor, by the screening of a sober series on BBC 2 (that is the Corporation's more intellectually and culturally driven terrestrial channel) and media coverage of Holocaust Memorial Day, does the British public en masse go from widespread ignorance to almost total and intricate knowledge of Auschwitz. To put this in perspective, James Parkes, when asked, by a potential funder, how long education would take to eradicate antisemitism, responded that it would require 'About three hundred years'. Parkes was too aware of the ingrained cultural and religious attitudes that had to be challenged and overcome to offer the conceit that it would be removed in his own lifetime.[31] Holocaust education cannot be expected to be an instant penicillin fix of

HISTORY, MEMORY AND HERITAGE, 1945-2005

ignorance, or, in relation to the specific subject matter of this article, the misunderstandings about the nature of Belsen. With regard to the opinion poll surveys on Auschwitz, neither the high nor the low total can be read as firm evidence other than to show, in combination, the fluidity and perhaps superficiality of engagement with the Holocaust in Britain. Whilst we live in a televisual age, Peter Cook was right to warn about simplistic and mechanistic readings of the '*power* it has over people'.[32] Furthermore, against the close reading of Auschwitz's past, as represented by Laurence Rees and his team, are other recent cultural references to it and Belsen that reveal very different levels of engagement and understanding.

Readings from the Twenty-First Century (1): P.G. Wodehouse

A good example is provided in the 500-page biography of the comic writer P.G. Wodehouse by the literary editor of the *Observer*, Robert McCrum, published in 2004.[33] The connection between Wodehouse and the Nazis is obviously a very sensitive area for any biographer of Wodehouse who spent the war in Germany and lent them minor, foolish but relatively innocuous propaganda support through a series of broadcasts. He was no Ezra Pound, or, for that matter, William Joyce. His supporters have the task of preserving what they see as the genius of Wodehouse, and particularly his articulation of Englishness, from the accusation of treachery or collaboration. McCrum, not surprisingly, has no truck with such dismissals of his hero and is wary of giving any ammunition to Wodehouse's critics.

There are two 'Holocaust' references in this biography, the first in relation to the brief internment Wodehouse suffered in a Nazi prison camp in Tost, Silesia in 1940. Probably to garner sympathy for his subject McCrum commented that 'Silesia concealed the Third Reich's grimmest secret: Auschwitz (Oswiecim) was barely thirty miles from Tost, and Belsen-Birkenau less than a day's drive'.[34]

The mixing up of Belsen and Auschwitz, especially in British and American press reports, occurred during the Belsen Trial, held under the jurisdiction of the British military authorities in autumn 1945. As Donald Bloxham concludes, at this trial 'The name of Auschwitz was introduced but there was certainly no consistent differentiation between the extermination camp and the concentration camp to counteract the barrage of photographs and reports of the latter at the close of the war in Europe'.[35] Inevitably, the fact that many of both the accused and the victims had been in both camps caused confusion to contemporaries.

The memory work of McCrum some 60 years later is equally revealing: his interfusion and jumbling of nomenclature is compounded by an absence of geographical precision: Belsen is over 400 miles from Auschwitz even as the crow flies. It took Anne and Margot Frank, for example, four days in a wagon truck to complete the train journey from one camp to the other and often many weeks for those forced to complete more of that distance on foot through the death marches.[36]

The second Holocaust reference, also labelled in the index under the heading 'Belsen-Birkenau', is to Wodehouse's decision to delay a book about his wartime experiences, *Wodehouse in Wonderland*, 'until this Belsen business has become a thing of the past'. McCrum states that this 'one reference to the Holocaust is Wodehouse's only acknowledgment of the horrors endured by the Jews during the Third Reich'. Defensively, however, he adds that 'charges of anti-Semitism [against Wodehouse] do not stick'. Compared to his contemporaries Wodehouse's work was, in McCrum's words, 'strikingly free from either racist or anti-Semitic prejudice'.[37] This absence of literary antipathy is indeed to Wodehouse's credit, although he was not alone in this respect. The alternative argument used by many recent biographers that their subject matter's racism/antisemitism was simply 'typical of the day' is both lazy and inaccurate. The 'litmus test' of judging individuals as prejudiced/not prejudiced also ignores that for most individuals in Britain during the nineteenth and twentieth centuries, including those within the literary realm, ambivalence towards the 'other' was the norm. It involved the construction of 'good' Jews and 'bad' Jews, justifiable and unjustifiable hostility towards Jews and so on.[38] Indeed, the evidence produced by McCrum to show Wodehouse's positive attitudes towards Jews is far from convincing. In 1947 Wodehouse outlined how not quite his best friends, but his next to best friends were Jewish. In classic ambivalent fashion, however, he prefixed this cliché by commenting that 'Aren't the Jews extraordinary people. They seem to infuriate all nations, as nations'.[39]

The simple truth is that Wodehouse did not refer to what later became known as the Holocaust because it would have involved reflections on the human capacity for moral wrongdoing which were anathema to his naive world view. His comments that 'If this is Upper Silesia what must Lower Silesia be like?' and 'Camp was really great fun' speaks volumes about the nature and limitations of Englishness.[40] To be fair, many in Britain were equally reticent for much of the post-war period. Auschwitz, according to a man interviewed for a 1990 television documentary on attitudes towards Germany, 'means a lot of very unpleasant things to a lot of people'. His response, according to one critic, was 'so schooled in English understatement that he lacked a vocabulary which could embrace the subject. In this naive undefiled state, the British are almost unique in Europe'.[41] More relevantly here, it must be stressed that Wodehouse's comments in 1945 were about 'Belsen' – that is a generic reference to images of Nazi atrocities, and *not* therefore specifically to Jewish suffering. It has to be viewed in the context of the increasingly non-specific usage of 'Belsen' as exemplified by the contemporaneous writings of James Lees-Milne and James Agate in 1945 and the immediate post-war period. At a general and idealist level it is possible that Wodehouse might have wished for reflections on atrocities to disappear and for his pre-war world of innocence to return. On a more basic level, he was aware that 'Belsen', as a metonym for Nazism's evil, was impeding any popular acceptance of German–British rapprochement and thereby his full rehabilitation at home. It led to his emigration to America. With regard to the actual history of this concentration camp, it seems that neither Wodehouse in 1945, nor his biographer at the beginning of a new century, had a clue what 'this Belsen business' was about (the latter, to coin a phrase, not knowing his Belsen from his Birkenau). It is significant, however, that McCrum in 2004 explicitly linked Belsen to *Jewish* victims of the Nazis – a connection that, as we have seen, was rarely publicly articulated in 1945.

It is understandable that McCrum and other admirers of this great, indeed iconic, comic writer should be wary of providing ammunition for those who would dismiss Wodehouse as either a pro-Nazi or an antisemite. The British comic writer and broadcaster, Stephen Fry, a leading fan of Wodehouse, has stated that 'In the salad of Wodehouse's otherwise perfect life there lurked one undoubted caterpillar. The Berlin Broadcasts Business (hereinafter referred to as the BBB) continues, quite wrongly, to affect and infect Wodehouse's status in the world'. Fry initially was concerned that McCrum was going to 'turn the blasted BBB into the defining moment of his life'. He was satisfied in the end that what McCrum has unearthed 'are far from caterpillars in the salad. Mere pips in a juicy grape'.[42]

Another reviewer, slightly less sympathetic to Wodehouse, confirmed some of Fry's fears, dwelling on the Belsen reference and referring to it as 'a chilling quote'.[43] Ironically, in this respect, by juxtaposing twenty-first-century understandings of the Holocaust on contemporaries from 1945, McCrum makes an unhappy connection between Wodehouse and Jewish suffering. This linkage appears utterly insensitive, indeed 'chilling' given the comic writer's wartime blunders, but was not, in fact, made at all. The rest of this essay will analyse another recent example within which collective memory from 'now' was imposed on the past – the Channel 4 series, *The 1940s House*. It resulted in an intriguing and complex matrix made up of the conflicting demands of firstly, history and heritage, and secondly, British and Jewish remembrance of the Second World War.

Readings from the Twenty-First Century (II): *The 1940s House*

It must be emphasised that what follows will not be a 'cheap' anti-heritage critique of *The 1940s House* but an opportunity to explore the multi-layered memory that emerges within it. In *Theatres of Memory* (1994), Raphael Samuel argued that 'In the present day, television ought to have pride of place in any attempt to map the unofficial sources of historical knowledge. Quite apart from drama documentaries, and such long-running series as 'Timewatch', it is continually travelling down memory lane and using the past as a backdrop'.[44] Samuel, in contrast to many who had dismissed the 'heritage industry' as reactionary and diversionary, welcomed its democratic potential in which all could participate in either creating representations of the past or in 'consuming' its products.

Writing over a decade later, Tristram Hunt, a leading public historian, warned that 'television's fascination with "reality history" is distorting our rich and vital national heritage'. Hunt referred specifically to *The 1940s House*, and its predecessor, *The 1900s House*, as examples of 'reality history offer[ing] a simple short-cut to empathy history; the past was no longer a foreign land requiring difficult explanation by boring academics. In fact, its inhabitants were just like us'. Reality television is 'all very fascinating' but it fails to 'offer any great depth of analysis', leaving only 'the past as theatre'.[45] In less judgmental fashion, David Lowenthal has argued that heritage is not 'bad' history or history at all – it is simply a different way of dealing with the past. History is, or should be, critical, and heritage is about celebration.[46]

Can history and heritage be so clinically separated as Lowenthal suggests? Are, as Hunt proposes, the differences between past and present collapsed in 'reality television history'? These questions will be analysed through *The 1940s House* and the place of Belsen within its narrative structure.

The series was broadcast in January 2001. It featured the Hymer family from West Yorkshire who were transported to a suburban house in Kent to experience life on the Home Front. In the fourth and last 'historical' episode as the conflict comes to a close, entitled 'the beginning of the end', the team of experts determining the experiences of the Hymers decided to bring the war 'closer to home' for the family. First, the Hymers' house suffers from the impact of a nearby exploding V2 bomb leaving the family to clear up without water and with its gas supply cut off. Second, the three adults in the family were, at this disorientating moment, given a message that they 'had to listen to a very important broadcast'.[47]

They gather round the radio to hear Richard Dimbleby describe the horrors of Belsen in an extract lasting just over a minute and a half: 'I have seen many terrible sights in the last five years but nothing approaching Belsen... I passed through the barrier and found myself in the world of a nightmare, dead bodies, some of them in decay, lay strewn about the road...' In the book version of *The 1940s House*, written by Juliet Gardiner, another extract is given of Dimbleby's broadcast, including the sentence

> it is hard to describe adequately what I have seen... there are 40,000 men, women and children in the camp, German and half a dozen other nationalities, thousands of them Jews... In the last few months alone, 30,000 prisoners have been killed or allowed to die.[48]

What is interesting here, as Judith Petersen has shown by careful dissection of the transcripts, is that neither the Dimbleby extract on the programme nor that produced in the related book were actually broadcast to the British public in 1945 – the former because of its graphic detail and the latter because of its reference to the Jewishness of the victims.[49]

It is significant that in McCrum's Wodehouse biography, the book of *The 1940s House* and in many more recent documentaries, the Jewish connection to Belsen is simply assumed. We have thus moved, in collective memory, from the universal horror at Nazi atrocities in 1945 to the awareness, if not complete, and not fully nuanced, that the Nazis committed specific crimes against the Jews as a whole. There is, therefore, an expectation that Dimbleby's broadcast *should* refer to Jews. Through the rare occurrence that the remaining historical evidence provides researchers with a choice, there is the possibility of enabling this to happen. A distortion occurs, however, if we impose *our* understanding, and *our* evidence on contemporaries. For example, few of the many hundreds of Mass-Observers in 1945 referred to Jews in their discussion of Nazi atrocities.[50] Their failure to do so reflects that there were few references to the Jews in the various reports on the concentration camps whether in broadcasts, newsreels or press articles. That absence was not accidental and the universalism imposed by the authorities in the Ministry of Information extended to the presentation of Dimbleby's broadcast.

It is also relevant, returning to *The 1940s House*, that the more populist representation through the television series frames Belsen within a largely British framework, including references within the broadcast to the liberating soldiers and then through Mrs Hymers' visit, immediately following this scene, to an idyllic church graveyard. The graveyard, filmed basked in sunshine as the epitome of Englishness, contains a war memorial for the 'five gallant auxiliary members of the Beckenham Auxiliary Fire Service', killed whilst on duty by enemy action on 19 March 1941 'in freedom's cause'. With the close juxtaposition of the Dimbleby broadcast and the visit to the war memorial, the horrors of Belsen, *The 1940s House* suggests, were what Britain was fighting against. In partial contrast, the book format is more critical and less within the world of heritage celebration. It is within this context that there is the space to refer to the Jewishness of Belsen's victims, allowing the narrative to be more complex and multi-layered.[51]

Finally, in terms of this series, we need to explore the reaction of the Hymers to the Dimbleby broadcast. They are clearly and genuinely moved by what they have heard. However contrived the situation, they were not consciously acting the scene – there is an honest attempt by all concerned to at least raise the issue of how the broadcast was received in spring 1945 when, as we have seen, many still remember where they were when they heard, read or saw the images of the liberated concentration camps.

But what the Hymers heard in summer 2000 is both literally and experentially *not* what the public heard and felt some 55 years earlier. Dimbleby's broadcast, even in its edited format, was powerful and evocative. He was the leading British broadcaster of his day. It is possible, but unlikely, that the older Hymers would have had memories of Dimbleby – they were young children when he died. But, as Juliet Gardiner confirms, 'they were all taken completely by surprise' and none of the Hymer family had heard Dimbleby's broadcast before.[52] Instead, the resonance of his broadcast, it must be suggested, and their response to it, reflects also the impact of later images, particularly visual images, that have now become iconic in British culture. In 1992, for example, the *Daily Mirror* had on its front page a photomontage of images from a Serbian camp for Muslims with the headline: 'Belsen 92: Horror of the New Holocaust'.[53] Most films on Nazi atrocities will use, rarely with any care for detail, images from the liberated camps – shots from one camp can stand in for another.

At the Imperial War Museum's hugely successful permanent Holocaust exhibition, a photograph of the bulldozers at Belsen is the biggest by far in the whole display. During the Nuremberg Trials the filmic compilation *Nazi Concentration Camps* ended with the bulldozer scene and helped confirm the moral guilt of the accused with regard to *all* the crimes for which they were accused. In the Imperial War Museum the bulldozer image is used as final proof of the horror and extent of the Holocaust.[54] In the twenty-first century, 'Belsen' and the imagery it evokes are as much common currency as in 1945, but the meanings associated with it have subtly and not so subtly changed.

Concluding Thoughts

In 2000 or 2005 we cannot recreate the responses to the concentration camp exposures as if it was 1945. As Lawrence Douglas argues, 'To view *Nazi Concentration Camps* today gives an imperfect idea of what the [Nuremberg] tribunal saw fifty years ago. The horror captured in *Nazi Concentration Camps* is now so familiar that it is difficult to imagine an *original* screening – that is, a screening that shocks not simply because of the barbarity of the images, but also because of their novelty'.[55] But does it matter if time is somehow suspended? In *The 1940s House*, Mrs Hymer (whose compassion and desire to engage seriously with the differences of 'then' makes her the pivotal figure in the series) recognises the time-related dissonance. After the Dimbleby broadcast, Mrs Hymer's reflections on the experience are voiced over the visit to the (real) war memorial where she is (as ever) tidying up and placing flowers: 'I don't suppose my generation will ever know the full trauma of war and the effects on people's minds because... how can we know?' In the book version she also recognised that it was only in the Anderson shelter 'where the war has seemed most real to us. It's brought us closer together and I think that it's in the Anderson shelter that we have been best able to envisage what it must have really been like for people in the Second World War'.

Yet in popular marketing of the series, the gap between reality and re-creation is removed. The cover of the second of the two commercially available videos of *The 1940s House* boasts that it 'contains 2 thrilling episodes'. In 'The Beginning of the End', the synopsis reads, 'With D Day comes "holidays at home" and the return of the odd luxury. Suddenly, the Blitz tests the family's morale to the full – will they survive to celebrate VE Day?'[56] Of course, unlike the vicious heritage recreations in the theme park that transformed the Isle of Wight in Julian Barnes' *England, England*,[57] we know that the Hymer family will still be there at the end of the series.

The perverse logic in which the locations within Krakow where *Schindler's List* was filmed have become tourist attractions themselves, often at the expense of visits to the actual sites of murder and rescue, is replicated in a minor and gentler way with *The 1940s House*. From December 2000 to June 2001 a highly successful exhibition was mounted at the Imperial War Museum re-creating 17

Braemar Gardens in Beckenham, which itself had been heritage-ised for the series. The exhibition was accompanied by 'publications and souvenirs'.[58] Here, in spite of all the efforts of the historians behind the series, and the Hymer family itself, critical perspectives are lacking, and heritage triumphs over history.

If it is evident that the cameramen at Belsen recognised the Jewishness of its victims, it is also clear from the researches of Toby Haggith that they went beyond filming them in a degraded and futureless state.[59] Such acknowledgment of the individuality of the former inmates and their portrayal in a humane way did not, however, generally meet the 'proof positive' requirements of atrocity imagery that was required for a British audience. Whether, 60 years on, it is appropriate to use the pure horror images today is debatable. *The 1940s House*, by its use of the radio broadcast, largely avoids this dilemma. As a prime example of historical 'reality television', however, it raises the question of what is, and is not, valid to portray.

Critics of a later example, *The Trench* (BBC2, March 2002), which dealt with life on the First World War 'western front', complained that no one would have the bad taste to do such a historical re-creation of Auschwitz.[60] In fact, the same point had been made over 30 years earlier by satirists on both sides of the Atlantic. In Britain, the Monty Python team, who possessed a keen eye for the nature of mass television presentation and the opportunities it offered through parody 'to plumb the depths of the absurd',[61] presented the 'Batley Townswomen's Guild' in a re-enactment of the 'Battle of Pearl Harbour'. Interested only in re-creating 'modern works', its leader, Mrs Rita Fairbanks (Eric Idle) before battle commences, tells the cameras that 'of course last year we did our extremely popular re-enactment of Nazi war atrocities', adding that 'this year we thought we would like to do something in a lighter vein'.[62] Two years earlier, *MAD* magazine had parodied the American situation comedy, *Hogan's Heroes*, set in an Allied prisoner-of war-camp with its quick-witted prisoners and hospitable guards and utter lack of menace. *MAD*'s version, 'Hochmann's Heroes', presented 'that gay, wild, zany, irrepressible bunch of World War II concentration camp prisoners... Those happy inmates of "Buchenwald"'.[63]

In 1992, Colin Richmond warned that there was a danger of the *Shoah* slipping 'entirely into that historical limbo which is half-

Heritage (it is happening, it is happening) and half-Entertainment (it has happened, it has happened)'.[64] Eight years later, and even more bleakly, Richmond suggested that 'In an Age of Popularism the next inevitable step will be Theme Park Auschwitz'.[65] The absurdist satire of Monty Python and *MAD* pointed out how popular, televisual, abuse of the past might be taken to its absolute extreme. But could it actually be realised, as in the nightmare heritage vision of Colin Richmond?

In 2002, critic Mark Lawson announced that:

> Later this year, a British television company will broadcast *Camp*, a four-part series in which a hundred volunteers relive the experience of the victims of the Nazi death camps. The participants will be shaved and starved and subjected to medical experiments modelled on those of Dr Mengele. At the end of each episode, 25 of the volunteers, randomly selected by the computer, will be given a card marked 'Oven' and escorted to replica cattle trucks.
>
> Responding to objections from Holocaust survivors, the producer said: 'This is a serious historical exercise intended to bring home to young viewers, in particular, the terrible daily horror of the Final Solution'.

Lawson quickly added that his readers need not worry: 'I just made up *Camp*'. The point he wanted to make was actually with regard to *The Trench* – why was it eagerly anticipated whereas 'most of us would feel instantly that an Auschwitz role-playing show is an impossible proposition; you couldn't get it commissioned'? Yet even Lawson was not fully convinced of his own argument of the impossibility of *Camp*: 'the quest for controversy and ratings in television is now such that one man's satire of television is another's pilot for Channel 5'.[66]

Lawson's *Camp* is not *The 1940s House*, which is an honest if flawed brief attempt to re-create being a bystander to Nazi atrocities. Nor is *Camp* to be found in the rather silly and unnecessary re-enactments of dialogue between Nazis in Laurence Rees' *Auschwitz*, acting which detracts from the chilling testimony of ageing perpetrators and moving accounts of the survivors around which the series is so powerfully constructed. So far, Lawson is right – Holocaust reality television can only be imagined as a sick joke and a moral trump card against the excesses of historical re-creation. It does not follow that Colin Richmond is therefore mistaken in his gloomy prognosis. The dangers are shown in a modest and no doubt utterly well-meaning 'Pastime Colouring Book' available across heritage sites in Britain.[67] In *Scenes from the Second World War*, children have the opportunity, as if sponsored directly by Python's Rita Fairbanks, of not only using their crayons to give life to 'The Japanese Attack [on] the American Fleet at Pearl Harbor' but also to 'The Liberation of a Concentration Camp' before finishing their artistic ambitions with 'Hiroshima: After the Atom Bomb' – all geared towards the national curriculum for history.[68] Heritage bad taste consumerism seems to know no boundaries – for example, in Southampton, a town devastated by the loss of men on board the *Titanic*, pens, which when inverted, portray the ship hitting the iceberg and then sinking, have been available from its historic Bargate. The point to be emphasised is that anything with regard to Holocaust representation is possible. It sometimes takes the sledgehammer humour of Monty Python, or works such as 'Hell', by the bad boys of 'Brit art', the Chapman brothers, to shock us into re-assessment.

Sixty years on from the liberation of Belsen, we have still not worked out how to deal with its imagery. Ultimately, there may not be a way of getting Belsen 'right'. Nevertheless, the world of heritage, with its general absence of critical self-reflection, has been particularly inept and insensitive in representing the Holocaust.

In a review of Donald Bloxham's remarkable dissection of memory and representation of the Holocaust in the war crimes trials, *Genocide on Trial*, the postmodernist historian Patrick Finney criticises the book's author for using vocabulary that talks of 'distortions', 'skewed representations' and 'rewriting history'.[69] Finney is right to stress the need to take seriously in its own right the memory processes by which past events are then constructed and re-constructed.[70] They tell us much about how later identities are themselves formed (and contested). Indeed, there has been valuable work in this respect with regard to Belsen in the past ten years. Yet there is the obvious danger of relativism in the postmodern critique if such distortions and rewritings are not recognised as having *political* implications. In the case of Belsen the most blatant is in the form of Holocaust denial. The much greater threat, however, in the re-telling of its liberation is that it falsely constructs the British war effort as officially and self-consciously fought against the antisemitism/racism of the Nazi regime. As Paul Gilroy and others have shown, British war memory has been instrumentalised to keep out post-1945 immigrants – those from the New Commonwealth and more recently asylum seekers.[71] Whilst images from Belsen have been utilised explicitly and with some success to show the true nature of neo-nazi organisations in Britain, including today's BNP in its attempt to claim respectability, attempts to use them against politicians such as Enoch Powell, as was tried by Tony Benn in the 1970 general election, have generally backfired.[72]

The Holocaust can even be used, retrospectively, to justify less edifying aspects of the British military effort during the Second World War. Thus a pilot, who was part of the Bomber Command force that destroyed Dresden in February 1945, told BBC News 60 years later that he 'didn't know the full meaning of Holocaust until after the war but if I had, I would have been even more proud of what I had done'.[73] In popular memory, another element has been added to the moral fortitude of the war effort by adding to it that Britain fought to save the Jews. The defeat of Nazism, in which Britain played such a massive role, was at a great cost. It is, however, the final insult to activists such as Eleanor Rathbone, James Parkes and others who wanted to make the rescue of the Jews a war aim, and were frustratingly and repeatedly thwarted in this ambition by the British government, to now say that it was indeed a key objective.

The past, whether historians like it or not, has been and will continue to be politicised. In Britain, the Second World War is still the focal point of collective memory, and the proximity of the (British) liberation of Belsen and the end of war has aided a narrative that further confirms, through its last months, that the country fought a 'good' war. It is significant that Colin Richmond's biography of James Parkes (2005), which focuses on Parkes' engagement with the Holocaust, either directly or indirectly, has been utterly ignored by critics, and that Susan Pedersen's biography of Eleanor Rathbone (2004) devotes only a brief chapter to her Jewish refugee rescue work, even though it increasingly dominated her subject matter's life after 1933. There is, as Pedersen concedes, a 'very extensive' literature on British responses to the Holocaust, both popular and governmental, but this comment is relegated to a footnote. Rathbone's rescue work is not the main thrust of her important biography.[74]

Furthermore, the literature on Britain and the Holocaust has failed to make an impact on the general historiography of the 'home front'. Indeed, it is possible, taking the two seminal books on this subject, that knowledge of contemporary British engagement with the plight of the Jews during the war is actually waning. In Angus Calder's *The People's War* (1969), mention is made of the parliamentary declaration of 17 December 1942 and there is brief discussion of what was known and believed about the destruction of European Jewry.[75] Yet Juliet Gardiner's *Wartime: Britain 1939–1945* (2004), universally praised as 'definitive and comprehensive', which includes chapters on domestic episodes such as alien internment as well as war-time antisemitism, fails to acknowledge that Jews outside Britain were also of public concern. *Wartime* does, however, include Dimbleby's broadcast and responses to it.[76] *Wartime* is a remarkable achievement and Gardiner succeeds in detailing 'people's varied experiences of war'.[77] Yet by focusing only on Belsen with regard to Nazi atrocities, the impression is given of an absolute lack of British knowledge, and therefore engagement, before April 1945. The significance of this absence in Gardiner's account is that it reflects a wider societal amnesia. Judith Petersen writes of BBC 1's coverage of the fiftieth anniversary of VE Day in 1995 that the 'few minutes ... devoted to the Holocaust ... did little to disturb the monolithic underpinnings of Britain's war memory'. She adds:

> this channel of 'broad appeal', which is regarded as a national institution suffused with authority, urged the British television-viewing public to remember the plight of European Jewry only insofar as it contributed positively to Britain's war memory: the only memorial trace of Britain's connection to the Holocaust was the liberation of Belsen by British servicemen.[78]

The nature of the images of concentration camps in spring 1945 was unprecedented and it is therefore hard to exaggerate the contemporary impact. Recognition of the shock and horror they induced, however, should not be at the expense of similarly recognising the information that was available about the Jewish plight throughout the war and contemporary reactions to it.

The final point to be considered in this article is why heritage and 'popular' history have yet to get to grips with the absence of Jews in the representation of Nazi atrocities in spring 1945. The ahistorical inclusion of Dimbleby's 'Jewish' Belsen broadcast in the book version of *The 1940s House* has already been commented on. A much more extravagant re-writing of the concentration camp footage to become part of a *Jewish Holocaust*, rather than an *atrocity* narrative, is to be found in the lavish American television mini-series *Nuremberg* (2000) which re-creates the tribunals with deliberate pedagogic intent.[79] What is striking, taking the decade from 1995 to 2005, is whilst there has been an abundance of subtle academic studies from a range of disciplines showing how atrocity images were framed in 1945 (and how they have been utilised subsequently), these works have made little or no impact on popular representation.[80]

To conclude: are we left with the pessimistic reading that heritage, as Lowenthal suggests, will ultimately exclude all that is problematic to a celebratory account of the past?[81] That British engagement with the plight of European Jewry during the Second World War was ambivalent and that the Jewishness of Belsen's victims was largely censored in 1945 are details not comfortably digested by 'heritage' – hence the success of the dominant war narrative which highlights, in sequence, Britain alone, military and civilian sacrifice, Belsen liberation and VE Day. And yet the re-connection of Belsen to the specific crimes committed against the Jews, and the belated respect granted to Holocaust survivors shows that more pluralistic readings of the Second World War have, by the end of the twentieth century, become possible.

If history, as has been suggested, might be 'the new rock 'n' roll',[82] then television is the main media through which it is consumed. In 2005 a six-part sober series solely devoted to the history of Auschwitz was broadcast on the BBC. Such programming would have been inconceivable just two decades earlier. *Auschwitz: The Nazis and the 'Final Solution'* was removed from either the Holocaust ignorance of Wodehouse's 1945 'Belsen business', or, largely, the potential to exploit the Holocaust through what has been dubbed (though not unproblematically), 'the Shoah business'.[83]

It would be wrong, however, to end too redemptively. However impressive, this series, screened on what is 'a minority channel... broadcast for "special interests" to a limited audience',[84] was not, on its own, going to overturn the lingering ignorance of the Holocaust in Britain. In this respect, the fluidity and instability of knowledge, as superficially revealed in opinion poll findings, is not aided by confusions in popular publications such as 'Belsen-Birkenau' and references to Richard Dimbleby standing 'outside the charnel house of Belsen' on 19 April 1945.[85] We may, or may not, all be postmodernists now, but there is still a basic need to get the details of 'where' and 'when' right. Furthermore, an overly optimistic reading of the situation now would also fail to acknowledge the lingering antipathy in Britain towards recognition of the particular plight of the Jews in Nazi Europe. Such anti-particularism has been manifested most recently in opposition to the annual Holocaust Memorial Day first instituted in January 2001.[86]

To sum up: the gulf between heritage and history is a real one and it has made and continues to make a huge impact on the representation of Belsen and the Holocaust generally. Heritage, as Raphael Samuel argued, can be progressive and inclusive. At its most thoughtful, the acute sense of place which it brings to our understanding of the past could be brought productively into dialogue with the critical approach of the historian. So far, as we have seen with Belsen and the evolution of British collective memory since April 1945, history has largely been the loser.

NOTES

My thanks to Judith Petersen for her helpful comments on an earlier draft of this paper.

1. Alan Bennett, 'Seeing Stars', in *Untold Stories* (London: Faber and Faber/Profile, 2005), pp.170–1, originally published in the *London Review of Books*, 3 January 2002.
2. Colin Richmond, 'Diary', *London Review of Books*, 13 February 1992.
3. John Horne and Alan Kramer, *German Atrocities: A History of Denial* (London: Yale University Press, 2001), p.430.
4. On the Armenians, see Joanne Laycock, 'Imagining Armenia: Orientalism, History and Civilisation' (unpublished PhD thesis, University of Manchester, 2005).
5. Memorandum, July 1941, in National Archives, INF 1/251 Pt 4.
6. Lias, 30 August 1942 in FO 371/30917 C7839 and Dixon to Martin, 16 May 1944 in PREM 4/51/8, National Archives.
7. For fuller development of all these factors see Tony Kushner, *The Persistence of Prejudice: Antisemitism in British Society during the Second World War* (Manchester: Manchester University Press, 1989), ch 5; and idem, *The Holocaust and the Liberal Imagination: A Cultural and Social History* (Oxford: Blackwell, 1994).
8. See, for example, Jon Bridgman, *The End of the Holocaust: The Liberation of the Camps* (London: Batsford, 1990), ch.2.
9. Hannah Caven, 'Horror in Our Time: images of the concentration camps in the British media, 1945', *Historical Journal of Film, Radio and Television*, Vol.21, No.3

(2001), p.209.
10. Jonathan Dimbleby, *Richard Dimbleby: A Biography* (London: Hodder & Stoughton, 1975), ch.5.
11. Judith Petersen is completing a PhD thesis at the University of Southampton on British television and the Holocaust.
12. Kushner, *The Holocaust and the Liberal Imagination*, pp.210–11.
13. Jeffrey Shandler, *While America Watches: Televising the Holocaust* (New York: Oxford University Press, 1999), pp.75–6, 112; and Lawrence Douglas, *The Memory of Judgment: Making Law and History in the Trials of the Holocaust* (New Haven, CT: Yale University Press, 2001), pp.56–63, 100–1.
14. Mass-Observation Archive: FR 2228, April 1945, University of Sussex.
15. Kushner, *The Holocaust and the Liberal Imagination*, pp.209–10.
16. David Cannadine, 'The First Hundred Years', in Howard Newby (ed.), *The National Trust: The Next Hundred Years* (London: National Trust, 1995), pp.21–2.
17. Entry, 6 January 1946, in James Lees-Milne, *Caves of Ice* (London: Chatto & Windus, 1983), p.4.
18. James Agate, *Ego: The Autobiography of James Agate* (London: Hamish Hamilton, 1935).
19. James Lees-Milne, *Prophesying Peace* (London: Chatto & Windus, 1977), p.192.
20. Ibid.
21. James Lees-Milne, *The Age of Adam* (London: Batsford, 1947), p.113.
22. Diary entry of 12 May 1945 in James Agate, *Ego 8: Continuing the Autobiography of James Agate* (London: George Harrap, 1946), p.113.
23. Martin Gilbert, *Auschwitz and the Allies* (London: Michael Joseph, 1981).
24. See, for example, David Engel, *In the Shadow of Auschwitz: The Polish-Government-in-exile and the Jews, 1939–1942* (Chapel Hill, NC: University of North Carolina Press, 1987).
25. Kushner, *The Holocaust and the Liberal Imagination*, p.209.
26. For one of these, see Colin Richmond, *Campaigner against Antisemitism: The Reverend James Parkes 1896–1981* (London: Vallentine Mitchell, 2005).
27. Laurence Rees, *Auschwitz: The Nazis and the 'Final Solution'* (London: BBC Books, 2005), p.334.
28. Bernard Josephs, 'Poll suggests rise in Auschwitz awareness', *Jewish Chronicle*, 25 March 2005.
29. Derek & Clive, *Ad Nauseam* (album, 1978).
30. Ibid.
31. James Parkes, *Voyage of Discoveries* (London: Gollancz, 1969), pp.128–9.
32. Derek & Clive, *Ad Nauseam*.
33. Robert McCrum, *Wodehouse: A Life* (London: Viking, 2004).
34. Ibid., p.288.
35. See Donald Bloxham, *Genocide on Trial: War Crimes Trials and the Formation of Holocaust History and Memory* (Oxford: Oxford University Press, 2001), pp.97–101.
36. Carol Ann Lee, *Roses from the Earth: The Biography of Anne Frank* (London: Viking, 1999), ch.8, esp. pp.179–80; and Willy Lindwer, *The Last Seven Months of Anne Frank* (New York: Pantheon, 1991); Daniel Goldhagen, *Hitler's Willing Executioners: Ordinary Germans and the Holocaust* (New York: Little, Brown, 1996), chs.13 and 14 provide the fullest account of the death marches though heavily influenced by his monocausal explanation of the Holocaust.
37. McCrum, *Wodehouse*, p.354.
38. Bryan Cheyette, *Constructions of 'the Jew' in English Literature and Society: Racial Representations, 1875–1945* (Cambridge: Cambridge University Press, 1993).
39. McCrum, *Wodehouse*, p.355.

40. Ibid., p.285.
41. *The Media Show*, Channel 4, 14 October 1990 and critical comment by Mark Steyn in *The Independent*, 15 October 1990.
42. Stephen Fry, 'Plum on target', *Observer*, 5 September 2004.
43. Nigel Williams, 'Plum Pudding', *Guardian*, 4 September 2004.
44. Raphael Samuel, *Theatres of Memory* (London: Verso, 1994), p.13.
45. Tristram Hunt, 'Whose story?', *Observer*, 19 June 2005.
46. David Lowenthal, *The Heritage Crusade and the Spoils of History* (Cambridge: Cambridge University Press, 1998 edition [1996]), p.121 and *passim*.
47. This episode was broadcast on 18 January 2002, Channel 4. The instructions to listen are reproduced in Juliet Gardiner, *The 1940s House* (London: Channel 4 Books, 2000), p.237, and are taken from Mrs Hymer's diary of the *1940s House*.
48. Ibid.
49. Judith Petersen, 'Belsen and a British Broadcasting Icon', unpublished paper, 2005.
50. See Kushner, *The Holocaust and the Liberal Imagination*, pp.209–12.
51. 'The Beginning of the End', *The 1940s House*; Gardiner, *The 1940s House*, p.237.
52. Juliet Gardiner, email to the author, 19 April 2005.
53. *Daily Mirror*, 7 August 1992.
54. Tony Kushner, 'The Holocaust and the Museum World in Britain: A Study of Ethnography', in Sue Vice (ed.), *Representing the Holocaust* (London: Vallentine Mitchell, 2003), p.27.
55. Douglas, *The Memory of Judgment*, p.27.
56. *The 1940s House* (VHS video vol.2: Channel 4/Wall to Wall/Contender Entertainment Group, 2001).
57. Julian Barnes, *England, England* (London: Jonathan Cape, 1998).
58. Tim Cole, *Images of the Holocaust: The Myth of the 'Shoah' Business* (London: Duckworth, 1999), p.75, writes of the success of *'Schindler's List* tours' where the tourists 'do not so much see sites of "Holocaust" history, as sites of *Schindler's List* history'; Imperial War Museum leaflet, 'The 1940s House Exhibition'. See also http://www.channel4.com/history/microsites/0-9/1940house/ for the full marketing of the series.
59. See his contribution in this volume.
60. Mark Lawson, 'The battle for ratings', *Guardian*, 11 March 2002. The first episode of *The Trench* was broadcast on 15 March 2002.
61. George Perry, *Life of Python* (London: Pavilion Books, 1986), p.127.
62. This was in episode 11 of the first series, broadcast on BBC 1, 28 December 1969 and changed slightly in the film compilation *And Now for Something Completely Different* (1971).
63. *MAD*, January 1967 referred to and reproduced in Shandler, *While America Watches*, pp.144–5.
64. Colin Richmond, 'Englishness and Medieval Anglo-Jewry', in Tony Kushner (ed.), *The Jewish Heritage in British History* (London: Frank Cass, 1992), pp.43–4.
65. Colin Richmond, 'Introduction: The Jews in Medieval England', *Jewish Culture and History*, Vol.3, No.2 (Winter 2000), p.2.
66. Lawson, 'The battle for ratings'.
67. Produced by Ultradesigns, each colouring book 'covers a particular period of history and illustrates major events of the time. These are periods indicated within the national curriculum for history'. See http://www.ultradesigns.co.uk, viewed 14 December 2005.
68. *Scenes from the Second World War* (Ultadesign, no place, no date) with illustrations by David Ochiltree. I am grateful to Elisa Lawson for alerting me to this text.
69. In *Rethinking History*, Vol.8, No.3 (Autumn 2004), pp.489–50.

70. See also Robert Eaglestone, *The Holocaust and the Postmodern* (Oxford: Oxford University Press, 2004).
71. See Paul Gilroy, *There Ain't No Black in the Union Jack* (London: Hutchinson, 1987); Patrick Wright, *On Living in an Old Country* (London: Verso, 1985); Tony Kushner, 'Remembering to Forget: Racism and Anti-Racism in Postwar Britain', in Bryan Cheyette and Laura Marcus (eds.), *Modernity, Culture and 'the Jew'* (Cambridge: Polity Press, 1998), pp.226–41.
72. Tony Kushner, 'Offending the Memory? The Holocaust and Pressure Group Politics', in Tony Kushner and Nadia Valman (eds.), *Philosemitism, Antisemitism and 'the Jews'* (Ashgate: Aldershot, 2004), pp.246–62.
73. On BBC 1, '10 o'clock News', 11 February 2005.
74. Susan Pedersen, *Eleanor Rathbone and the Politics of Conscience* (New Haven: Yale University Press, 2004), p.440 note 43.
75. Angus Calder, *The People's War: Britain, 1939–1945* (London: Jonathan Cape, 1969), pp.499–511.
76. Juliet Gardiner, *Wartime: Britain 1939–1945* (London: Headline, 2004), p.674.
77. Ibid., p.xi.
78. Judith Petersen, 'How British Television Inserted the Holocaust into Britain's War Memory in 1995', *Historical Journal of Film, Radio and Television*, Vol.21, No.3 (2001), p.270.
79. *Nuremberg (2000)*, directed by Yves Simoneau, was broadcast on American television in a two part series. See James Jordan, 'Bearing Witness to the Holocaust in American Fictive Film' (unpublished PhD thesis, University of Southampton, 2003), ch.6.
80. See, for example, Jo Reilly, *Belsen: The Liberation of a Concentration Camp* (London: Routledge, 1998); idem *et al.* (eds.), *Belsen in History and Memory* (London: Frank Cass, 1997); Barbie Zelizer, *Remembering to Forget: Holocaust Memory Through the Camera's Eye* (Chicago: University of Chicago Press, 1998); Caven, 'Horror in Our Time', pp.205–53; Cornelia Brink, 'Secular Icons: Looking at Photographs from Nazi Concentration Camps', *History and Memory*, Vol.12, No.1 (Spring/Summer 2000), pp.135–50; Shandler, *While America Watches*; Douglas, *The Memory of Judgment*; Bloxham, *Genocide on Trial*; Ben Flanagan and Donald Bloxham (eds.), *Remembering Belsen* (London: Vallentine Mitchell, 2005).
81. Lowenthal, *The Heritage Crusade*, pp.156–62.
82. Peter Mandler, *History and National Life* (London: Profile Books, 2002), p.1.
83. Cole, *Images of the Holocaust: The Myth of the 'Shoah' Business*, which, whilst full of astute observations, does not query the appropriateness of the term itself.
84. Petersen, 'How British Television Inserted the Holocaust', p.270.
85. Gardiner, *The 1940s House*, p.237.
86. Tony Kushner, 'Too Little, Too Late? Reflections on Britain's Holocaust Memorial Day', *Journal of Israeli History*, Vol.23, No.1 (Spring 2004), pp.116–29.

Forgetting and Remembering: Memories and Memorialisation of Bergen-Belsen

RAINER SCHULZE

Sixty years after the liberation of Bergen-Belsen concentration camp, annual commemorations of the liberation, meetings of survivors, scholarly conferences and a number of publications dealing with the camp and its history could suggest that the process of memory formation and memorialisation has been a long and continuous process since the end of the Second World War.[1] However, this is only partly so. It is true that a rich cultural memory of Bergen-Belsen developed relatively early outside Germany, and among the survivors, but it focused on the concentration camp and mostly disregarded the prisoner-of-war camp, which existed there from 1940 until January 1945. At the historic site itself, and in Germany generally, the process was even more chequered and protracted. Memory formation is linked with the prevailing public discourse, and Bergen-Belsen was no exception to this. In the first two decades after the liberation, Bergen-Belsen reflected the overall amnesia that overtook Western Germany in this period with regard to its recent Nazi past.[2]

The Establishment of the *Gedenkstätte* Bergen-Belsen: Concealing Memory

When British troops liberated Bergen-Belsen on 15 April 1945, following a local ceasefire, disease was rampant in the main concentration camp. Therefore, the survivors were evacuated as quickly as possible to the German *Wehrmacht* barracks, which were a little more than a mile away (for an aerial view, see plate no.13). The dead were buried in huge burial pits on the site of the concentration camp, and most of the wooden huts were torn down and all the remains torched as soon as the inmates had been moved out in order to prevent a further spread of disease (see plate no.14).[3] Although done for good reasons, the burning-down of the prisoners' huts in April and May 1945 contributed to the process of getting rid of the evidence as to what had happened at Bergen-Belsen – a process which had begun shortly before the liberation, when the SS destroyed all papers relating to the camp, including the register of the prisoners.

The survivors set up their own memorials very quickly. Only one day after their liberation, (Catholic) Polish survivors erected a provisional cross made from birch wood. Likewise, Jewish survivors put up their own provisional memorial next to the mass graves on 25 September 1945. However, it was not until October 1945 that the British Military Government ordered the German Provincial Government in Hannover to set up an appropriate memorial 'to ensure that the memory of the infamy of the concentration camps does not fade'.[4] Even though most of the prisoners' huts had already disappeared, the fences around the former camp, the watchtowers, the crematorium, and the buildings of the SS compound still remained, and the topography of the camp continued to be recognisable despite the mounds of the mass graves. As a first step, the German authorities arranged for the mass graves to be provisionally hemmed in by a stone lining and to be labelled with wooden plaques indicating the approximate number of dead buried there. They also decided to clear the site, which meant removing the last structural remains of the concentration camp, covering it with a layer of topsoil and surrounding it with a belt of shrubs and trees native to the region, the Lüneburg Heath.[5] During the winter of 1945–46 work began on dismantling the watchtowers, tearing down the fences, and taking away the crematorium. Even the stone foundations of some of the huts were dug out. Much of what was recovered in this way was sold off as building materials to local firms and individuals. Other structural remains were ploughed under and thus concealed. This was done in general agreement with the British authorities. In July 1946, the zonal headquarters of the British Military Government in Germany instructed the regional Military Government office in Hannover that the proposed memorial for those who had died at Bergen-Belsen 'should not, by intention, invoke painful memories of the manner of their death'.[6]

The landscape architect Wilhelm Hübotter, who had been asked by the German Provincial Government in Hannover to draw up a plan for the layout of the proposed memorial site at Bergen-Belsen, resigned from his commission in the spring of 1946. He had been attacked by the Central Committee for the Liberated Jews in the British Zone, which had its headquarters at the Displaced Persons Camp Bergen-Belsen, because of his involvement in a number of high-profile landscape design projects during the Nazi period. Most notoriously, he had collaborated on the landscape design for the so-called Sachsenhain (Grove of the Saxons), a memorial site situated 50 kilometres west of Bergen-Belsen for 4,500 Saxons allegedly killed there by Charlemagne in the year 782, which was used by the SS for rallies and ceremonies. However, Hübotter's release from the commission did not mean that the main principles of his plans were given up as well. Hübotter had wanted to turn Bergen-Belsen into a site 'of eternal significance', set out in a way that drew 'a final line under a time which must never return... We must succeed in burying the "sensation" Belsen and turn it into a permanent and enduring warning'.[7] These ideas were also pursued by Hübotter's successors.

The landscape design of the memorial site which was eventually approved reflected Hübotter's dictum that 'the design solution can only lie in a landscape direction'.[8] It involved a massive change to the original camp topography by superimposing a completely new layout of circular pathways. The memorial site became, as set out at an earlier planning meeting, 'a place of beauty, and of reverence, where those who had died could rest in peace',[9] but it became at the same time a place that showed no more traces of the crimes that had been committed there. It thus contributed to the process of concealing and forgetting the historical events as much as it was a reflection of this process.

In 1946, it had been decided to erect a monument in the form of a high obelisk and a wall of remembrance.[10] All nations that had suffered losses at Bergen-Belsen were invited to mount a plaque on the wall with an inscription 'of a non-religious nature' and of no more than 200 letters.[11] However, even these inscriptions made only a vague reference, if any, as to why people were buried there. The

British plaque, for example, reads 'To the memory of all those who died in this place'.[12] The other plaques are similarly non-specific.

Owing to numerous problems, the actual construction and landscaping work only began in mid-1948, and the dedication ceremony of the memorial did not take place until 30 November 1952. On the advice of the British government, representatives of countries of the Soviet bloc were not invited to the inaugural ceremony, despite the fact that their nationals had formed a significant proportion of those incarcerated at Bergen-Belsen.[13] With the inauguration, the British handed over the responsibility for the administration and upkeep of the memorial to the *Land* Lower Saxony (Niedersachsen).

Only a few years after the end of the Nazi regime it had become all but invisible to an uninformed visitor that Bergen-Belsen had been the site of a prisoner-of-war camp and a concentration camp. This was reinforced by the fact that in the end the memorial site only comprised the area where the mass graves were located, which was the section of the camp where the concentration camp prisoners had been incarcerated. The remaining part of the original camp – the commandant's offices and the SS compound – were separated from the memorial site and initially used to accommodate German refugees and expellees from central, eastern and south-eastern Europe who had come to the area after the Second World War. After they had been rehoused elsewhere in 1953–54, the remaining wooden huts were sold and the stone buildings, among them the delousing facilities and the confinement building, torn down. The site became incorporated into the adjacent NATO military training ground and remained part of it until the early 1990s.[14]

The Evolution of the *Gedenkstätte* since the 1950s: The Slow Process of Recovering Memory

In the early 1960s, the political debate in West Germany slowly shifted, and the Holocaust – at that time still generally referred to as the 'Final Solution' – gradually became included into the public discourse. It was at this time, and following the desecration of several Jewish cemeteries in West Germany by the daubing of swastikas, that the first scholarly research on the history of Bergen-Belsen was commissioned.[15] In the wake of the publication of this study, a small documentation centre was set up in 1966 at Bergen-Belsen which provided some basic information about the concentration camp.[16] However, it focused mainly on the fate of the Jews, and included next to nothing about the prisoner-of-war camp or the displaced persons camp.

In the 1980s, citizens' initiatives, made up mainly of local teachers and amateur historians who were unhappy about the continuing lack of information provided at the former camp site, demanded a more critical discussion of the role of Bergen-Belsen.[17] As a result of this pressure, and following the announcement by US President Ronald Reagan that he would also visit Bergen-Belsen during his tour of Europe to commemorate the fortieth anniversary of the end of the Second World War, the *Landtag* (state parliament) of Lower Saxony (Niedersachsen) unanimously passed a resolution in April 1985 requesting the state government to update and expand the existing memorial at Bergen-Belsen.[18] In April 1990, on the forty-fifth anniversary of the liberation of the concentration camp, a new and larger documentation and information centre was opened. For the first time, a small permanent staff was now available to welcome visitors, look after survivors and their relatives who came to the site, and engage in educational work and some academic research. The centre also included an updated exhibition on the history of Bergen-Belsen, based on the limited range of research available at the time, which meant that the focus remained on the history of the concentration camp.[19] In 1992 work began to recollect names and biographical details of those incarcerated at Bergen-Belsen concentration camp. The first *Gedenkbuch* (Book of Remembrance), published on the fiftieth anniversary of the liberation, comprised some 25,000 names; the second edition, published ten years later, already included 50,000 names.[20] This is an impressive achievement, but it is still well short of the total of c.120,000 prisoners estimated to have been at Bergen-Belsen concentration camp at some point over the two years of its existence.

The current endeavour to recover memory was instigated by the Final Report of the Select Committee on German Unity, which was passed by the German *Bundestag* (Federal parliament) in 1998. This report included a passage on the role of concentration camp memorials in the formation of a cultural memory in the recently unified Germany, and set out the basic tasks these memorials were expected to fulfil: to maintain and preserve the memory of the victims; to secure traces at the historic sites; to collect sources and do research in order to document the history of the sites in exhibitions and other forms; and finally, to engage in educational work.[21] Bergen-Belsen was identified as one of the concentration camp memorials of international importance on German soil because it was unique in that it had been a prisoner-of-war camp, a concentration camp and a reception camp for the death marches from the east.[22] Since 2000 it has received funding from the Federal government to carry out research on the history of the camp(s), to update and expand the permanent exhibition, and to build a new museum and information centre to present the findings and make the newly obtained knowledge available to the general public.

Bergen-Belsen as a Site of Conflicting Memories

However, the memorial site at Bergen-Belsen does not only reflect the changing public discourse. Bergen-Belsen is also very much a site of contested memory. There is no single universal memory of Bergen-Belsen. Different groups have different memories of Bergen-Belsen, which have evolved over time, and there were points when these memories seemed almost incompatible.

For the Jews, Bergen-Belsen marks the final stage of the Holocaust, murder by wilful neglect, but it also marks the rebirth and new beginnings of Jewish life after the Holocaust in the displaced persons camp which was set up in the nearby *Wehrmacht* barracks.[23] This camp was an important centre of rehabilitation and re-orientation and a critical battleground in the fight with the British authorities over the Jewish demand for free emigration to Palestine. For the (non-Jewish) Poles, likewise, Bergen-Belsen is a place of their political and physical persecution and destruction on the one hand and of cultural rebirth after liberation on the other. For the British, the liberation of Bergen-Belsen by their troops constitutes one of their finest hours in the Second World War, and one which visibly justified the long and costly battle against Nazi Germany. And the list continues – Sinti and Roma, Soviet prisoners-of-war, Italian military internees, Jehovah's Witnesses, homosexuals all have their own memories of Bergen-Belsen, as do all the other groups of people persecuted by the Nazis who were detained at Bergen-Belsen.[24] There was often little or no space for these different memories to co-exist side-by-side.

The survivors were united in their opposition to the removal of the structural remains of the concentration camp, which they regarded as the final act of the breach of the rules of civilisation which they had suffered under the Nazis.[25] They were not against the establishment of a memorial at Bergen-Belsen, quite the opposite, but they demanded a memorial that would preserve the memory of what had happened there, rather than one that would destroy or conceal it. However, their protests were in vain, and as a result they focused their memories on their own memorials. The provisional Polish cross was replaced by a permanent large wooden cross on 2 November 1945, All Souls' Day. Likewise, on 15 April 1946, the first anniversary of the liberation, the Jewish survivors established a stone memorial in place of the earlier provisional monument. Both the wooden cross and the Jewish memorial still stand today and serve as the place of remembrance for these survivors and their relatives and friends.

The memory of Bergen-Belsen became additionally blurred by the fact that the photographs and film footage of the concentration camp, produced by the British Army Film and Photographic Unit (AFPU) immediately after the liberation, have become almost iconic images of the twentieth century. Their usage in world media since 1945 has contributed in many ways to a memory of Bergen-Belsen which became detached from the actual historic site and the actual historical events. In the public perception, Bergen-Belsen has come to symbolise and exemplify all the atrocities of Nazi rule: the very model of a Nazi 'horror camp',[26] whereas in fact it was not the prototype of a Nazi concentration camp at all.

The Redevelopment of the *Gedenkstätte*: Towards a Comprehensive Memory

Bergen-Belsen is a place where some historical events are still far from clear. Obviously, the basic chronology has long been established, but many questions have remained open and might never be fully answered. It is all but impossible to reverse fully the long process of destruction of memory which began with the SS destroying all the papers relating to the camp and which continued in the first decades after the liberation.

This fact has informed the work on the redevelopment of the *Gedenkstätte*, which has been guided by three main principles:

- Openness: there will be no definitive memory of Bergen-Belsen that will be decreed and no definitive reading; instead, visitors will be invited, on the basis of the available evidence, to reach their own conclusions.
- Comprehensiveness: all groups who were held and incarcerated at Bergen-Belsen, from the first prisoner-of-war camp onwards, will be commemorated.
- Acceptance of the tortuous process of memory-formation: there will be no attempt to reverse the often radical intervention into the topography of the historic site which has taken place since the summer of 1945, in order to allow visitors to appreciate how memory was formed, and changed, over time.

The new *Gedenkstätte* consists of three elements, which are integrally linked, and together will help to recover lost memory, and make the historic site 'speak' again: the Documentation and Information Centre, the permanent exhibition, and the landscape design for the historic site.[27]

The New Documentation and Information Centre

The new Documentation and Information Centre was specifically commissioned to house the new permanent exhibition, the new archive, a reading room, and other facilities such as seminar rooms, a bookshop and a small cafeteria. The concept of the new building is based on the idea of a sculpture through which the visitors walk on their way to the historic site. In order to take the visitors out of their normal everyday reality, the floor of the building is not level, but ascends slightly as they move along the 'historical path', which runs from the forecourt through the building and on to the centre of the historic site, ending at the former *Appellplatz* of the Star Camp (the exchange camp).

The long and narrow building of fair-faced concrete is set in a break in the forest which is densely wooded today. The actual building remains outside the site of the former concentration camp and today's cemetery, but a seven-metre extension 'floats' freely over the former camp boundary. A large window at this point of the building allows a view outside and directly on to the former *Appellplatz* of the Star Camp, which is also the site of one of the mass graves (see plate no.15). By looking out of this window, the visitors will be confronted by the duality of the historic site: concentration camp and cemetery. The window almost draws the historic site into the building and makes it part of the exhibition. In turn, the exhibition is rigorously focused on what the visitors see but would not understand without the exhibition providing them with the information which the site itself cannot do any more.

The New Permanent Exhibition

Up until 1990, the *Gedenkstätte* did not have any archive and was neither authorised nor equipped to collect and preserve documents and historical artefacts. As a result, there was no systematic collection of sources on the history of Bergen-Belsen at the historic site itself. Instead, records on Bergen-Belsen are scattered all over the world and can be found in the national archives of all those countries that were involved with Bergen-Belsen in one form or another, as well as in the more specialist archives set up in many countries to document Nazi crimes. Survivors of Bergen-Belsen donated their artefacts, diaries, letters or other personal documents to archives, libraries and museums in the countries where they settled after their liberation, to Yad Vashem in Israel, or to the United States Holocaust Memorial Museum. Some groups, such as the Association of Survivors of Bergen-Belsen in Tel-Aviv (Irgun Sherit Hapletah Bergen-Belsen) set up their own documentation centres. A solid cultural memory of Bergen-Belsen developed from relatively early on, but it developed away from Bergen-Belsen, and quite independently of the *Gedenkstätte*, and for a long time it was more or less unknown or unacknowledged within Germany by those responsible for the site of the former concentration camp.

In order to reverse the process of the destruction of memory at Bergen-Belsen, the first task was, therefore, to trace sources and artefacts concerning the history of the prisoner-of-war camp, the concentration camp and the displaced persons camp all over the world. The next step was to return as many of them as possible to the place from where they originated, even if only in the form of facsimiles, photographs or temporary loans. For that purpose, co-operation agreements were concluded with archives and museums in Israel, the United States, Great Britain, France, Russia and Poland, and close contacts have been formed with survivors' associations, individual survivors and people involved in the rescue and rehabilitation operation.

As a result of this extensive search, it became possible to document the multi-dimensional history of Bergen-Belsen in a much more detailed and comprehensive manner. This applies both to the organisational history and the role which Bergen-Belsen played in the broader context of the Nazi system of racial, social and political persecution, as well as to the history of the people who were incarcerated at Bergen-Belsen. The result is presented to the public in the new permanent exhibition. Its master narrative is shaped and determined by the key aim to explain the historic site. The focus throughout is on Bergen-Belsen as, first, a place of crime and, later, a place of rehabilitation for the survivors. The exhibition follows a broadly chronological approach, documenting first the prisoner-of-war camp (1940–45), then the concentration camp (1943–45), and finally the displaced persons camp (1945–50).

The exhibition is source-driven, meaning that the sources are the main carrier of the narrative and are not just mere illustrations. This applies equally to all the different kinds of sources available: documents, photographs, film footage, artefacts, and video interviews. The decision as to which source is used is determined solely by which one is most suited to document and visualise specific aspects of the story of Bergen-Belsen. As the actual horror can never be recreated, and as it cannot be adequately described either, all the exhibition aims to do is to provide the visitors with the available evidence upon which they will then have to draw their own conclusions and form their own images as to what the conditions at Bergen-Belsen had been like. Both archive and exhibition are closely linked, with the exhibition showcasing the findings held in the archive. In this way, it is intended to encourage visitors to the exhibition to consult the archive for further information.

The history of Bergen-Belsen is told as far as possible from the perspective of those who were imprisoned there, or for whom it became the place of rehabilitation after their liberation. The narrative focuses on the conditions under which human beings existed at Bergen-Belsen. Within this focus, there are a number of common themes which accompany the visitors on their 'historical path' through the exhibition and which serve as an underlying texture for the exhibition:

- the juxtaposition of the hope of rescue and the prospect of death which ruled over the daily existence of all those who were detained both at the prisoner-of-war camp and the concentration camp, and which continued into the DP period for those who survived the imprisonment;
- the international character of Bergen-Belsen, where the prisoners and survivors have come from almost all European countries and included members of all political, social and ethnic groups persecuted by the Nazi regime;
- the strong Jewish impact owing to the fact that in contrast to all other concentration camps in the territory of the German *Reich*, the largest group of prisoners and, later, survivors of Bergen-Belsen were Jews (this will enable visitors to appreciate why Bergen-Belsen has held such an important position in Jewish cultural memory to the present day);
- the singular and often contradictory position which Bergen-Belsen held in the system of Nazi camps of which it was simultaneously an integral part;
- the racist ideology of the Nazi state forming the common denominator of what occurred at Bergen-Belsen and underpinning the conscious and systematic violation of human rights and international law and conventions which the SS and the *Wehrmacht* committed in collusion with, and in knowledge of, other state and Nazi institutions on all levels as well as a wide range of private firms, organisations and individuals.

One reason why Bergen-Belsen has become so widely known is due to the photographs and film footage of the AFPU from the first days after the liberation. Most, if not all, visitors to Bergen-Belsen will have seen some of these images, and will expect to learn more about what they show. This footage is, therefore, extensively documented and set in its historical context. The photographs are shown in the open exhibition but in a form that leaves it to the visitors to decide whether they want to step closer and view them in detail. In contrast, the historic film footage is shown in an enclosed space at the centre of the building, and thus at the centre of the exhibition. Both are shown as historical sources which rather than recording the Nazi crimes as such, record the results of the final phase of Bergen-Belsen when it had become a death camp where tens of thousands of prisoners were left to die by starvation, disease and general neglect.

In a way, these images documenting the end of Bergen-Belsen concentration camp form the counterpart to the only existing film clip of the deportation of prisoners from a holding camp to their annihilation in the death camps in eastern Europe. This film clip is shown at the beginning of the concentration camp exhibition. The train which left the Dutch camp of Westerbork on 19 May 1944 transported 208 Jews and 245 Sinti and Roma in crowded cattle wagons to their death in Auschwitz. However, at the front of this train there were some (third class) passenger coaches, and the 240 prisoners travelling in these were deported to Bergen-Belsen.[28] This innocent-looking act of passengers boarding the train at Westerbork, on the one hand, and the unburied corpses and thousands of survivors barely alive who were uncovered by the British troops in April 1945, on the other hand, exemplify the story of Bergen-Belsen concentration camp.

Bergen-Belsen will also be known to many visitors as the place where Anne Frank died shortly before the liberation of the camp.[29] The story of Anne Frank has become part of the cultural memory of the Holocaust, and the exhibition needs to document how she and her sister Margot came to Bergen-Belsen and what happened to them there. This is done by showing that Anne Frank was one of many thousands of female concentration camp prisoners who were transported from Auschwitz-Birkenau to Bergen-Belsen in the autumn of 1944 in order to do slave labour and who perished in the final phase of the camp.

The design of the new Documentation and Information Centre accentuates and underscores the general tenor of the exhibition. The left-hand side of the long building forms the area of individual and subjective remembrance. The concrete wall remains empty apart from video screens which show excerpts from biographical interviews with survivors of Bergen-Belsen. In the past five years, some 230 survivors have recounted on video their lives before and after Bergen-Belsen and the specific experiences of their incarceration there.[30] These personal testimonies form the audio-visual counterpart to the historical photographs and film footage of the liberated concentration camp, in which the individual is hardly recognisable in the anonymous mass of the dead and the nearly dead. The sight of survivors as they look some 55–60 years later on video screens, and the process of listening to what they have to tell about their experiences and their journey to Bergen-Belsen, are intended to underline the 'dehumanization' which the prisoners suffered at Bergen-Belsen. It is also intended to make it easier for the visitors to relate to the people who went through the 'hell of Belsen' in a way which the historical images cannot do.[31]

The right-hand side of the building accommodates the historical exhibition. The three main parts each emphasise specific aspects which are seen as essential within the general conceptual framework outlined above: the mass death of some 14,000 Soviet prisoners-of-war in the winter of 1941–42 in the prisoner-of-war camp; the desperate and mostly illusory hope of rescue of those Jews who were deported to Bergen-Belsen in the initial phase of the concentration camp; the mass death in the final phase of the war when tens of thousands of concentration camp prisoners were transported to Bergen-Belsen from Auschwitz and other camps in the east; rescue on 15 April 1945 by British troops from the certain death assigned to them by the Nazi state, even though the dying continued for a long time; the rebirth of Jewish life in the Jewish DP camp from 1945 onwards, and the parallel, from 1945 to 1946, of Polish life in the Polish DP camp. Excerpts of interviews with survivors also feature in the historical documentation, as do interviews with liberators and those involved in the rescue effort after the liberation.

The exhibition walls and showcases are kept simple and as minimalistic in their design as possible. Their appearance is intended to make the visitor think of archival shelves and containers which display what is known about Bergen-Belsen but at the same time indicate that many questions remain unanswered. They are also meant to express a degree of openness. More sources may yet be found in the coming years, in which case they can still be included in the exhibition; other questions might be asked in a few years' time, in which case the exhibition can be rearranged in order to address them.

The exhibition forms an essential part of the pathway to the historic site, and after walking through the exhibition it is hoped the visitors will see the actual site with different eyes and realise that the peaceful and pleasant-looking landscape covered in heather and interspersed with birch trees and junipers is deceptive. Beneath the soil the dead lie in mass graves. Close to the mass graves stand the memorials which the survivors set up as reminders of their own suffering and the suffering of those who died there. In the distance on the one side is the Soviet prisoner-of-war cemetery and on the other side are the barracks where the displaced persons camp was set up. The historic site confronts the visitors again with the themes of rescue and death, and of the singularity of Bergen-Belsen while being an integral part of the Nazi racial state which they already encountered as underlying themes in the historic exhibition.

The New Landscape Design

In the early 1990s, the section of the former concentration camp which had been incorporated into the military training ground in the 1950s was finally handed over to the *Gedenkstätte*. In contrast to the original memorial site, this section had not undergone systematic clearing and garden-like landscaping. Archaeological digs have shown the existence of structural remains of the former camp closely under the topsoil, such as stone foundations of some of the huts, watchtowers, water reservoirs, the old delousing facilities, and even remains of the main camp road. The task facing the landscape planners was to integrate the two sections of the historic site which had been separated for over 40 years into one coherent and meaningful place without disturbing the mass graves or removing any of the elements set up at the cemetery since the liberation, such as the memorials erected by the survivors, the wall of remembrance and the obelisk.[32] In order to help visitors understand the historic structures of the camp, strategic clearings in the woods on the site of the memorial and in the surrounding forest provide glades and groves to indicate the boundaries and the different areas covered by the prisoner-of-war camp and the concentration camp. The most important orientation is provided by a central corridor which traces the entire length of the former main camp road (see plate no.16).

The principal task of the *Gedenkstätte* is to remember those who died and suffered there, and to try, as far this is still possible, to give them back their identity and their personal history which the Nazis had set out to destroy together with their physical existence. Until now the names of the dead are missing in the cemetery, but a new 'Place of Names' which will be created in the new central corridor of the memorial site will serve as a special place of remembrance for all the people who died at Bergen-Belsen concentration camp. With their names, the dead will at least in death regain their individuality and dignity at the very site where some 60 years ago the attempt was made to take both away from them. The many thousands of dead whose names are not known will each be honoured symbolically as well until such time as their names might be recovered. The redesign of the landscape is a long-term undertaking, and it will take a number of years before it will be fully completed. As the site is now a (predominantly Jewish) cemetery, the work has to be done with utmost caution and sensitivity and with respect to the dead buried there.

The Future of the *Gedenkstätte*: Preserving the Memory

More than 60 years after the liberation of the concentration camp and 55 years after the closure of the displaced persons camp, a comprehensive memory of Bergen-Belsen is returning to the historic site.[33] This marks a major change in the way Bergen-Belsen is remembered after the long phase of suppression and destruction of the memory. When the first memorial was set up, it was basically about the dead buried in the mass graves. In recent years, this has been gradually widened to tell the story of Bergen-Belsen as a prisoner-of-war camp, concentration camp, and displaced persons camp, and of the people in these camps and, in the case of the survivors, their lives both before and after Bergen-Belsen. At the same time, the political and social contexts of remembering Nazi crimes and the victims of Nazi persecution and genocide have changed dramatically. On the one hand, the Holocaust has moved from the margins to the centre of historical consciousness, on the other hand more and more visitors to Bergen-Belsen have no direct connection with the history of the place.[34]

The new *Gedenkstätte* has to fulfil two very different tasks. First and foremost, it must be accepted by the survivors and their descendants, and by the relatives and friends of those who perished, as a dignified and truthful place of their own remembrance. However, it is just as important that the *Gedenkstätte* links the past with the future so that the younger generation can relate their own experiences in a meaningful way to what happened at Bergen-Belsen. This means that the political and educational functions of the *Gedenkstätte* are becoming more important than ever before. With the newly acquired documents, artefacts, photographs and video interviews, a new and much better resourced study centre will be able to broaden the educational work and put it on a much wider footing. The *Gedenkstätte* will have to transform itself into a place which is just as much a centre of education, information and research as it is a site of remembrance.

The fact that in a few years' time hardly any survivors of Bergen-Belsen will still be alive will have a dramatic impact on the work of concentration camp memorials including Bergen-Belsen. It will be the task of the *Gedenkstätte* to ensure that Bergen-Belsen keeps a place in public memory. This means that it has to address not only the question of what to remember at Bergen-Belsen, and how, but equally the reasons why we and future generations should remember.

NOTES

I would like to thank all my colleagues at the *Gedenkstätte* Bergen-Belsen, in particular Diana Gring, Bernd Horstmann, Klaus Tätzler and Karin Theilen, without whose help I would not have been able to write this article.

1. Two recent publications are B. Shephard, *After Daybreak: The Liberation of Belsen, 1945* (London: Jonathan Cape, 2005); B. Flanagan and D. Bloxham (eds.), *Remembering Belsen: Eyewitnesses Record the Liberation* (London: Vallentine Mitchell, 2005).
2. For the general context, see J. Herf, *Divided Memory: The Nazi Past in the Two Germanys* (Cambridge, MA: Harvard University Press, 1997), esp. chs. 7 and 8.
3. On the liberation of Bergen-Belsen and the ensuing rescue and relief operation, see P. Kemp, 'The British Army and the Liberation of Bergen-Belsen April 1945', in

J. Reilly, D. Cesarani, T. Kushner and C. Richmond (eds.), *Belsen in History and Memory* (London: Frank Cass, 1997), pp.134–48; K. Margry, 'Bergen-Belsen', *After The Battle*, No.89 (1995), pp.8–25; J. Reilly, *Belsen: The Liberation of a Concentration Camp* (London: Routledge, 1998), pp.19–49.

4. The National Archives of the UK, formerly the Public Record Office (hereafter TNA), FO 1010/168: CCG (BE), Office of the Chief of Staff (British Zone), to 229 'P' Mil Gov Det Hannover, 10 October 1945. This instruction was passed on to the *Oberpräsident* of Hannover, Hinrich Wilhelm Kopf, on 19 October 1945, who in turn passed it on to the German authorities in *Landkreis* Celle, the administrative district where Bergen-Belsen is situated.

5. For this and the following, see J. Wolschke-Bulmahn, 'The Landscape Design of the Bergen-Belsen Concentration Camp Memorial', in J. Wolschke-Bulmahn (ed.), *Places of Commemoration: Search for Identity and Landscape Design* (Washington, DC: Dumbarton Oaks Research Library and Collection, 2001), pp.269–300; J. Wolschke-Bulmahn, '1945–1995: Anmerkungen zur landschaftsarchitektonischen Gestaltung der Gedenkstätte Bergen-Belsen', *Die Gartenbaukunst*, Vol.7 (1995), pp.325–40; J. Woudstra, 'Landscape: An Expression of History', *Landscape Design: Journal of the Landscape Institute*, No.308 (March 2002), pp.42–9; R. Schulze, '"Germany's Gayest and Happiest Town"? Bergen-Belsen 1945–1950', *Dachauer Hefte: Studien und Dokumente zur Geschichte der nationalsozialistischen Konzentrationslager*, Vol.19 (2003), pp.233–7; A. Pohle, 'Die Gedenkstätte Bergen-Belsen: Zum Umgang mit dem historischen Erbe', *Schulverwaltungsblatt für Niedersachsen*, Vol.52 (2000), pp.300–2; W. Wiedemann, 'Vom Vergessen und Erinnern: Zur Geschichte der Gedenkstätte Bergen-Belsen', in Landesjugendring Niedersachsen e.V. (ed.), *Spuren suchen, Spuren sichern: Das Projekt – Die Ausstellung – Die Patenschaften* (Hannover: Buchdruckwerkstätten, 1997), pp.13–18.

6. TNA FO 1010/168: M.F.A.& A. Section, Zonal Executive Office, CCG Bünde to HQ Mil Gov Hannover Region, 30 July 1946.

7. Kreisarchiv Celle (hereafter KA-C) N 3 Nr. 3a: Hübotter to Landrat Wentker, 28 November 1945. The German term for the final line was written in capital letters by Hübotter: *SCHLUSS-STEIN*.

8. KA-C N 3 Nr. 3a: Hübotter to Landrat Celle, 4 December 1945.

9. TNA FO 1010/168: HQ Mil Gov Hannover Region, note on Belsen Memorial meeting, 13 August 1946.

10. TNA FO 1010/168: Minutes of a meeting held to consider designs for and the location of an International Memorial in Camp I Belsen, held at Hohne at 11.00 hrs 5 Sept. 1946.

11. TNA FO 1010/170: Note by PW/DP Branch, HQ Military Government, Land Niedersachsen, 13 January 1947.

12. The texts of all the plaques can be found in an information leaflet issued by the Gedenkstätte Bergen-Belsen: 'Gedenkstätte Bergen-Belsen', typescript, undated, pp.14–16.

13. TNA FO 1010/169: Note on Belsen Concentration Camp, undated (c.Nov. 1952).

14. See Schulze, '"Germany's Gayest and Happiest Town"?', pp.236–7.

15. E. Kolb, *Bergen-Belsen: Geschichte des 'Aufenthaltslager' 1943–1945* (Hannover: Verlag für Literatur und Zeitgeschehen, 1962). The monograph has seen a number of updated and revised editions and was translated into several languages; the most recent edition is E. Kolb, *Bergen-Belsen: Vom 'Aufenthaltslager' zum Konzentrationslager 1943–1945* (Göttingen: Vandenhoeck & Ruprecht, 1985, 6th edn. 2002). English translation: E. Kolb, *Bergen-Belsen: From 'Detention Camp' to Concentration Camp, 1943–1945* (Göttingen: Vandenhoeck & Ruprecht, 1984, 3rd edn. 2002).

16. F. Bischoff (ed.), *Das Lager Bergen-Belsen: Dokumente und Bilder mit erläuternden Texten* (Hannover: Verlag für Literatur und Zeitgeschehen, 1966).
17. J.H. Kriszan, 'Bergen-Belsen: Menschen und ihre Schicksale', *Celler Zündel*, special issue (1985), see esp. p.3.
18. See Archiv der Gedenkstätte Bergen-Belsen (hereafter GBB), 'Gutachten der Sachverständigenkommission zur Neugestaltung der Gedenkstätte Belsen', typescript, Hannover, January 1987.
19. Niedersächsische Landeszentrale für politische Bildung (ed.), *Bergen-Belsen: Texte und Bilder der Ausstellung in der zentralen Gedenkstätte des Landes Niedersachsen auf dem Gelände des ehemaligen Konzentrations- und Kriegsgefangenenlagers Bergen-Belsen* (Hannover: Niedersächsische Landeszentrale für politische Bildung, 1990; 2nd rev. edn. 1991). There are translations in a number of other languages including English, French, Russian and Hebrew.
20. *Gedenkbuch: Häftlinge des Konzentrationslagers Bergen-Belsen* (Bergen-Belsen: Niedersächsische Landeszentrale für politische Bildung – Gedenkstätte Bergen-Belsen, 1995); *Gedenkbuch: Häftlinge des Konzentrationslagers Bergen-Belsen*, 2 vols. (Bergen-Belsen: Stiftung Niedersächsische Gedenkstätten – Gedenkstätte Bergen-Belsen, 2005). Both the preface and introduction have an English translation. The data register of prisoners of the concentration camp at the *Gedenkstätte* comprises additional information which has not been included in the publications.
21. 'Schlußbericht der Enquete-Kommission "Überwindung der Folgen der SED-Diktatur im Prozeß der deutschen Einheit"', in Deutscher Bundestag (ed.), *Die Enquete-Kommission 'Überwindung der Folgen der SED-Diktatur im Prozeß der deutschen Einheit' im Deutschen Bundestag – Besondere Veranstaltungen* (Baden-Baden: Nomos Verlagsgesellschaft, 1999), pp.142–803, here pp.616–30.
22. Deutscher Bundestag, 14. Wahlperiode, Drucksache 14/1569 (27 July 1999): 'Konzeption der künftigen Gedenkstättenförderung des Bundes', here section 2, p.4. The other concentration camps thus singled out for their international and national importance were Neuengamme, Dachau and Flossenbürg in former West Germany, and Buchenwald, Ravensbrück, Sachsenhausen and Mittelbau-Dora in the former German Democratic Republic.
23. H. Lavsky, *New Beginnings: Holocaust Survivors in Bergen-Belsen and the British Zone in Germany, 1945–1950* (Detroit: Wayne State University Press, 2002).
24. In the final months before the liberation, the prisoners incarcerated at Bergen-Belsen concentration camp comprised members of all groups persecuted by the Nazis and more than 20 nationalities.
25. For the Jewish survivors, see 'A Garden in Belsen', *Our Voice: Organ of the Liberated Jews in the British Zone*, 12 July 1947; see also 'Über das Belsen-Denkmal im Lager I', *Wochenblatt*, No.22 (71) (1949) (Yiddish, German translation by Nicholas Yantian).
26. See, for example, T. Kushner et al., 'Approaching Belsen: An Introduction', in Reilly et al. (eds.), *Belsen in History and Memory*, esp. pp.3–16. For a discussion of the images, see also T. Haggith and J. Newman (eds.), *Holocaust and the Moving Image: Representations in Film and Television Since 1933* (London: Wallflower Press, 2005), esp. section 3; J. Struk, *Photographing the Holocaust: Interpretations of the Evidence* (London: I.B. Tauris, 2004), esp. ch. 6; C. Brink, *Ikonen der Vernichtung: Öffentlicher Gebrauch von Fotografien aus nationalsozialistischen Konzentrationslagern nach 1945* (Berlin: Akademie Verlag, 1998); H. Caven, 'Horror in Our Time: Images of the Concentration Camps in the British Media, 1945', *Historical Journal of Film, Radio and Television*, Vol.21 (2001), pp.205–53; M. Caiger-Smith (ed.), *The Face of the Enemy: British Photographers in Germany, 1944–1952* (London: Dirk Nishen Publishing, n.d. [1986]). An early example of the general use of these images is *Lest*

We Forget: The Horrors of Nazi Concentration Camps Revealed for All Times in the Most Terrible Photographs Ever Published, compiled by the *Daily Mail* (London: Daily Mail, 1945).
27. The information that follows is based on the internal working papers produced in the past two years by the members of the international team of researchers and the management group for the new permanent exhibition. See also Gedenkstätte Bergen-Belsen, *Newsletter*, No.1 (2002) and No.2 (2003).
28. Nederlands Instituut voor Beeld en Geluid (Netherlands Institute for Vision and Film), Film Westerbork Transport. See also, in their archive, Collectie RVD Filmarchief, Kamp Westerbork (overs) (Acte 1), Archiefnr. 02-1167-01. For further information, see also K. Broersma and G. Rossing, *Kamp Westerbork gefilmd: het verhaal over een unieke film uit 1944* (Assen: Van Gorcum, 1997).
29. W. Lindwer, *The Last Seven Months of Anne Frank* (New York: Anchor Books, 1992).
30. The interviews follow a uniform conceptual and technical format; they cover the whole life of those interviewed, are conducted in identical settings, and are digitilised throughout. See K. Theilen, 'Zeitzeugeninterviews in der neuen Dauerausstellung', unpublished paper given at the symposium in honour of Henry Friedlander's 75th birthday, Celle, 24 September 2005.
31. On the role of oral testimony of survivors, see L. Langer, *Holocaust Testimonies: The Ruins of Memory* (New Haven, CT: Yale University Press, 1991); U. Baer (ed.), *'Niemand zeugt für den Zeugen': Erinnerungskultur und historische Verantwortung nach der Shoah* (Frankfurt am Main: Suhrkamp, 2000). See also H. Greenspan, 'The Awakening of Memory: Survivor Testimony in the First Years after the Holocaust, and Today', Occasional Papers, Center for Advanced Holocaust Studies, United States Holocaust Memorial Museum, Washington, DC (2001).
32. For a more detailed discussion of the task facing the landscape planners, see E. Benz-Rababah, S. Burmil and J. Wolschke-Bulmahn (eds.), 'The Bergen-Belsen Design Workshop: Memory, Design and Friendship', typescript, Hannover, 2001. For the broader context, see S. Milton, 'Holocaust-Memorials: Ein amerikanisch-europäischer Vergleich', in R. Steininger (ed.), *Der Umgang mit dem Holocaust: Europa – USA – Israel* (Vienna: Böhlau, 1994), pp.433–43, as well as the contributions in D. Hoffman (ed.), *Das Gedächtnis der Dinge: KZ-Relikte und KZ-Denkmäler 1945–1995* (Frankfurt am Main: Campus, 1998) and in Bulmahn (ed.), *Places of Commemoration*.
33. At the time of writing (October 2005), the new Documentation and Information Centre with the new permanent exhibition is scheduled to open in 2007. The new landscape design for the memorial site is expected to take at least another three to five years before it is completed.
34. For the broader context, see, among many others, P. Novick, *The Holocaust and Collective Memory: The American Perspective* (London: Bloomsbury, 2000); J.E. Young, *The Texture of Memory: Holocaust Memorials and Meaning* (New Haven, CT: Yale University Press, 1993); L.S. Dawidowicz, *The Holocaust and the Historians* (Cambridge, MA: Harvard University Press, 1981).

Abstracts

A Brief History of Bergen-Belsen
DAVID CESARANI

Bergen-Belsen was not typical of any Nazi concentration camps. But its history reflects the development of Nazi racial policy and, especially, anti-Jewish policy. The first camp on the site held French and Belgian POWs. Thousands of Soviet POWs were sent to Stalag XIC/ 311 at Bergen-Belsen, of whom most perished due to neglect, disease and malnutrition. It is more familiar as a camp where Jews were held as bargaining counters in Nazi schemes to exchange Jews for Germans interned in Allied countries, a project rooted in anti-Semitic fantasies that only had relevance in the context of a genocidal policy. While conditions in the exchange camp were relatively good in 1943–44, more and more Jews were sent there as the Nazis expanded their genocidal campaign. Typhus, combined with the breakdown of food and water supplies, led to a massive death rate in early 1945. The new SS camp commandant, Josef Kramer, did little to stem the suffering despite Himmler's wish to use the Jews as a last bargaining counter.

The Medical Relief Effort at Belsen
BEN SHEPHARD

Over 14,000 inmates of Bergen-Belsen camp died in the first few weeks after the camp was liberated by the British in April 1945. This has provoked continuing debate as to whether those deaths were inevitable or could have been avoided had the medical problem of Belsen been better managed. This essay looks in outline at the evidence and shows how the British struggled to handle a humanitarian crisis for which they were quite unprepared.

ABSTRACTS

British Relief Teams in Belsen Concentration Camp: Emergency Relief and the Perception of Survivors
JOHANNES-DIETER STEINERT

Based on a research project on 'British Humanitarian Assistance in Germany after the Second World War', this essay focuses on the work of British relief teams, provided by the British Red Cross and the Society of Friends, who entered Bergen-Belsen just one week after liberation. The essay concentrates on the main objectives of British wartime planning and the training of relief workers, and goes on to examine the actual deployment of the teams and their perception by the survivors. Written sources traced include documents from the British Government, the Society of Friends and the Jewish Committee for Relief Abroad.

The Filming of the Liberation of Bergen-Belsen and its Impact on the Understanding of the Holocaust
TOBY HAGGITH

This essay is an examination of the film shot at Bergen-Belsen by British Army cameramen. It describes how these men recorded the unfamiliar and horrific scenes they encountered in the camp and offers some explanation for the often-controversial images that resulted. There is also a brief history of how the Belsen film has been used since the war and some thoughts on its contribution to wider public awareness and understanding of the German concentration camp system and the Holocaust.

What Wireless Listeners Learned: Some Lesser-Known BBC Broadcasts about Belsen
SUZANNE BARDGETT

Patrick Gordon Walker took a radio van into Belsen five days after the liberation. In his detailed and frank diary he described obtaining interviews from survivors and guards, and several harrowing episodes. The recordings he made were heard by millions in two programmes broadcast on the Home Service several weeks later. The following year the BBC marked the first anniversary of Belsen's liberation with an ambitious 'drama-documentary', based on Jerseyman Harold Le Druillenec's experiences in Neuengamme and Belsen. These programmes show that – although the full history behind Belsen was not appreciated – the BBC nonetheless made it a priority to convey the 'concentration camp story' to its listeners.

'And I was only a child': Children's Testimonies, Bergen-Belsen 1945
BOAZ COHEN

This essay tells the story of child and teenage inmates of Bergen Belsen. In a unique set of testimonies, taken in the camp in 1945 and 1946, young survivors told the stories of their recent ordeal. They were collected by Helena Wrobel (later Wrobel-Kagan), herself a Belsen survivor, in the high school she established in the camp. She asked her pupils to write on the theme 'My Path from Home to Bergen Belsen'. The essay describes the make-up of the camp's child survivor population, the environment in which the testimonies were taken and the issues which they confront.

The Liberation of the Bergen-Belsen Camp as seen by Some British Official War Artists in 1945
ANTOINE CAPET

Debates now taking place on the impact of the images of Belsen tend to neglect the drawings and paintings made by the Official War Artists. It is not clear why, while a lot of attention is devoted to photographs and films, these other visual testimonies are left aside. One reason might be technical: to reproduce colour art faithfully used to be a major difficulty before the introduction of computer-assisted processes, but it seems that these works of art may be deemed too demanding. The essay concludes that by neglecting these graphic documents, historians and educators are depriving themselves of a major source of visual representation of what took place in Belsen in the days following the liberation of the camp.

ABSTRACTS

From 'This Belsen Business' to 'Shoah Business': History, Memory and Heritage, 1945–2005
TONY KUSHNER

Belsen has a particular significance in British collective memory since the liberation of the camp in 1945. This essay traces the evolution of that memory, comparing and contrasting initial responses with those at the end of the twentieth and start of the twenty-first centuries. In particular, it explores the problems of representing Nazi atrocities through Belsen liberation imagery and analyses the tensions between history and heritage in the representation of the past.

Forgetting and Remembering: Memories and Memorialisation of Bergen-Belsen
RAINER SCHULZE

A rich cultural memory of Bergen-Belsen developed immediately after its liberation by British troops in April 1945. However, at first this happened primarily outside Germany. At the site of the former camp itself visitors saw little more than the mass graves of those who died there. It was only in the early 1960s that the slow and difficult process of recovering memory began. In October 2000 work began on a major transformation of the *Gedenkstätte* (memorial). A new Documentation and Information Centre will house a permanent exhibition documenting not only the history of the concentration camp, but also that of the prisoner-of-war and displaced persons camps which existed there. At the same time, a new landscape design will aid understanding of the historic layout of the site.

Notes on Contributors

Suzanne Bardgett studied Modern History at Durham University. She was the Founder Editor of the *Imperial War Museum Review*, a journal of articles by the Museum staff on aspects of its collections. In 1995 she was appointed Project Director of the Imperial War Museum's Holocaust Exhibition, which opened in 2000 after five years of planning and research, and subsequently led the team which created the adjacent exhibition, *Crimes against Humanity: An Exploration of Genocide and Ethnic Violence* (opened 2002). She continues to represent the interests of both these exhibitions and to oversee the Holocaust Exhibition's acquisitions programme.

David Cesarani is Research Professor in History at Royal Holloway, University of London. He served on the advisory board of the Imperial War Museum's Holocaust Exhibition, has made a number of radio documentaries for the BBC and acted as consultant for several historical programmes on television, including *The Irving Trial* (Channel 4, 2000) and *I Met Adolf Eichmann* (BBC2, 2001). His most recent publication is *Eichmann: His Life and Crimes* (2004).

Anita Lasker-Wallfisch grew up in Breslau, Germany. She and her sister Renate were deported to Auschwitz, where Anita joined the camp orchestra, and was able to save her own life and her sister's. After the war, Anita Lasker-Wallfisch became a cellist of world-renown. In the mid-1990s she was one of the first Holocaust survivors in Britain to tell her story on radio, when she read a memoir of her ordeal during concert intervals on BBC Radio Three. Her autobiography – *Inherit the Truth* – was published in 1996. Mrs Lasker-Wallfisch's papers are held in the Imperial War Museum's Department of Documents.

Dick Williams joined the Territorial Army as a driver in a unit of the Royal Army Service Corps, and by 1944 had been appointed Staff Captain 8 Corps HQ. He landed in France on the evening of D-Day, and entered Bergen-Belsen under a white flag with Brigadier Glyn

NOTES ON CONTRIBUTORS

Hughes. Major Williams has addressed many audiences about his memories of the relief effort at Belsen and contributed to the Holocaust Memorial Day commemoration held at Westminster Hall in 2005. His letters describing conditions in Belsen and the subsequent relief effort are held by the Imperial War Museum's Department of Documents.

Ben Shephard is the author of *A War of Nerves: Soldiers and Psychiatrists in the Twentieth Century* (2000) and *After Daybreak: The Liberation of Belsen* (2005). A former television producer, he has held visiting fellowships at Yale, New York and Oxford universities and will give the Lees-Knowles Lectures on Military History at Cambridge in the autumn of 2006. He is currently working on a study of the Displaced Persons problem after the Second World War.

Johannes-Dieter Steinert is Reader in History at the University of Wolverhampton and member of the History and Governance Research Institute (HAGRI). His research interests focus on German, British and European social and political history, with special emphasis on migration and minorities, survivors of Nazi persecution, and international humanitarian assistance. His publications include *Beyond Camps and Forced Labour: Current International Research on Survivors of Nazi Persecution*, Proceedings of the First International Multidisciplinary Conference, held at the Imperial War Museum London, 29–31 January 2003 (ed. with Inge Weber-Newth, 2005).

Rainer Schulze is Head of the Department of History at the University of Essex. He has specialised in twentieth-century German history, the history of Bergen-Belsen and the history of forced migration after the Second World War. Since 2000 he has worked as one of the project leaders of the international team of researchers preparing the new permanent exhibition at the Gedenkstätte Bergen-Belsen, and in 2005 he became a member of the International Experts' Commission for the Redevelopment of the Gedenkstätte Bergen-Belsen, the only representative from Britain.

Eva Macourková was born in Pilsen, Czechoslovakia, in 1931. Her father was arrested on 1 September 1939 and perished in Auschwitz in late 1942. In January 1942 Eva was deported, together with her elder sister Hana and their mother, Růzena, to Theresienstadt (Terezín), from where they were sent to Auschwitz and then to Christianstadt, a sub-camp of Gross-Rosen. All three were liberated in Belsen in April 1945, but Růzena Macourková died ten days after the liberation. Eva and Hana returned to Pilsen, where Eva resumed her education and eventually became a translator.

Toby Haggith works in the Film and Video Archive of the Imperial War Museum, where he is head of Public Services and devises the cinema programme. He studied history and politics at the University of York, and then later the economic and social history of Britain at Birkbeck College, University of London. He completed his doctorate at the Centre for Social History in the University of Warwick. He is currently writing a book about British films on slum clearance and town planning. He is the co-editor, with Joanna Newman, of *Holocaust and the Moving Image: Representations in Film and Television Since 1933* (2005).

Boaz Cohen received his PhD from the Department of Jewish History in Bar Ilan University for his thesis on 'Holocaust Research in Israel 1945–1980: Characteristics, Trends, Developments'. He teaches Jewish Studies in Sha'anan College, Haifa, and Holocaust Studies in Western Galilee College, Acre. His current research is on early children's Holocaust testimonies. Recent publications include 'Holocaust Survivors and the Genesis of Holocaust Research', in Johannes-Dieter Steinert Dieter and Inge Weber-Newth (eds), *Beyond Camps and Forced Labour: Current International Research on Survivors of Nazi Persecution* (2005).

Antoine Capet is Professor of British Studies at the University of Rouen, France. He did his Doctorat d'État on *Le poids des années de guerre: Les classes dirigeantes britanniques et la réforme sociale, 1931–1951* (1991). He was General Editor of the *Revue française de civilisation britannique* (2003–06) and is currently 'Britain since 1914' Section Editor of the Royal Historical Society Bibliography, sitting on the Editorial Committees of Cultural and Social History and Twentieth-Century British History. Work in progress includes a comprehensive bibliography of Britain at war, 1939–45.

NOTES ON CONTRIBUTORS 243

Tony Kushner holds the Marcus Sieff Chair in the Department of History and is the Director of the Parkes Centre at the University of Southampton. His research interests are modern Jewish history, especially British Jewish history, the history of antisemitism and immigration and ethnic history.

Index

Numbers in italics refer to illustrations

6th Airborne Division, 115
8th Corps, 1, 27, 35
11th Armoured Division, 35, 36, 51, 94
11th Field Ambulance, 66
15th Scottish Division, 51
30th Field Hygiene Section, 66
32nd Casualty Clearing Station (CCS), 36, 39, 41, 45, 66, 76
49th Parallel, The (film), 114
63rd Anti-Tank Regiment, 65
76th Field Hygiene Section, 65
224th Military Government Detachment, 27, 66, 128, 218
606th Field Artillery Regiment, 156
1940s House, The (British tv series), 202–5, 206–7, 208, 212

Abrahams, Ruth, 75
Adam, Robert, 195
AFPU (Army Film and Photographic Unit), 89–122, 192, 223, 227–8
Agate, James, 194, 196, 201
Allied Declaration on behalf of European Jewry, 191–2
Alwyn, William, 132
American Joint Jewish Distribution Committee, 34
Angel of Bergen-Belsen, The (tv documentary), 92–3
Argyll and Sutherland Highlanders, 115
Army Film and Photographic Unit *see* AFPU
Arnhem, 115
Ashberg, Margery, 68
Asher, Irving, 114
Association of Survivors of Bergen-Belsen, 225
A.T.S., 114
Auerbach, Rachel, 167
Auschwitz-Birkenau, 17, 19, 31, 35, 80, 110, 113, 127, 128, 177, 196–9, 199–200, 201; and Belsen inmates, 1, 6, 18, 22–3, 85, 90, 93, 125, 126, 129, 133, 139–40, 154, 158, 159, 161, 162, 163, 164, 192, 228, 229
Auschwitz: The Blueprints of Genocide (film), 113
Auschwitz: The Nazis and the 'Final Solution' (BBC tv documentary series), 197–8, 208, 212

Bamber, Helen, 1, 74–5
Bark, Evelyn, 69
Barnett, Major Ben, 4, 237; eyewitness account, 51–4
BBC (British Broadcasting Corporation), 1, 6, 25, 123–52, 192–3, 197, 198, 210, 211
Beardwell, Myrtle, 56, 67
Becher, Kurt, 20
'Belsen Concentration Camp: Facts and Thoughts' (BBC radio programme), 128–30, 134–5, 137–41, 228
Belsen Trial, Lüneberg, 89–90, 131, 175, 199
Bengal Famine Mixture, 40, 42
Benn, Tony, 210
Bennett, Alan, 189, 193, 196
Bermuda Conference (1943), 14
Bernstein, Sidney, 91, 98–9, 103, 109
Birnbaum, Solomon A., 64
Bitburg, 8
Blackman, Muriel, 69
Bloxham, Donald, 199–200, 209
BNP, 210
Boder, David, 45
Bourke-White, Margaret, 91
Boy Scouts Association, 63
Brand, Joel, 18
BRC *see* British Red Cross
Breslau (now Wroclaw), 22
Britain, and discussions about Jewish refugees, 14; and Gedenkstätte Bergen-

INDEX

Belsen, 220, 226; German nationals interned by, 15; history, memory and heritage in, 1–2, 190–213; liberation of Belsen, 25–6, 27–30, 84, 222; liberation of Belsen depicted by war artists, 7–8, 170–85; liberation of Belsen filmed by army film and photographic personnel, 5, 89–122; medical relief effort in Belsen, 3–4, 31–61, 84–5; Nazi views on influence of Jews in, 14; radio broadcasts about Belsen in, 6, 123–52; relief teams in Belsen, 4–5, 62–78
British Army Bulldozer pushes Bodies into a Mass Grave at Belsen, A (photograph), 171, 172–4, 182
British Red Cross (BRC), 62, 63, 64, 66, 67, 73, 79; *see also* Red Cross
British Zone Review, 46
Bronka S., 164
Broughton, Bill, 68
Broughton, Kit, 68
Brownlow, Kevin, 91–2
Brunswick, 124, 125
Buchenwald, 16, 35, 80, 91, 110, 134, 192, 197

Calder, Angus, *The People's War*, 211
Cannadine, David, 194
Cartagena, Gitta, 126, 128, 139–40
Catholic Committee for Relief Abroad, 63
Caven, Hannah, 93, 192
Celle, 79, 94, 96, 99, 102, 125
Central Committee for the Liberated Jews, 219
Charlemagne, 219
'Children's Hour' (BBC radio programme), 130
Christianstadt, 80–1
Churchill, Winston, 34
Clarkson, Beth, 68
COBSRA (Council of British Societies for Relief Abroad), 4–5, 63
Cole, Leslie, 7, 174–5, 181, 182; *Belsen Camp: The Compound for Women*, Plate 9; 175, 178–9; *Malta: No Time to lose – Soldier Dockers unloading a Convoy during a Raid*, 174–5; *One of the Death Pits, Belsen: SS Guards collecting bodies*, Plate 10; 174, 175, 176–8, 179
Colonial Office (Britain), 34
Cook, Peter, 198, 199

Cosenza, 100
Cottrell, Leonard, 6; 'The Man from Belsen' (BBC radio play), 131–4, 135, 142–52, 238
Council of British Societies for Relief Abroad *see* COBSRA

Dachau concentration camp, 31, 39, 91, 103, 134, 192, 197
Daily Mirror, 205
Davis, Captain W.A., 39, 40, 43
DDT, 33–4, 37–8, 43, 54, 65
Death Marches, 24, 160–1
Delage, Christian, 92
Dimbleby, Richard, 25, 123, 192–3, 203, 204, 205, 206, 211, 212, 213
Dora-Mittelbau concentration camp, 17
Douglas, Lawrence, 206
Dresden, 81, 210
Drummond, Sir Jack, 33, 40
Dutch prisoners, 1, 2, 14, 17, 39, 154
Dyall, Valentine, 132

Eden, Anthony, 191
Edyta R., 154–5, 159, 164
Edzia J., 158
Eichmann, Adolf, 15, 18
Eichmann Trial, 193
Eisenhower, Dwight D., 102
Estera (Edzia) Z., 159, 162
Evian Conference (1938), 14

Falmouth, Lady, 64, 70
FAU (Friends Ambulance Service), 63
Fenelon, Fania (Fania Perla), 128, 137
Final Report of the Select Committee on German Unity, 221–2
Finney, Patrick, 209
Fira P., 162
Flossenberg, 160
Frank, Anne, 1, 18, 200, 228
Frank, Margot, 18, 200, 228
Freedman, Barnett, *The Landing in Normandy: Arromanches, D-Day plus 20, 26th June 1944*, 176
French prisoners, 13, 14, 22, 39
Friends Ambulance Unit (FAU), 63
Friends Relief Service (FRS), 63, 66, 68
Fry, Stephen, 201–2

Gardiner, Juliet, 203, 205; *Wartime Britain 1939–1945*, 211

Gaumont British News, 110
Gedenkbuch (Book of Remembrance), 221
Gedenkstätte Bergen-Belsen, 8–9, 217–35
Geneva Conventions, 13
German medical workers, 43, 57
German Provincial Government, Hannover, 218, 219
Gilbert, Martin, 196
Gilroy, Paul, 210
Gluck, Captain, 42
Goben, 161
Goldstein, Helen, 192
Gollancz, Victor, 197
Gonin, Lieutenant Colonel Mervin, 66–7, 72–3
Gordon Walker, Patrick, 6, 38, 123–30; *The Lid Lifts*, 128, 129; 'Belsen Concentration Camp: Facts and Thoughts', 128–30, 134–5, 137–41, 238
Goslar, Hannah (Hannah Pick), 1
Gould, Louisa, 131
Grant, Sergeant Ian James, 96
Greenberg, Rabbi Irving, 31, 32, 46
Grese, Irma, 28
Groß-Rosen, 80–1, 154, 160
Guards Armoured Division, 115
Guide International Service (Girl Guides Association), 63
Gutka, F., 155

Haas, Adolf, 16, 19
Haifa, 17
Hamburg, 126, 131, 140
Hamm, 128
Hannover, 218, 219
Hardman, Rabbi Leslie (Jewish chaplain), 27, 30, 38, 129, 140
Hardy, Bert, 91
Harris, Sergeant, film shot by, 108
Haywood, Sergeant Harold, 94, 111
Hebrew Gymnasium, Bergen Belsen camp, 155–8
Himmler, Heinrich, 15, 19, 20
Hinton, Michael, 68
Hirsch, Joshua, 92
Hirtz, Senta, 75
Hitchcock, Alfred, 91, 103, 114
Hitler, Adolf, 13, 15, 32, 134
Hochberg-Marianska, Maria, 163
Hogan's Heroes, American tv sitcom, 207
Holocaust, 166, 167, 171, 174, 220, 222, 228, 232; and history, memory and heritage, 189–216; impact of filming of liberation of Bergen-Belsen on understanding of, 89–122
Holocaust (Hollywood mini-series), 198
Holocaust Education Trust, 198
Holocaust Memorial Day (Britain), 1–2, 198, 213
Hopkinson, Sergeant Peter, 100; film shot by, 100
Horne, John, 190
Horsey, Peter, 42
Horwell, Arnold, 126
Hosler, Franz, 102
Hübotter, Wilhelm, 219
Hughes, Brigadier Glyn, 4, 27, 28, 36, 37, 39, 41, 45, 52
Hungarians, 18, 23, 40, 42
Hunt, Tristram, 202–3
Hutchinson, Charles Ronald, 110
Huxley, Julian, 32
Hymer family, 203, 204, 205, 206, 207

Imperial War Museum, 2, 26, 90, 170, 180, 206–7; Film Archive, 112; Holocaust Exhibition, 23, 101, 205; 'Women and War' exhibition, 180–1
Impey, Lilian, 68
Insdorf, Annette, 90, 91
Intelligence Corps, 126
International Voluntary Service for Peace, 63
Isbica, 22
Istanbul, 18, 34, 35
Italian prisoners, 14

James (née Matthews), Joanna, 82, 85–6
JCRA *see* Jewish Committee for Relief Abroad
JDC (American Jewish Joint Distribution Committee), 17
Jenkins, Hugh, 68
Jenkinson (member of SAS), 35
Jewish Agency, 15
Jewish Brigade, 155, 156
Jewish Chronicle, 198
Jewish Committee for Relief Abroad (JCRA), 34, 63, 65
Jews, Allied indifference to fate of, 31, 32; and Allied relief agenda, 34; and British attitudes, 46–7, 190–2, 193, 200, 210, 212, 213; children's testimonies, 7, 153–69; form majority of inmates at

INDEX

Belsen, 6, 93, 109, 125, 172, 192, 227; and history, memory and heritage, 8, 190–2, 193, 197, 200, 201, 204, 210, 211–12, 213; and memories and memorialisation, 222, 223, 227, 229; and Nazi policies, 2, 13–18, 19–20; *see also* Holocaust; names of individuals
Johnston, Lieutenant Colonel James, 36, 37, 41, 43–4, 44–5, 56, 57, 67
Jona B., 161, 162, 163

Kadziolka, Father, 104
Kahn-Minden, Eva, 75
Kaplan, Israel, 167
Kasztner, Rudolf, 18
Klein, Fritz, 102
Klüger, Ruth, 75
Korda, Alexander, 114
Krakow, 206
Kramer, Alan, 190
Kramer, Josef, 19, 20, 28, 52, 108, 111
Kulker, Helen, 126

Lasker, Marianne, 127
Lasker, Renate, 126, 127
Lasker-Wallfisch, Anita, 3, 29, 74, 126, 127; essay, 22–6
Laski, Harold, 32
Lawrie, Sergeant William Fairlie, 94–5, 95, 96, 98, 100, 101, 107, 109, 111, 115; film shot by, 103, 106
Lawson, Mark, 208
Lea H., 154, 155, 157, 160
Leatherbarrow, Sergeant Richard, 100
Le Druillenec, Harold, 6, 131–3, 142–51, 175, 239
Lees-Milne, James, 194–6, 201; *The Age of Adam*, 195–6
Lehman, Herbert, 33
Leiser, Erwin, 90
Leverson, Jane, 68, 69, 70–1, 73
Levi, Primo, 71
Levy, Dr, 35
Levy, Rabbi Isaac, 27, 30
Lewis, Sergeant Mike, 94–5, 96, 99, 99, 101, 106, 107, 111, 114–15; film shot by, 104, 105
Light Anti-Aircraft regiment, 113th, 39
Lipscomb, Lieutenant Colonel F.M. (Martin), 39, 45, 76
Lisbon, 34
Littman, David, 156

Liverpool, 34–5
Lodz Ghetto, 162
London, 1, 2, 41, 110; Eaton Square, 196; Landsdowne House, 195–6
London, Louise, 32
Lowenthal, David, 203, 212
Lower Saxony, 8, 220; Landtag, 221
Lüneberg, 89–90, 131, 133, 142, 150
Lüneberg Heath, 13, 218
Luxembourg, 124
Lyotard, Jean-François, 47

MacAuslan, Alan, 42
McCrum, Robert, 199, 200, 201, 202, 204
McFarlane, Jean, 54, 69
McLuhan, Marshall, 173, 174, 182
Macourková (née Sachselová), Eva, 5, 80–2, 238; essay, 84–6
MAD magazine, 207, 208
Magnum photographic agency, 91
Majdanek, 35, 62, 110
'Man from Belsen, The' (BBC radio play), 131–4, 135, 142–52, 239
Marrus, Michael, 73
Mass-Observation survey, 193, 204
Matthews, Andrew, 5, 79–82, 85, 86
Matthews, Joanna (later Joanna James), 82, 85–6
Matthews, Sally (later Sally Harris), 82
Medical Research Council, 41, 43
Meiklejohn, Dr Arnold, 39–40
Memory of the Camps, 91, 93, 111
Miller, Dr Emmanuel, *The Psychological Aspect of Relief Work*, 65
Miller, Lee, 91
Ministry of Defence (Britain), 35
Ministry of Information (Britain), 190, 204
Miriam B., 160–1, 163–4
Mitchell, Leslie, 110
Mobile Bacteriological Laboratory, 7th, 66
Monty Python (British tv comedy series), 207, 208
Moore, Dudley, 198
Morris, Sergeant, 175; *The Liberation of Bergen-Belsen Concentration Camp, 1945: One of the Mass Graves partially filled with Corpses*, 175, 176, 178
Morrison, Father, 104
Movietone News, 102, 110
Munich, 165; Central Historical

Commission, 167
Murray, Gilbert, 32
'My Way from Home to Bergen-Belsen' (children's testimonies), 153–69

Naples, 34, 40
National Trust, The 194
Natzweiler, 16
Neuengamme, 131, 132, 142, 150
Neusalz, 160, 163, 164
Niederhagen, 16
Night and Fog (film), 92, 113
Nolbandov, Sergei, 99
Normandy landings, 114, 131
Nuremberg, 212
Nuremberg Trials, 112, 193, 205

Oakes, Sergeant Harry, 91, 94, 95, 95, 99–100, 106–7, 192
Office IVB4, 15
Oppenheimer, Paul, 1
Order of St John of Jerusalem, 63
Oxford Committee for Famine Relief (Oxfam), 34
Oxford Yeomanry, 51, 126, 128, 138

Panzer Training School, 4, 19, 36, 37, 38, 39, 41, 42, 43, 44, 54
Parkes, James, 197, 198, 210
Parkinson, Joyce, 68
Parkinson, Sergeant, 107–8
Passover Remembrance, A (tv programme), 112
Paton, Alex, 42
Payne, Driver Mechanic, 128, 138
Pedersen, Susan, 210
Perla, Fania (Fania Fenelon), 128, 137
Petersen, Judith, 193, 204, 211
Peterswaldau, 160
Pick, Hannah (Hanneli Goslar), 1
Picture Post, 91
Pilsen, 80, 82, 86
Pinewood Studios, 90, 97, 108, 114, 115
Pini, Eugene, 132, 133
Pitt-Rivers, Rosalind, 43
Plaszow, 18, 164
Pnina J., 160
Pola Z., 157, 163
Poles, 16–17, 40, 222, 229
Polish Central Historical Commission, 165–6
Pollock, Karen, 198

Pollock, Susan, 1–2
Pommer, Eric, 114
Porrins, Leslie, 151
Powell, Enoch, 210
Powell, Michael, 114
Prague, 82, 86
Princie, Sergeant, 124–5, 128
Psychological Warfare Department, 98–9, 123

Quakers *see* Society of Friends/Quakers

Radio Luxembourg, 123–4
Rahe, Dr Thomas, 86
Rankin, Bill, 68
Raperport, Gerald, 4, 237; eyewitness account, 57–61
Rathbone, Eleanor, 197, 210
Ravensbruck, 19
Reading, Anna, 93
Reading, Lady, 46
Reagan, President Ronald, 8, 221
Red Cross, 5, 17, 19, 34, 41, 54, 68, 180; *see also* British Red Cross; Swiss Red Cross
Rees, Laurence, 197, 199, 208
Regina G., 154
Reilly, Joanne, 90, 172, 174
REME (Royal Electrical and Mechanical Engineers), 125
Remember: Richard Dimbleby at Belsen (BBC tv programme), 112
Resnais, Alain, 90, 92
Reynaud, Colonel, 131, 133, 142, 143, 144, 146, 147
Richmond, Colin, 189, 207–8, 210
Rodger, George, 91
Roosevelt, President, 33
Rosensaft, Josef, 74, 156
Royal Army Medical Corps, 29
Royal Army Service Corps, 27, 95
Royal Artillery, 114
Royal Electrical and Mechanical Engineers (REME), 125
Royal Engineers, 27, 28, 29, 30
Royal Fusiliers, 115
Royal Holloway, Research Centre for the Holocaust and Twentieth-Century History, 2
Royal Scots Dragoon Guards, 2
RSHE (SS head office), 19–20
Ruby Loftus screwing a Breech-Ring, 182

INDEX

Ruita S., 164
Russian prisoners, 2, 14; see also Soviet prisoners

Sachsel, Alfred, 80
Sachselová, Eva (later Eva Macourková), 5, 80–2, 238; essay, 84–6
Sachselová, Hana, 80–2, 84–5, 86
Sachselová, Růžena (mother of Eva and Hana), 80–1, 84, 85
Sachsenhain (Grove of the Saxons), 219
St John's Ambulance, 64
Sala R., 164
Salonika, 17
Salvation Army, 63; *European Relief Study Paper*, 64–5
Salzwedel, 125
Samuel, Raphael, 202, 213
Sara G., 161, 164
SAS, 35, 51
Save the Children Fund, 63
Scenes from the Second World War colouring book, 209
Schindler's List (film), 206
Second Army, 35, 36
Sephardi Jews, 17
Sewell, Brigadier E.P., 53
SHAEF (Supreme Headquarters Allied Expeditionary Force), 98; Psychological Warfare Department, 98–9, 123
Silva Jones, Molly, 4, 67, 237; eyewitness account, 54–7
Sington, Derrick, 38, 133, 149
Smith, Lilian, 68
Smith, Marcus, 39
Society of Friends/Quakers, 5, 39, 62; *Relief Worker's Vocabulary*, 64; *see also* Friends Ambulance Service; Friends Relief Service
Soper, Fred, 33
Southampton, 209
Soviet prisoners, 13–14, 229; *see also* Russian prisoners
Stalag XIB, 96
Stalag XIC/311, 13–14
Stela L., 162, 164
Stern, Frank, 73–4
Stern, Henri, 74
Stewart, Colonel Hugh, 98, 108, 114
Stockholm, 35
Streep, Meryl, 198
Street Fighting (film), 114

Swiss Red Cross, 84; *see also* Red Cross
Syma G., 158, 162, 164

Tanner, Mrs H., 107
Taube, W., 159, 160, 161
Taylor, Lieutenant Colonel, 53
Templer, General Gerald, 46
Theresienstadt (Terezín), 19, 80
Todesmühlen, Die (film), 111
Trench, The (British tv series) 207, 208
Tritton, Ronald, 89
Trnopolje, 89
True Glory, The (film), 110, 111
Trysanska, Luba, 92–3

United States Holocaust Memorial Council, 31
United States Holocaust Memorial Museum, 25
United States Typhus Commission, 33–4
UNRRA (United Nations Relief and Rehabilitation Administration), 33, 63

Vaughan, Janet, 43
Vittel, 15
Volkenrath, Elizabeth, 127, 129

Walker, Sergeant 'Jock', film shot by, 97
War Artists Advisory Committee, 174
War Office (Britain), 35, 99
Wasserstein, Bernard, 32
Weindling, Paul, 33
Werkendamm, Hetty, 126
Westerbork, 228
Westminster Hall, London: Holocaust Memorial Day ceremony, 1–2
Whitbourn, James, 1
Wilhelmshaven, 131, 142, 150
Wilkinson, Ellen, 100
Williams, Major Dick, 1, 2, 3, 95–6, 236; essay, 27–30
Williams, Eryl Hall, 68
Wilson, Lieutenant Martin, 94, 98, 98, 99, 101; *The Bodies of Victims in Bergen-Belsen Concentration Camp*, 180, 181
Wilton, John, 195
Wodehouse, P.G., 199–202, 212; *Wodehouse in Wonderland*, 200
Wolfenbüttel, 124
Woolf, Leonard, 32
Wrobel (later Wrobel-Kagan), Helena, 7, 153, 155–6, 158, 165, 166, 167

WVHA (Economic and Administrative Head Office of SS), 16, 18
Wyand, Paul, 98

Yad Vashem, 165, 225

Young Women's Christian Association, 63

Zinkeisen, Doris, 7, 179–80, 182; *Belsen: April 1945*, Plate 11; 179, 180–2
Zionists/Zionism, 34, 156, 157, 191